# Reclaiming Lives ...

# Reclaiming Lives ...

## Rediscovering Myself
## While Educating Kolkata's Poor

By

**Rosalie Giffoniello**

With

**Robert M. Weir**

ISBN: 978-1500929442

Library of Congress Control Number: 2014915410

CreateSpace Independent Publishing Platform,
North Charleston, South Carolina, USA

Printed September 2014

*Reclaiming Lives* is also available as an e-book. Photographs in this printed book appear as black-and-white. Those same photographs appear in color in the e-book version. To order an e-book, search online for keywords: "Reclaiming Lives Giffoniello"

Other books by Robert M. Weir
   *Cobble Creek*
   *Peace, Justice, Care of Earth:*
     *The Vision of John McConnell, Founder of Earth Day*
   *Brain Tumor: Life · Love · Lessons*
   *Dad: a diary of caring and questioning*

This book is dedicated to
the disadvantaged and disabled children
of Kolkata, India,
who inspired me to reach my potential
while they struggled to reach theirs

In *Reclaiming Lives,* Rosalie Giffoniello, an American teacher, overcomes her personal struggles of insecurity and dependency and finds her identity by providing educational opportunities for destitute children who live in the slums of Kolkata (Calcutta), India. Each page abounds with hope, inspiration, and fulfillment for countless children who reclaim their lives through Rosalie's determination ... as she joyously reclaims her own.

In 2001, Rosalie Giffoniello co-founded Empower The Children, a 501(c)3 nonprofit, based in New Jersey, USA. Empower The Children funds educational, vocational, and lunch programs for slum-dwelling children and women. Rosalie lives and works in Kolkata six months each year.

Robert M. Weir writes and speaks about people, peace, social justice, environment, and adventures. He also edits book manuscripts for emerging and established authors. He is among—and a contributor to—humanity's spiritual and metaphysical leaders. When not traveling, he lives in Michigan, USA. **Robertmweir.com.**

Fifty percent of your purchase price will be donated to Empower The Children. **Empower-children.org.**

Robert Weir and Rosalie Giffoniello stand in the doorway of Preyrona 2, a school operated and funded by Empower The Children.

# Contents

India covers 1.15 million square miles. Its population is 1.237 billion people, the world's second most populated nation, not far behind China and four times more than the United States, which ranks third. Most of these people live in the three largest cities of Delhi, Mumbai, and Kolkata.

Kolkata lies on the nation's east side, near the Bay of Bengal, which also borders Bangladesh and Myanmar. Nepal is relatively close to the north.

The population density of Kolkata is 2,500 per square kilometer (4,000 per square mile). In the slums, families of five to ten live in a room the size of an average bedroom in a more affluent nation. In non-formal schools, up to 70 children sit on the floor in a room the size of a two-car garage.

This is the arena in which Rosalie Giffoniello and people associated with her nonprofit, Empower The Children, provide educational, vocational, and lunch programs.

The children are generally happy; their religious beliefs and sense of community are strong. The students are well behaved and motivated; they know that doing well in school is their ticket out of the slums.

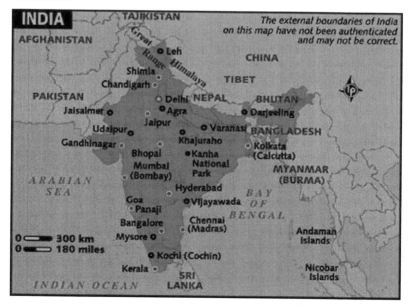

And that's when I realize that so many of us are here doing exactly the same thing: stopping at nothing. I'm bent on empowering children, reclaiming their lives. But, of course, I'm also, really, reclaiming my own.

The journey hasn't been easy. At each juncture, I was beset with fears and doubts, never given room for complacency or ease. Though scarred by mistakes and misgivings, the journey has been made and I can look back with consolation that not a single step has been wasted.

I like to think that I made the journey willingly.

—Rosalie Giffoniello

# Remembering Rosalie's 13th Birthday
**By Renee Drucker**

## June 7, 1959

Whenever anyone in the family had a birthday, we celebrated by going to some place special and having dinner out afterward. This time, it was Rosalie's birthday, her 13th. She chose to see the outdoor art show at Greenwich Village, then to Milano's restaurant.

It was a bright, sunny day and we were all dressed up for the occasion. Dave parked the car a few short blocks from our destination. Roy and Rosalie walked ahead of us; we were a few yards behind. Suddenly, we saw Rosalie stop, as she bent over a child who was lying on the sidewalk, kicking and screaming hysterically. From where we were, we could read Rosalie's lips saying, "Sh. Sh. Tell me what's the matter." She repeated it several times, but the child continued screaming and kicking. Without hesitation, Rosalie picked up the child who looked about four, cradled her in her arms, saying, "Everything is going to be all right, don't cry." By that time, Roy had stopped and was surveying the scene. I quickened my steps thinking I could help. Dave held me back, saying, "Don't. She's managing well on her own."

No sooner had he said that, a woman came flying out of the house in front of where we were standing, pulled the child from Rosalie's shoulder, and said, "If you pee your pants again, you'll be outside forever." And then dragged her up the steps.

The woman then turned, pointed to Rosalie, and shouted, "And you, you should learn to mind your own damn business." To which Rosalie countered, "You, you should be arrested for the way you treat this child!" The woman slammed the door.

We were all in a state of shock. Roy went up to Rosalie and said, "You did a *mitzvah*. G–d will bless you for it." Dave said, "My gut feeling is Rosalie will never change. She'll always think of others before herself."

I just stood there looking at her. Her blouse was soaked with urine; her skirt, soiled from the child's dirty shoes; her face, the look of disgust. But, to me, she never looked more beautiful.

And Dave's prophesy was right. She never did change.

*People say to me,*
*"Rosalie, this is India."*
*And I say to them,*
*"This is about children's lives."*
—Rosalie Giffoniello, co-founder
of Empower The Children

> *The important thing is this:*
> *to be able at any moment*
> *to sacrifice what we are*
> *for what we can become.*
> —Charles Du Bos, essayist

# Book Off the Shelf
### June 1999–September 1999

I'm lying on the bed in the downstairs guest room.

"What should I do this summer? What should I do this summer? What should I do this summer?"

My mind feels relaxed, neither urgent nor imploring.

"What should I do this summer? What should I do this summer?"

Suddenly, I hear a most curious sound: bumpity, bumpity, bump.

"What in the world is that?"

I get off the bed and walk cautiously into the living room. Lying on the floor is a slim book that had somehow fallen off a shelf from an upstairs bookcase and cascaded down *the entire flight of stairs* into the living room. I pick up the book and recognize it immediately: *Something Beautiful for God.*

> *I keep saying,*
> *"Calcutta is killing me."*
> *But I can't leave without a sign.*
> *A sign dropped me here,*
> *and only a sign will whisk me*
> *away.*
> —Rosalie Giffoniello, co-founder of Empower The Children

I open the book and remove a letter I had placed there six years earlier, in 1993—a letter from Mother Teresa inviting me to come to Calcutta to work with disabled children in one of her orphanages.

Without hesitation, I go to the phone and call my travel agent. "Peggy, book me a flight to Calcutta."

"Calcutta in the summer? Are you crazy?"

"Yes, Calcutta in the summer. No, I'm not crazy."

"Can't you go someplace that's fun?"

\* \* \*

Calcutta in the middle of summer means monsoon. The plane lands at 1:00 a.m. The pilot announces that the temperature is eighty-six degrees. The heat and humidity are oppressive, but I soon learn that the flooding is worse, blocking traffic and making walking almost impossible.

Monsoon season is the reign of the *rickshaw wallahs* who pull their heavy, hand-drawn, two-wheeled carriages over potholes and through thigh-high water rife with floating garbage and, very likely, sewage. The *rickshaw wallahs* get paid handsomely in monsoon season. As they pull, they sing.

"What have you done this time, Rosalie?" I ask myself as I climb into the taxi at the airport. When friends heard I was going to Calcutta, many of them said, "Rosalie, you're brave. You're really brave." "I'm not brave," I insisted. "I'm a coward. If I were brave I wouldn't be so scared."

I can't help but remember that, years ago, I didn't go to Calcutta because Art wouldn't go with me. And years after that, I had to seek courage from a healer before going to Tibet. But now I'm in Calcutta, in the middle of the night, sitting in a taxi that's taking me to a guesthouse on Sudder Street whose name and address I found in a ten-year-old guidebook.

Suddenly I change my mind. I say aloud, unconcerned if the taxi driver might hear or understand. "Yes, Rosalie, you're brave. You're really brave. It's time to acknowledge that."

The guesthouse is old and spooky. A single bulb hangs from the ceiling and casts eerie shadows on the water-stained walls. I can't sleep. I can't even lie down on the sheets because they look so dirty. I sit up all night and study the guide book. I'm not worried. There are many guesthouses on Sudder Street. I'll shift in the morning.

I doze and suddenly it's 8:00 a.m. I haven't unpacked, so it's easy to make a move. I pay the bill and step into the sunlight.

I'm immediately approached by a teenage boy. He's nicely dressed, clean, and looks well-fed—not like a beggar. "Do you need any help?" he asks in perfect English.

"I need a room."

"I'll help you."

We search up and down Sudder Street, and I settle on a small guesthouse that's newly opened so it's still unblemished by the peeling walls, water marks, and mold that the rainy season inflicts on buildings throughout India. I'm grateful for the help and offer the boy *baksheesh*.

"No, thank you. Just buy milk for my baby sister."

"How old is your sister?"

"Four years old."

We find a vendor selling milk powder. It's expensive, far more than the amount I have in mind. But, after all, the milk is for his sister—how sweet. After both the boy and vendor attempt to convince me to buy a large container, I buy a smaller size. I feel miserly, like I'm taking food out of the little girl's mouth. With these conflicting feelings, I start to walk toward my hotel. I turn briefly to say thanks just in time to see the boy selling the milk back to the vendor. There's no smirk on their faces; it's just business as usual.

Now I really wonder why I came to Calcutta! But I'm here, and I start to unpack. My summer address is the Gulistan Guest House, room 103. What I don't know then is that the Gulistan Guest House, room 103, will be my home for the next three years!

Clutching Mother Teresa's letter, I head for Mother House, the headquarters for the Missionaries of Charity and the final resting place of the modern saint so many revere. I'm not Catholic, but I'm moved by the sacredness of the place.

It's an imposing building of slate-grey concrete with four tiers of neatly stained brown wooden shutters, depicting the number of levels within. Located on a major thoroughfare, A.J.C. Bose Road, a small but prominent blue sign with white letters proclaims that I'm in the right place. My heart agrees.

Entering the front gate, I find a small waiting area with a few benches and a life-size statue of Mother Teresa holding a rosary in one hand, with her other hand turned palm downward as though touching the top of someone's head.

Around a corner is a surprisingly spacious courtyard with a statue of the Blessed Virgin and another of Mother Teresa kneeling and bending to cradle an infant in the hem of her habit. Looking up, I see that the courtyard is actually an open-air atrium.

The upper levels of the building feature wide balconies where a few nuns walk or sit. It's all very neat and clean, almost pristine. I see a sister looking down in my direction. She and the other sisters have a bird's-eye view of all visitors, as do the birds that fly through.

Over time, I would come to know that hundreds of nuns, clad in the easily recognizable white *saris* with blue-striped trim, live in Mother House. Most come from Indian villages to join the order, often to escape an otherwise tedious or abusive domestic family life. They may know little about Catholicism, but they know they're safe with the Missionaries of Charity.

> *If you can't feed a hundred children, then just feed one.*
> —Mother Teresa, founder of the Missionaries of Charity

The courtyard is filled with volunteers, people with physical characteristics that represent cultures from around the world. They speak to one another in their mother tongue or English. Through brief conversations, I learn that many have come because of religious convictions, others to offer service, and some just out of curiosity.

Mother Teresa is enshrined in a white marble tomb. A marble plaque on top is engraved with her name, date of birth (1910) and death (1997), the words, "our dearly beloved mother foundress of the Missionaries of Charity," and a line from the Gospel of St. John: "Love one another as I have loved you."

The marble and the tomb's large size, much larger than Mother Teresa's diminutive frame, strikes me as odd, given her well-promoted vow of poverty. I'm not a particularly cynical person, yet I can't help but wonder if Mother Teresa is "resting in peace," entombed in marble, while millions of people in Calcutta are living in wooden- and tin-shack poverty.

But I quickly push this thought out of my mind. I'm excited to be here and ready to help.

I meet Sister Nirmala Maria, a bespectacled Irish nun, who is in charge of volunteers. She greets me warmly. After asking a few questions regarding my background and interests, she suggests that I work at Daya Dan, an orphanage for disabled children. "I think you'll be happy there," she says in her lilting Irish brogue. "Sister Innocencia, from Africa, is very forward-thinking, and Sister Bosco is easy-going. Sister Maria Santa is quiet but loves the children with all her heart and soul," she adds, describing the sisters who serve at Daya Dan.

"How do I get there?"

"Come back tomorrow morning. We serve breakfast at 7:00. And you can join others who are going."

I'm not a morning person, but I relish the idea of meeting like-minded people and being part of their efforts to help the poor.

\* \* \*

I can barely sleep from excitement, so getting up at 6:00 a.m. proves to be easy. I take a *rickshaw* to Mother House and join other volunteers for a breakfast of tea, bread, and a banana. This will be my morning food for the next eight weeks.

I chat with people from all over the world and each has a story to tell. Some are travelers passing through Calcutta with a day or two to spare, others are planning to stay six months or whatever their visa will allow. Everyone wants to feel part of something bigger than themselves.

I join a few Japanese volunteers who think they know the way to Daya Dan, about five kilometers away. We walk to a nearby bus stop, but everyone seems a bit confused, and bus after bus passes us by. Suddenly, out of nowhere, I hear a voice ask, "Are you going to Daya Dan?" How would anyone know that? A middle-aged woman with a shaved head emerges from a shadow. Silently, I nod toward her, and she very confidently guides us by bus and *autorickshaw* to our destination.

The bus is old, rickety, dirty, and banged up. All the windows are open and there are no doors. It seldom stops, so people come and go on the fly. Fortunately, it never moves very fast. The *autorickshaw* is a three-wheeled, doorless vehicle with a small air-cooled engine. It's designed to carry five: three cramped in a tiny rear seat and two sitting in front on partial seats on either side of the driver, who steers with a handlebar.

Daya Dan is a tall building, maybe six levels, judging from the outside, located on a narrow alley off a secondary road. The entryway holds a steel accordion security gate and a double-paneled wooden door.

We step into a modest-size foyer with a high ceiling that makes it seem like a mini atrium. A winding stairway with multiple landings ascends to the upper levels.

The Japanese volunteers ascend the stairs. I, instead, follow our guide through a set of small, somewhat hidden doors that I could have missed if not for her lead and emerge into a surprisingly spacious downstairs area.

In the bedroom, there are thirteen steel crib-like beds, all the same design and size. Thirteen boys between the ages of three and ten are being dressed after their bath. My guide, Joan from Australia, introduces me to Sister Innocencia whose bright smile reflects in her warm, brown eyes and whose ebony skin starkly contrasts the white *sari* that envelopes her.

"This is Patrick," says Joan, pointing to a boy with such an infectious laugh that you almost don't notice his intestines hanging out the side of his body. "He was born that way, but we're taking him to Bombay for surgery next month. They're promising he'll be fine." Patrick, completely unaware of his upcoming surgery, gleefully accepts the attention being showered upon him. Impulsively, he grabs a large tub of talcum powder and tosses it at us. We are instantly covered with aromatic white dust. Joan and Sister Innocencia laugh good-naturedly as we brush ourselves off. I am not impressed!

After everyone is dressed, mats are unrolled, and the children are put on the floor. I've seen a lot of unusual children in my twenty-six years as a special educator in New Jersey public schools, but I notice something that strikes me as very odd: all the kids are shaking their hands in front of their faces, a "self-stimulation behavior" typical of autistic children. Is it possible that all these kids are autistic?

The volunteers are told to play with the kids, but there aren't any toys, so each volunteer approaches the task in his or her own way. One man throws the kids up in the air, which, if a child has a seizure disorder, could prove dangerous. A young woman rocks an eight-year-old as if he were an infant. An older man allows a ten-year-old to climb onto his back. The child slowly entwines himself around the volunteer like a vine. The volunteer is sweating and uncomfortable but doesn't try to disentangle the boy.

I don't do anything but remain a silent observer.

At lunchtime, volunteers feed the children. Those who don't want to eat are force-fed. The whole thing is very disconcerting. Finally—this doesn't take very long—I can't hold myself back. I ask Sister Innocencia, "Why don't these boys feed themselves?"

"Some of them are blind."

"If they're blind, that means there's something wrong with their eyes, not their hands."

Sister gives me a very long look, and I think, "Oh, God, I've gone too far. On my very first day at Daya Dan, I've alienated the nun in charge of the downstairs children."

"What do you do at home?" she asks.

"I'm a learning consultant and speech teacher."

"How long will you stay in Calcutta?"

"Eight weeks."

Sister Innocencia is African. In Nairobi, she received a good education, drove a car, experienced freedom. She strikes me as a happy person, ready to embrace new ideas, and willing to do anything for the children. Smiling that sunshine of a smile I will see often in the next two months, she declares, "We have a lot of work to do."

* * *

The next day, I observe the boys more carefully, determined to help them as much as possible in the coming weeks. The way the boys eat really bothers me. They are totally passive. Even though some are ten years old, they sit at a table in the dining area with bibs around their necks and open their mouths like baby birds waiting to receive a worm from their mothers. They can't control the amount of food that the volunteers spoon into their mouths or the speed at which they put it in.

And then, as I saw yesterday, there are the boys who don't want to eat. Because they don't speak, we can't ask them why they don't want to eat. But they let us know by screaming and kicking and turning their heads from side to side to avoid the food.

These children are held down, some in chairs and some on the floor. Their heads are forced back, their mouths are forced open, and the food is shoveled in. Of course, pulling their heads back closes off their esophagi, so the food is blocked from going down. As if it were

> *The proverb warns that, "You should not bite the hand that feeds you." But maybe you should if it prevents you from feeding yourself.*
> —Thomas Szasz, psychiatrist, academician

going to help, the volunteers pour water into the kids' mouths, which then gurgles back up in giant bubbles, like they're gargling.

I'm even more alarmed than I was the day before. Someday, somebody is going to choke. "Sister, please," I say in an exasperated tone. "We must teach these boys to feed themselves. They must become independent."

"What do you suggest?"

"I suggest spoons. They're easy to use. Get a bunch of spoons, different sizes, and let's see who can manage."

Of course, I'm not blind to the fact that Indians eat with their hands, but, as an American, I can only teach what I know.

Sister Innocencia buys the spoons. We distribute them to the volunteers who place the spoons in the children's hands and then wrap their hands around the children's hands. We chant in unison, "Scoop the food, bring it up, put it in your mouth. Scoop, up, in. Scoop, up, in." We say the words as we go through the movements so the boys have auditory cues. After days of helping them, we let them hold the spoons to see what they will do. They drop the spoons. We put the spoons back into their hands, and again they drop them.

"I think we need a way to temporarily attach the spoons to their hands." I suggest. "What can we use?"

"Tape. We will tape the spoons to their hands."

"We'll need a lot of tape, but it's worth a try."

We get rolls and rolls of tape from a local shop and tediously tape a spoon to each boy's hand. It must be uncomfortable because the boys shake the spoons madly, trying to dislodge them.

"What else?" I ask.

"String?"

"Okay, let's try."

This isn't easy. We can't tie the string too tightly or it'll cut the skin. And if it's loose, it's too unstable. So, string isn't the answer.

"Sister, we need something else, something quick and easy and not consumable. We can't keep buying tape and string every day."

"Velcro. Velcro opens and closes easily. It can be used again and again and should be comfortable."

So we give the local carpenter spoons and Velcro. He takes a block of wood, makes a slit, inserts the handle of the spoon into it and attaches the Velcro. The design enables the boys to hold the block of wood rather than the spoon, and the Velcro, wrapped around their hands, prevents them from dropping it. It works. Most of the boys are eating independently. I feel much better. Now what?

\* \* \*

The next day, I say, "Sister Innocencia, I think we should teach these boys to walk."

"Good idea. Can you do that?"

"Sure. Is there any physical therapy equipment here?"

"No."

"What about parallel bars?"

"No."

"What about walkers?"

"No."

"Canes?"

"No."

*"Oy vey!"*

*"Oy vey?"*

"Never mind."

"How about bamboo?" she suggests. "There is plenty of bamboo in Calcutta. We can take long pieces and attach them to the opposite ends of the walls. The boys can walk across the room."

"Sister, you're a genius." So the carpenter constructs makeshift parallel bars across the room. The only thing we hadn't considered is that bamboo is flexible, very flexible, so when you apply pressure, it bends.

> *It is always the simple that produces the miraculous.*
> —Amelia Barr, novelist

"Not quite as stable as I'd hoped," I say doubtfully.

But Sister Innocencia, always positive, says, "Let us try. Who shall go first?"

"Someone easy."

"How about Peter? He is even-tempered."

Well, even-tempered Peter is screaming his head off as the bamboo poles shake like pudding. He refuses to walk. They all refuse to walk.

"We need an incentive at the beginning and a reward at the end. Everyone responds to rewards. Sister, do you have any toys?"

"No."

"Any sweets?"

"No."

"What do you have?"

"Water."

"Water?"

"Yes, water. It is monsoon season, and hot, and the boys are thirsty."

So we give Peter a teaspoon of water at the start and another teaspoon of water at the end. Seeing that this "journey" is possible—coupled with the reward—the other boys are also willing to try. Up and back they go, their legs as wobbly as the bamboo poles.

"Sister," I say, extending my hand for a handshake, not sure if she knows how to high five, "It's a pleasure to know a genius."

After a while, the boys no longer need the parallel bars but walk around Daya Dan independently. Instead of lying on mats all day, bored, they discover their curiosity and begin to explore. And, eventually, the autistic-like self-stimulation disappears.

\* \* \*

I've been at Daya Dan only three weeks and already many of the boys are feeding themselves and walking. What about the next five weeks? Can I accomplish anything else before I go home? I'm feeling insecure. The sisters now have a high expectation of me, and I don't know if I can meet it. But I'm determined to try.

"Sister Innocencia, there's a basic tenet in special education that I think isn't being applied at Daya Dan."

"What is that?"

"Well, you do different activities in different places with things that have different functions."

"It sounds complicated."

"No, actually, it's simple. You eat at the dining room table and you use a spoon. You study in the classroom and you use a pencil. You go to potty in the bathroom and you use the toilet."

"That does make sense."

"But here everything is done in the dining room, except, of course, the potty part."

"When the boys have accidents, then even the potty part is done in the dining room," Sister says with a smile.

"True."

"So what do you suggest?"

"Let's make a classroom and have lessons there. I'll donate chairs that have a tray and could serve as desks. Then, whenever the boys go into the classroom and sit in the chairs, they'll know it's school time."

"I like that."

We get into the ambulance, which is nothing more than an empty van—no emergency personnel, no equipment, no oxygen, not even a first aid kit. But it does have a little siren on top. The driver is about twenty-five, with no medical experience.

All of that doesn't seem to matter. We have a clear idea of what we want—oversized highchairs. For the eight-, nine-, and ten-year-olds, *very* oversized highchairs.

We go from shop to shop, but, of course, highchairs are for small children. It's hot and humid, so the ambulance windows are down. Pollution blows into our faces, our hair, our clothes. The first time I took a shower in Calcutta, I was puzzled by black liquid running down my body. I thought, somehow, the dye was running out of my hair, and it took me a few minutes to figure out that it was pollution.

"Sister, this shopping is exhausting."

"It is monsoon season."

"Does that mean it isn't exhausting the rest of the year?"

"It is exhausting all the time."

"Then I should be grateful I won't be here after August?"

"You should be grateful."

We're still driving and looking. We try baby shops, toy shops, furniture shops, hobby shops, rental shops. But no luck.

"I'm finished," I tell Sister. "I can't do another thing. Maybe we should give up."

"Let us try one more shop, a medical shop. Maybe they have an idea."

So we go to a medical shop, which is well equipped with wheelchairs, walkers, canes, oxygen tanks, and other apparatuses, all well organized and neatly arranged.

"What is your good name?" asks the salesman.

"Rosalie," I reply.

"How can I help you?"

"I have a very specific request."

I don't see any oversized highchairs, so I describe what we're looking for.

He has a simple suggestion: have a carpenter make them. "I can arrange everything," he says. "I will do my level best."

"There should be a vertical peg between the boys' legs, so they don't slip forward. And a ledge for their feet, so their legs don't dangle. That will improve their posture," I suggest.

"I understand completely," he assures us. "My carpenter will make them exactly as you have described."

"When will they be ready?"

"On Saturday."

"Saturday? How is that possible? Eight chairs with trays and pegs and ledges?"

"Don't worry, Madame, we will have the chairs ready by Saturday. You have my word."

On Saturday, we go to the medical shop to pick up the chairs.

"Sorry, Madame, they aren't ready," the shopkeeper says.

"When will they be ready?"

"On Wednesday."

"Are you sure?"

"One hundred percent sure. It is our duty."

We return on Wednesday, and the chairs aren't ready. "In due course of time—isn't that what they say in India?" I ask Sister Innocencia in frustration.

I'm getting worried. I'm leaving in a month and want to have the classroom prepared for the volunteer teacher who will follow me. Unfortunately, it's looking less and less likely. Back again to the shop on Saturday and we receive yet another assurance.

"The shopkeeper must think we're awfully gullible," I whisper sarcastically. "Why would we believe him when he says the chairs will be finished next Wednesday?"

> *Hasten slowly*
> *and you shall soon arrive.*
> —Milarepa, yogi, poet

But, sure enough, they are.

Back at Daya Dan, the handyman takes a great interest in the chairs. "I think I should paint them," he recommends.

"Why?" I ask.

"They will look nicer."

"I think they look all right. They're functional, not for display."

"They can be washed more easily if they are painted."

"The seats and trays are Formica. They can be washed easily."

"But the wooden parts," he persists. "They will get ruined."

"It's a school chair. It'll soon be covered with stains from markers, crayons, and glue. Then it'll look authentic."

"But the pee. You know that some of the boys are not yet toilet trained. What about the pee?"

"Yes, the pee. There's always the pee to consider," I concede reluctantly.

The handyman paints the chairs sky blue, and I'm really pleased. The classroom looks very cheerful, and I congratulate him. "Is there anything else I could do, Madame?"

"Not at the moment. Thank you."

The kids and volunteers are ready for the first day of school. We've hung up vegetable, fruit, and animal charts and a few blackboards. I distribute lessons, individually tailored to each child. The volunteers patiently guide the children as best they can, and, despite a couple of mishaps, the atmosphere is one of productivity and learning. I have to admit I'm *kvelling*. After about an hour, we end with a song and everyone seems happy. "That wasn't so hard," I tell myself. "After waiting so long for the chairs, it was worth it."

"Time to go now," I announce. "Everyone get out of the chair and go to the dining room. It's almost time for lunch."

Volunteers help the children out of their chairs, but suddenly there's a great clamor. Some kids are screeching, others crying, a few laughing, but all share one thing: their backs are covered with blue paint. "Of course," I moan. "Why didn't I realize it? It's the monsoon season and the paint won't dry for months!"

"Where's the paint remover? Where's the solvent? What should we do?" All the volunteers are shouting at me.

"I don't know."

"But you have to tell us. You're the teacher."

"Yes," I agree weakly. "I'm the teacher. But I'm not a carpenter. I'm not a handyman. I'm not a painter."

\* \* \*

Yes, *I am* a teacher, I remind myself.

And as I watch these children come to life with new skills—basic skills of walking, feeding themselves, exploring their environment—I think about the decision on that first day to stay with Joan on the ground floor. I could have followed the Japanese volunteers upstairs. But the children upstairs are severely disabled, while, downstairs, I see kids who have greater potential. Their progress motivates me to do more. Joan may have been my guide on that first day, but my teacher's heart is guiding me now.

Sister Innocencia suggests, "Now that the boys eat so nicely, we can take them to a restaurant."

One Japanese volunteer points to Paul and says, "We cannot take him to a restaurant—bad customer." He's referring, of course, to the pee.

"Paul is the ultimate pee-er," I put forward one afternoon to the other volunteers as we eat lunch together. "He was the first to use the new trampoline, and he duly christened it. He understands his duty!"

"Paul may be dutiful, but Patrick is the ultimate gentleman," interjects Sissel, a volunteer from Norway. "He was standing in front of the volunteer room and realized he had to pee. Instead of peeing into the room, he politely moved his pecker to the side and peed sideways. Of course, he hit Sahdev standing next to him, but he missed the volunteers. He has his priorities!"

After Sissel finishes, I continue with my story. "I wanted Paul to show off for Sister Innocencia after he learned to undress himself without help so, after lunch, I told him to remove his clothes for his nap, like the boys always do. He complied immediately and then peed all over the place."

This conversation happens often. All the volunteers like to tell pee stories. This makes no sense, of course. The pee stories aren't as gross as poop stories, but, nonetheless, you'd think we'd find more erudite topics to discuss.

Though spoken in jest, this preoccupation with bodily functions illustrates an underlying problem. The boys, even the older ones, aren't toilet trained, and they wear no diapers, only shorts. A couple of times each day, the boys are made to sit on plastic potties that are much too small for them. The bigger boys so overhang the potties that they practically sit on the floor. They look around with no idea as to why they are forced to sit there and, of course, seldom do they pee or poop in the potty.

> *Your present circumstances don't determine where you go; they merely determine where you start.*
> —Nido Qubein, businessman, motivational speaker

Eventually, they do pee or poop—but always after the volunteers have bathed and dressed them. Their shorts are then immediately removed, and the boys are bathed and given yet another clean change of clothing. They might be bathed three, four, five times a day. You can imagine how good a bath feels during the summer season when it's hot and humid—it's like a reward for *not* being toilet trained. So, they receive a lot of positive reinforcement for behavior we're trying to eradicate.

I tell Sister Innocencia, "If you spent as much time teaching these kids as you do bathing them, they'd all be brilliant scholars."

Sister Innocencia has decided to bring the five blind boys to the clinic to have their eyes examined, and I agree to come along to help. These children need a lot of assistance. They can't walk independently. Most of them aren't toilet trained and need to be diapered when out in public. And their level of cooperation is limited because they don't understand what's happening.

The ambulance isn't available, so we pile into two taxis with volunteers holding kids on their laps. It's very hot and humid in the taxi. The kids are blanketing us, and, I have to admit, I'm worried about the other volunteers. I've worked with disabled children my entire life and have a special feeling toward them, but Calcutta, especially in the monsoon season, stretches everyone's endurance.

We arrive at the facility, a large building, modern by Calcutta standards, with many small examination rooms.

"Sister Innocencia, the kids are very well-behaved," I comment as we sit in the spacious waiting room.

"Yes, they are," she says with some degree of pride. Truth be told, the kids are more passive than cooperative, sitting like rag dolls on the volunteers' laps. We wait a long time for clinic staff to appear, but they don't. The room is filling up. Twenty people. Thirty people. Fifty people. The seats are occupied. Some people are standing along the walls.

Finally, a staff person appears behind a counter, and then everything happens. From every corner of the room, there's a dash to the counter to obtain a necessary form. There's no order whatsoever, just pushing and shoving and shouting. I don't get it. Wouldn't it be more efficient to line up and wait patiently for the form? But that isn't what happens. No, it's a scramble, and we join in. We finally get a form for each child and fill it out. Then we're given a queue number.

And we wait again. Now the children are getting hungry and restless, and their diapers are dirty. But no one comes to check on us or assist us. We wait four hours until our number is called. We're led into a small room—utilitarian and empty except for a few chairs, with no pictures or any aesthetics on the wall—and wait again. But at least we're out of the waiting room.

Then we're moved again. This room is even smaller but equally bare. Because there's no equipment, I assume this is the room where the doctor will take the case histories. No, it's where an aide takes the case histories. There's no table, so he writes on his lap.

We're moved to a fourth room and wait more.

The doctor finally appears and our sigh of relief is palpable. He is dressed in a Western-style shirt and trousers, not covered by a lab coat. "Hello," he says. "Who are these children?"

"They are orphans living at Daya Dan Orphanage," replies Sister Innocencia.

"Can you tell me about them?"

"They cannot see."

"Did they have a normal birth?"

"I do not know. They came to us after they were born."

"Did the mothers have prenatal care?"

"We do not know who the mothers are. Most of the children were abandoned."

"What about after their birth? Did they thrive or were they sickly?"

"They were at Shishu Bhavan, an orphanage for newborns and younger disabled children, so I cannot answer that question."

"Do they have normal intelligence?"

Sister Innocencia looks at me.

"It's possible, but we can't tell," I reply. "Their intelligence might be masked by lack of stimulation."

"Oh, I see."

Like the other rooms we've been in, this one is also barely furnished. There's no examination table, no optical examination equipment, only a couple of chairs. The doctor has a small pen flashlight in his breast pocket. He removes it and looks into each child's eyes. "They are blind," he says.

"Yes, we know they are blind. That is why we brought them here. We want to know what can be done for them," replies Sister Innocencia.

"Take them home and give them love and attention for the rest of their lives. There is no hope."

We're back in the taxis, and Sister and I aren't saying anything. I have no idea what she's thinking, but my thoughts aren't particularly charitable. Then the inevitable happens: Sahdev vomits all over a Japanese volunteer sitting next to him. The volunteer is outwardly calm, but I can sense that he is inwardly repulsed, which is understandable. After all, he doesn't know Sahdev. Even a father covered with his own son's vomit might feel repulsed.

We stop the taxi, and everyone jumps out. I pour my bottle of water all over the volunteer and wipe him down as best I can. When the bottle is empty, we get back into the taxi.

The volunteer, completely depleted, asks weakly, "Do you do this every day?"

"Not every day," replies Sister Innocencia, "but next week, we will go to the neurologist and then the audiologist and finally the speech therapist."

She's not easily defeated, encouraged by the boys' progress so far and hopeful for even greater potential than we've been able to discern. Good for her.

> *For a gallant spirit there can never be defeat.*
> —Wallis Simpson, Duchess of Windsor

\* \* \*

The ambulance is available to take children to the neurologist. So a dozen of us—seven children, four nuns, and I—pile into a vehicle that's designed for seven. Due to heavy rain, we can't roll the windows down, and we sit like lobsters boiling in a pot. The roads are flooded, and traffic is crawling. The children, unaccustomed to being outside the orphanage, show no interest in the sights and sounds of Calcutta. They're hot and cranky and bored, increasingly restless, and we're almost passing out from the heat and humidity.

The driver, believing that a timely arrival is more important than a safe arrival, decides to remedy the situation by driving recklessly. This is considered a viable solution? He drives over a small grassy divider to the wrong side of the road, directly into oncoming traffic.

"*Aste, aste,*" I shout, using one of the few Bengali words I know. "Slowly, slowly," I entreat. The driver hears me but doesn't respond.

"Sister Innocencia, tell the driver that he's on the wrong side of the road," I cry.

She tells him, and the driver nods. "He knows," she replies.

"Sister, please tell him Rosalie doesn't want to die in Calcutta."

She doesn't tell him. Instead, the nuns take out their rosary beads and start to pray aloud.

Talk about life in the absurd. Here I am, a Jewish girl from Brooklyn, sitting in an ambulance in Calcutta with seven Hindu kids, a crazy Hindu driver, and four Catholic nuns saying Hail Marys.

In an effort to appease me, the driver puts on the siren, imagining that its tiny wail, almost inaudible in the cacophony of taxis and cars *horning*, will make the oncoming cars part like the Red Sea. To his apparent disbelief, the cars don't part. With a sudden jerk, he steers the ambulance onto the sidewalk. The pedestrians there don't exactly part but scatter in all directions as the ambulance screeches to a halt.

Now we're sitting on the sidewalk on the opposite side of the road, facing the opposing traffic. Undaunted, the driver puts the ambulance back on the road again and maneuvers it so that other vehicles have to stop or steer past as he turns it around. But now we're going away from the hospital. At some point, the driver jumps the divider, turns the ambulance around, and heads in the right direction.

This whole scenario is an assault to my sensibilities. Wouldn't it be easier and quicker to just stay in your lane and follow the traffic rather than wasting time with all these reckless maneuvers? But no one is asking my opinion.

We finally arrive, senseless and frazzled, only to discover that the hospital, a full-service facility, is as flooded as the streets. The water in the lobby is ankle deep. The nuns walk directly toward the elevators. I'm aghast, but no one else is the least bit bothered. "Wait," I protest. "Water and electricity don't go together. The children could get electrocuted!" Ultimately, I win this debate, but that means carrying the six children who can't climb on their own up three flights of stairs. Many people pass us on the stairs, but no one offers to help.

When we reach the third floor, we collapse in the chairs outside the neurologist's chamber to wait our turn. But our turn will never come on this day. There, ominously, a sign hanging outside the neurologist's office clearly states: "The neurologist sees patients on Monday, Wednesday, Friday." Today is Tuesday.

"Sister, did you call to make an appointment?" I ask.

"No," she replies. "Next time I will know better."

* * *

Back at Daya Dan, I ask the ambulance driver about his t-shirt, which has a full-color artistic rendering of Aung San Suu Kyi and the words:

FEAR IS A HABIT<br>
I AM NOT AFRAID<br>
AUNG SAN SUU KYI<br>
1991 NOBEL PRIZE WINNER

Aung San Suu Kyi is a woman I admire. She was a brave, successful politician in Burma in 1990 and chairperson of the National League of Democracy party when it won a majority of Parliamentary seats in a general election. But she was not allowed to serve because the controlling military junta placed her under house arrest. This led to her winning the Nobel Peace Prize a year later. *

"What do you know about Aung San Suu Kyi?" I ask the driver.

He doesn't speak English, so someone translates that he knows nothing of her.

"Where did he get the shirt?"

"Someone gave it to him."

To him, it's just a shirt. I want the shirt.

He wants a radio so he can listen to music while he drives. "It calms my nerves," he tells the translator.

I don't have a radio but I do have a cassette player that I rarely use.

We swap. He's delighted. I'm delighted. I sleep in the t-shirt each night to give me courage for the next day.

*\* Aung San Suu Kyi remained under house arrest until November 13, 2010, after which she successfully re-entered politics and assumed a governmental leadership role in Myanmar.*

I'm feeling panicky. My time in Calcutta is drawing to a close, and there's so much left to do. I want to make more of a difference. But how?

I lie on my bed at the Gulistan at night and ask, "So how am I holding up?" The truth of the matter is: Not very well. Everybody's expectations are all so high, and I feel unequal to the task. Most of the time I feel isolated: No one to turn to, no one to complain to, no one to consult with. I feel helpless. That's really the word—so completely helpless to fulfill the goals that I had set for myself this summer.

> *When you decide to follow a certain path, you should follow it to the end and not be diverted from it for personal reasons.*
>
> —Aung San Suu Kyi, politician, Nobel Peace Laureate

But, in spite of my helplessness, I do not have a feeling of hopelessness. Every morning when I get up and leave for the orphanage, I have renewed hope, which energizes me and supports my motivation.

At Daya Dan, we have only two choices: to laugh or cry. When I'm with Sr. Innocencia, we laugh, but when I'm alone, I cry. I cry an ocean of tears. The only time I ever cried so much was when I got my divorce. I cried the Atlantic Ocean then, and I cry the Pacific Ocean now. Or maybe it's the Indian Ocean.

Why? Because there is nothing here in terms of an educational program except potential—the potential of minds that have never been stimulated, their qualities hidden from the world. So, what am I to do? What do I do about helping these children discover their hidden qualities?

I won't be here for the rescheduled neurological evaluations, but I could be here for the speech and hearing assessments. This possibility buoys my spirits. Speech therapy is my background, and I'm eager to meet Indians in my field. Maybe through them I can do more.

Sr. Innocencia sets an appointment at a new speech and hearing institute in Calcutta. It's a university, housed in a contemporary building where young, enthusiastic students are studying.

We warn the evaluators that our children are very complex cases. They had been abandoned, are socially isolated, receive little stimulation, and haven't developed speech or self-help skills. The trainees work in teams and say they are undaunted by the challenge. They escort the children away and leave Sister Innocencia and me to sit and chat with the director, a middle-aged man who has the chubby physique of someone who spends most of his day sitting at a desk, talking with parents and writing reports.

"This university has thirty speech therapists and audiologists in training," he says philosophically. "They are all Indian. And do you know what all these trainees are going to do when they have completed their studies? They will go to America. That is why there are no services available for disabled children living in Calcutta."

Knowing the evaluations will take time, he ultimately excuses himself, leaving Sister and I on our own. We wander around a bit and then sit quietly and wait. Finally, at the end of four hours, the trainees present their findings to the director, and he calls us back into his office to pass on the results.

"So please tell us, what is the diagnosis and what is the prognosis?" Sister Innocencia asks expectantly.

The director sits back in his chair, stares at the ceiling, and thinks for a long time, obviously choosing his words carefully.

"Very unique cases," he replies.

We try to elicit more information. "What's the prognosis? What's the treatment? What should we do?"

But that's all he has to say. "Very unique cases."

Sister and I laugh over the diagnosis all the way back to the orphanage. Once there, she hangs up a blank poster board and attaches each child's picture. On the bottom she writes, "We are very special."

I'm heart-broken. I have to leave. When I confirm my flight with Air India, I'm crying on the phone. I'm sure the person at the other end thinks I'm flying home for a funeral.

I hope my last day will be memorable, but why should it be? I've been at the orphanage only eight short weeks. Compared to others who come for months and do so much more, I'm no one special.

But Sister Innocencia gives me unexpected news. "The day before you leave is Mother Teresa's birthday and Daya Dan's first anniversary."

"That's reason to celebrate," I agree, secretly congratulating myself on my good luck.

"What shall we do that is special?" she asks. "The boys can do a lot more now, as compared to two months ago."

"Can we have a small performance? The boys could play instruments. You know, a violin, baby grand piano," I add, smiling at the audacity of this grandiose thought.

"They could shake tambourines, bang drums, and ring bells," replies Sister Innocencia undaunted.

"But we need background music. Any suggestions?"

"Of course. It must be 'The Sound of Music,'" she says. "My favorite."

I have to smile because, on my very first day at Daya Dan, I repeatedly heard "Bridge Over Troubled Water" being played on a small tape recorder. No doubt a volunteer at the orphanage that day was a fan of Simon and Garfunkel. Music in one form or another has always been present at the orphanage, but, interestingly, it's always Western music, never Indian music.

On the day of the performance, about thirty of the nuns from Mother House stream into Daya Dan. With their white *saris*, trimmed with blue, they all look alike and appear to have sacrificed their personal identity to the dictates of the order. The boys are wearing their Sunday best even though it's Friday.

We don't want the boys to become tired or restless, and we hope to start on time. But Sister Nirmala is late, so we have no choice but to wait.

Sister Nirmala is Mother Teresa's successor but is similar to the foundress in only one way: they're both tiny. Unfortunately, Sister Nirmala doesn't possess the superior stage presence of her predecessor, made evident in a famous photo of Princess Diana holding hands with the modern saint. The image of Diana towering like a giant over the diminutive sister has the opposite effect of what you might expect; it gives Mother Teresa a kind of vicarious largeness that supports the fact that she was feared as well as loved.

Finally, Sister Nirmala arrives. The children are sitting in their new blue chairs. The volunteers are squatting behind them, holding onto their elbows, ready to assist them in an unobtrusive way. The recording of "The Sound of Music" plays. The boys bang drums, shake tambourines, and squeal delightedly. And in ten minutes, the performance is finished. But the *bigger* performance is yet to come.

The children are assisted out of their chairs but then walk, unaided, to the dining room. They sit at the table and eat independently, scooping food with their Velcro-adapted spoons.

*Nothing is impossible; the word itself says, "I'm possible!"*
—Audrey Hepburn, actress, humanitarian

The nuns are amazed. Sister Nirmala spontaneously sits next to Paul who, though blind, eats very neatly, using the spoon to carefully scrape away any food left around his mouth—and he doesn't pee. Sister Nirmala, with ever-erect posture and a wizened face, smiles broadly, and someone snaps a photo.

"That picture will hang on our wall," Sister Innocencia says, "right here in the dining room. I will never forget this day."

"I will try to forget this day," I whisper to myself. "Otherwise, I'll never be able to leave Calcutta."

"It wasn't just the book falling off the shelf that brought me to Calcutta," I tell the sleepy man who's sitting next to me in the airplane that's carrying us from Calcutta to New Jersey. "It was a whole lifetime of events, maybe even former lifetimes."

My fellow passenger is Japanese and probably speaks limited English, but, ever polite, he smiles in agreement. Of course, he has no idea what I'm talking about. How can he? I'm struggling to make sense of it myself.

"Where does a life begin?" I ask him. "For some, it begins at birth. For others, it's a life-changing event or a life-threatening illness." I'm aware that he's falling asleep, but I continue. "For me, I'd have to say, it all began when Russia invaded Afghanistan."

# Buddhism Finds Us
## 1980–1984

It's 1980. Art and I have been married five years. We're both special educators in New Jersey public schools. Art's specialty is learning disabilities, and I'm certified in speech therapy and learning disabilities. We love to travel, so we leave at the end of each school year and don't come back until Labor Day weekend, just in time for the first day of fall classes.

Art's afraid to fly, so we've booked passage on a Russian ocean liner headed for Southampton, England. With an entire summer ahead of us, we don't feel like the five days on board a ship will be wasted. On the contrary, we look forward to the leisurely crossing, a slow prelude to sightseeing and hiking through England, a trip meant to satisfy our restless natures.

To our active imaginations, a Russian boat seems more exotic than taking the *Queen Elizabeth 2,* which conjures up images of formal dining rooms, a captain's table, and the need for fancy clothes. Everything we plan to take is stuffed into two backpacks with our hiking boots, too bulky to pack, permanently on our feet.

So what put the *kibosh* on our plans? Russia invades Afghanistan.

The United States orders an immediate embargo. And the Russian ocean liner is prevented from docking in New York harbor.

We're disappointed, but not deterred. We decide, instead, to explore Alaska, which we manage to reach quite cleverly, without ever boarding a plane: a bus to Montreal, a train across Canada, a bus to Seattle, and then a ferry through Alaska's Inside Passage. Art's good at arranging these kinds of things. He studies the guidebooks, finds the rooms, and carries the money. He's resourceful, adventurous, and brave. And I consider myself lucky to be his appendage on these trips, a silent partner in the planning, a hanger-on during the journey.

Our tiny stateroom on the train seems akin to the tiny stateroom we would have had on the Russian ocean liner, now at sea somewhere off the coast of New York. But Alaska turns out to be very expensive, and we soon grow tired of paying top dollar for fish that's caught locally. So, when an elderly couple spontaneously offers us a lift in their VW van to San Francisco, we readily agree. We hadn't planned on going to California, but ask very few questions.

I had not yet learned to ask introspective questions like "How is it that this opportunity has manifested itself?" Later, I would ask that question again and again and again, but only when enough *coincidences*—like the book falling off the shelf—had nudged me to Calcutta and I could no longer ignore them.

On our first day in San Fran, we wander into a bakery that's almost empty except for a middle-aged woman dressed in black, sitting alone. Art and I have a choice of tables. We

> ***All journeys have secret destinations of which the traveler is unaware.***
> —Martin Buber, philosopher

could easily leave her alone. Yet, I feel oddly drawn to this woman. I approach her and the words, "May we sit with you?" just pour out of my mouth.

"I'm waiting for a friend, but until she comes … please."

Her friend never appears, and we sit with this woman, Lola, for hours.

She owns a fine arts gallery in Chinatown, and, after we visit there, she invites us to her apartment. She gives us books and tells us about the Zen Center in the heart of San Francisco.

Art and I are capable of introspection and analysis, but this is our summer vacation, and our itinerary doesn't come with a syllabus. So, when it comes to travel, we're open to new experiences, not chained down by fears or suspicions. We just think, "How sweet, someone's being friendly to us on our very first day in San Francisco." Months later, a Buddhist monk would matter-of-factly tell us, "Lola was your guide. She was preparing you for your spiritual journey." But, of course, we don't know it at the time.

Based on Lola's recommendation, we visit the Zen Center. There, we learn of Rashi Gempil Ling, a Tibetan Buddhist monastery located in a small community called Freewood Acres in Howell, New Jersey. This is only a few miles from one of my schools! We write down the address.

But back in New Jersey, we discover that it isn't easy to contact Rashi Gempil Ling. Art sends a letter to the monastery, but it comes back with no forwarding address. So we take a ride. I think I know this area well, but entering Freewood Acres feels like visiting a foreign country.

The people here are Kalmyks, Buddhists of Mongolian origin, who came from their homeland in the 1950s. Kalmykia, located in Eastern Europe on the northern edge of the Caspian Sea, was once part of the Soviet Union. During World War II, the Kalmyks sought independence by aligning with Germany. But when Germany was defeated, they feared reprisals and fled to West Germany. There, they became political refugees, living for six years in displaced persons camps. Then, after legal wrangling, the first Kalmyks arrived in the U.S., settling in Philadelphia and in Freewood Acres.

Few people speak English here. The population is older, the younger generation having left long ago for lucrative jobs elsewhere. Those who remain are dressed in old-fashioned clothing and, with their round, ruddy faces and kindly expressions, look a lot like smiling Buddhas.

"Rashi Gempil Ling. Rashi Gempil Ling," we entreat and receive encouraging nods as red, chapped fingers point us in what we hope is the right direction.

After many wrong turns, we find a small driveway and happen upon a tiny temple in a beautiful garden. Nearby is a small house. We tentatively step into the temple and see statues of Buddha of all sizes and styles tucked into every corner, the Wheel of Life and various deities painted on silk *thangkas*, meditation cushions on the floor, Tibetan sacred books wrapped in cloth and stored flat on shelves, drums, cymbals, and other Tibetan instruments. But a swastika on the teacher's throne? I'm shocked! Why? Although I find it offensive and confusing, I'm willing to wait for an explanation.

In the garden is a Tibetan monk, head shaved, wrapped in red robes, sitting on a bench with an American man. They're intently examining a text. With my gregarious nature too untamed to control, I approach the monk and launch into a detailed explanation of how we were supposed to go to England but Russia invaded Afghanistan, so we went instead to Alaska and ended up in San Francisco and found the Zen temple through Lola, that we want to study Tibetan Buddhism, how difficult it was to find Rashi Gempil Ling, and now at last we're here. The American fellow, Michael, who would later become a monk and also the first foreigner to earn the status of *Geshe*, a degree awarded to Tibetan Buddhist monks that's equivalent to a PhD in the Western world, laughs heartily.

"That's a bit off-putting!" I think.

Michael points to the monk, who has been smiling sweetly throughout my regurgitation, and says good-naturedly, "Lotar doesn't speak English."

I glance down at what I thought was their Buddhist text and see it's an alphabet book. Lotar is learning to read and is up to the letter F.

"What a clumsy introduction to Buddhism," I think, but no one seems to mind.

Michael invites us to attend "the rookie class" on Wednesday evenings. "There are many Westerners and a few Kalmyks in that class," he says.

Before we leave, we notice an older monk rolling a ball to a dog who brings it back to him. "He's our abbot, Geshe Tharchin," Michael says. "He'll be your teacher."

As luck would have it, the first class we are to attend in September 1980 is cancelled—in favor of an incredible opportunity. Ling Rinpoche, the Dalai Lama's senior tutor, is visiting Rashi Gempil Ling. We're stunned by the hoopla until we realize that people wait a lifetime to meet this renowned man whose title, *Rinpoche,* means "incarnate lama." And we're being presented with this opportunity even before we've attended our first Buddhist class!

We remove our shoes and step inside the temple. The deities, including fierce demons, stare at us from the *thangkas.* But, again, my confused Western mind is most shocked by what appears to be the swastika draped over the throne. It gives me quite a start! In all the excitement, there's no one free to explain, and only later would I learn that this stylistic geometric form is actually an ancient religious symbol that originated in India from the Sanskrit words "to be good." For thousands of years, it was used by Hindus, Buddhists, Jains, and many cultures from the Orient to Southern Europe to represent life, sun, power, strength, and good luck. It didn't become a sign of hate and death until it was rotated forty-five degrees and corrupted by the Nazis in 1920.

Ling Rinpoche speaks to us, now a part of this group of devotees sitting cross-legged on the floor. Michael translates. Although I can't grasp the concepts, they nevertheless seem sacred, coming from a high lama and spoken in a holy space.

Without any apparent signal, everyone suddenly rises and approaches Ling Rinpoche. People are presenting him with *khatas*, which are long white greeting scarves that he ceremoniously drapes over their necks. Someone hands a *khata* to me and, although it feels a bit odd, I approach Ling Rinpoche, extend the *khata* with both hands as though I were holding a tray. He takes it and places it over my head and around my neck. I bow with my hands at my heart in prayer position.

We then "take refuge"* by reciting the Refuge Prayer: "I go for refuge to the Buddha, the Dharma, and the Sangha." Throughout it all, Art and I just watch and do what others do. Yet, it's bewildering—all this is just a few miles from my school!

*To "take refuge" is to have an understanding of suffering and to have confidence that the Three Jewels—the Buddha, Dharma, and Sangha—can help. To "take refuge" is not an attempt to avoid problems in this life but to avoid karmic problems in future lives or, better yet, to avoid future uncontrolled births. The Refuge Prayer can be spoken, sung, or chanted. Source: "Going for Refuge," View on Buddhism, http://viewonbuddhism.org/refuge.html, cited October 21, 2012.*

* * *

For the next several months, we faithfully attend the rookie class, learn to read and write Tibetan, and get a superficial understanding of *karma,* meditative equipoise, and wisdom. Tibetan Buddhism is a very detailed, precise study—perhaps more philosophy than religion. It has categories and subcategories and sub-subcategories. And, to make the challenge even tougher, His Holiness the Dalai Lama advises, "Do not accept Buddhism on faith. Investigate it. Study it. Come to your own conclusions." It seems like I will be in the rookie class for life.

As the summer of 1981 approaches, the only definitive benefit we can see from our study is that Art is no longer afraid to fly.

That's inexplicable! But again, without questioning it, without thinking that there might be larger, unseen, future implications, we do what any young, restless couple would do—we book a trip to Europe. Brimming with excitement and expectation, we ignore the request by Geshe-la that everyone in the rookie class go to the University of Wisconsin in Madison to hear the Dalai Lama speak.

Why give up a ten-week holiday in Europe for a week in the Midwest? We've been studying Buddhism for only one year. We haven't made a lifelong commitment to it. That line of reasoning assuages our guilt, and off we go for a summer of hiking and sightseeing. But guilt has a way of lingering, especially because Art is Catholic and I'm a Jew.

In the fall, Geshe Tharchin is summoned to teach at Sera Mey Monastery, a large and prestigious institution in southern India. This is an honor, and everyone is proud.

Classes continue under Michael's tutelage, but everyone misses Geshe-la's traditional style. He would read the scriptures in Tibetan, translate them, and then call on different people to re-read and explain. I would sit in terror, palms sweating and mind blank, as my turn approached. The feeling of not wanting to disappoint my teacher was even stronger than not wanting to disappoint myself or looking foolish in front of the others.

But interestingly, in the Tibetan system, it's perfectly fine for students to assist each other and call out answers. That isn't considered cheating, as it is in American classrooms. Years later, while teaching at Sera Mey, I had to keep reminding myself of this—that when my students call out an answer, they aren't being undisciplined but helping each other learn.

When Geshe-la returns, his students are ecstatic. I forget about my sweating palms and mind gone blank; I'm just happy to have my teacher back. Art and I buy flowers and fruit as offerings and drive to the temple to greet him. We're invited to his room. We'd never been in Geshe-la's room before, so being there seems sacred.

We prostrate at his feet, give him a *khata,* which he drapes around our necks, and welcome him back. Art, as usual, takes the lead. He asks Geshe-la to tell us about Sera Mey.

"It is a teaching university. Many monks who had been studying in Tibet fled after China took rule in the 1950s," he replies. "Now they study at Sera."

Unfortunately, China is suppressing Tibetan Buddhism and attempting to systematically eradicate Tibetan culture. In Tibet, for example, it's a crime to carry pictures of the Dalai Lama or the Potala, the thirteen-story palace monastery, with more than 1,000 rooms, that had been his home before he fled to India in 1959. The major Buddhist monasteries in Tibet are now mere tourist attractions. Every year, monks and nuns risk their lives fleeing over the Himalayas to reach neighboring Nepal and ultimately cross into India. They find their way to McLeod Ganj and Dharamsala,* the Dalai Lama's residence and site of the Tibetan Government-in-Exile, often arriving broken physically and mentally but never spiritually.

Years later, when in McLeod Ganj, I asked a nun who had fled from Tibet to India by foot, "What kept you going on your journey all those months?"

She replied, "I never took my mind off of the Dalai Lama."

"And what did you do when you finally met him?"

"I fell at his feet and wept uncontrollably."

* *In March 1959, Tenzin Gyatso, the 14th Dalai Lama, fled to India after the failed uprising in Tibet against the Communist Party of China. The Indian Government offered him refuge in Dharamsala where he set up the Government of Tibet in exile in 1960. McLeod Ganj became his official residence and also home to several Buddhist monasteries and thousands of Tibetan refugees. Source: "McLeod Ganj," Wikipedia, http://en.wikipedia.org/wiki/ McLeod_Ganj, cited October 21, 2012.*

\* \* \*

Art asks Geshe-la, "How many monks live at Sera Mey?"

"Eight hundred."

"Is there a school?"

"Yes."

"Do they teach English?"

"Yes."

"Oh, then Rosalie and I will go to Sera Mey and teach."

I almost fall off my chair. I've always wanted to go to India, but that's a place Art said he never wanted to see. As we leave Geshe-la's room, I ask incredulously, "Why did you ever make that offer?"

"Well, we didn't go to hear the Dalai Lama teach in Wisconsin when Geshe-la asked us to, so I thought we would make it up to him by going to India instead."

Ah, the power of guilt!

Art easily gets a leave of absence from his job for the 1982 school year. I have to fight for mine. The director resists and resists, insisting, "Whenever we grant a leave for a reason like this, the person comes back and resigns."

I'm indignant. "You know how committed I am to my work here. You know how much I love the special needs kids. How can you think such a thing? I will never resign." These are famous last words!

During the past two years, a lot has changed for Art and me. We consider ourselves practicing Buddhists, and I call myself a Jew/Bu. Because Art is

> *Great adventures await those who are willing to turn the corner.*
> —Chinese fortune cookie

no longer afraid to fly, my dream of visiting India is about to be realized. We are, in Lola's prophetic words, "embarking on an incredible journey."

Art's colleague, Henry, who is usually jovial and easy-going, is overwhelmed with a mixture of admiration and anxiety. "Arthur," Henry admonishes, "do you realize what you are doing? You are going into the great unknown."

And Art teasingly replies, "Henry, it's not the unknown I fear; it's the known."

\* \* \*

It's August 1982, 3:00 a.m., and we arrive in Bombay with no room reservations. Bombay is a big city, so we aren't particularly concerned until a tourist information agent at the airport informs us, "Sorry, all the guesthouses are full. What about a hotel?" The hotels cost mega-bucks, so we start to panic. We're on a tight budget. We need to stretch our money if it's going to last an entire year. When we don't answer immediately, the tourist agent hesitatingly inquires, "Would you be willing to stay with a family?" We jump at the opportunity.

After a few phone calls and a short taxi ride, we're in Juhu Beach, a famous and popular Bombay suburb a few miles from the airport. By now, we're almost drunk with happiness and lack of sleep. We hate the idea of waking up our host family and even worry that they won't hear us ring their bell or knock on their door. But, to our surprise, the entire D'Souza family—commercial airline Captain Otis D'Souza and his wife, their two sons, and two daughters—is awake and ready to chat. They serve tea, and we thank them for their hospitality. They graciously reply, "If you are a guest in India, *you are our guest*." Many times over the next seven months, these words would flow into our ears.

The D'Souzas are a Christian family in a country populated primarily by Hindus, Muslims, and Sikhs. Their faith is strong, made stronger by a miracle performed by their youngest daughter. Her cousin, a boy, was suffering from leukemia, and all medical attempts to cure him had failed. He was discharged from the hospital to die at home. Desperate, the family begged a priest to perform an exorcism. Everyone gathered around the boy, gently laid their hands on his body, and started to pray. The young girl, a small child at the time, was distracted and played by herself in the corner. The priest encouraged her to join the others and touch her cousin. She did so innocently and was suddenly hurled across the room where she lost consciousness. After several minutes, she was revived but remembered nothing. Sometime later, the sick boy returned to the hospital for additional testing, and, to everyone's amazement, the disease was completely gone. The oncologist delivered the astounding news to the family and humbly acknowledged, "Your God lives."

Juhu Beach becomes vibrant at night. The white sand is studded with small stalls where vendors sell everything from snacks to bangles. Each stall has a candle flickering amongst its wares, and the vendors, regardless of what they're selling, sit cross-legged behind the candles like meditating gurus. They treat each sale as a ceremony. An attendant with a pony gives children a ride along the ocean. People walk slowly. No one is in a hurry.

Away from Juhu Beach, we're confronted with a different reality. In downtown Bombay, throngs of people crush together, each trying to reach the head of an infinite line. Art and I are both from big cities, but we feel totally unprepared for this. With a population of eight million people[1] compressed into 233 square miles,[2] the volume of human beings is overwhelming. I grip Art's shirt desperately.

"If we ever get separated, I'll never survive. I'm not confident enough. I'm not smart enough. I'm not even carrying any money!"

"You'll survive," he says. His tone is matter-of-fact, which I interpret as insensitivity. But maybe it's just my own fear, an overreaction to deep-rooted insecurity.

We see an endless stream of people lining the road. "Maybe it's a parade or procession," I surmise.

"That might be interesting," Art agrees.

So we merge with them. Suddenly, a traffic light changes from red to green and everyone starts moving forward.

"Where's the parade?" I ask Art.

"There is no parade," he shouts. "They've been waiting to cross the street."

The masses board buses, trains, trams, and trolleys in a likewise chaotic manner, with no regard for the ease and expediency of boarding that would be possible by forming a queue. Yet, once on board, passengers form a cohesive whole that sways to an unconscious rhythm that enables a ticket collector to pass from front to back even though there doesn't seem to be an inch of space between them.

A bus ride is an assault on my senses. The Indian women's rich, thick, black hair is braided with leis of bright orange or yellow marigolds whose odor is *overwhelmingly pungent*. The press of bodies feels *suffocating* in summer heat. The radio, at full blast, is *deafening*. The erratic driving is *terrifying*. And, of course, the Indian snacks freely passed around are *killingly spicy! Can I really spend a year in India?*

Within a few days, we leave Bombay for Sera Mey Monastery in the small town of Bylakuppe, 660 miles to the south.

Traveling through India by train and bus brings surprises every day, some pleasant and some not so pleasant. Most not so pleasant surprises are associated with diarrhea and stomach cramps. So it makes sense to be very cautious when it comes to food. Art and I are staying at a youth hostel, and we order dinner: the usual rice and *dal,* a lentil soup served in various consistencies, depending on the cook. We've been eating rice and *dal* almost every day since arriving in India, and it's always on the safe list. So I feel a bit suspicious when I get a bowl of rice that has more than a fair share of ants. Of course, the ants are dead, boiled to death.

"What about these ants? You're not going to eat them, are you?" I ask Art.

"No."

"Let's send the rice back," I suggest.

"Just pick them out."

"Pick them out? We paid for this rice. It should be ant-free."

"Don't make a big deal out of it. Just pick them out." Art sounds condescending, which always makes me feel insecure.

"I'm not making a big deal out of it." Now I'm sounding defensive. "I just want rice that's clean and appetizing."

"Pick out the ants, and it'll be clean and appetizing."

"I'm going to the kitchen to ask for new rice."

"Do what you want, but I think it's a mistake." Art is very patiently picking out ants from his bowl of rice. A Japanese man sitting next to him is also picking out ants.

"How can it be a mistake to ask for new rice?" I persist. "It's not an unreasonable request."

"Do what you want." By now Art and the Japanese man have finished fishing out the ants and are beginning to eat.

I go to the kitchen and find the cook. "Excuse me. There are ants in my rice."

"Yes, you are right," the cook says as he swirls his finger around and around in my rice. "There are ants in your rice." Then he very patiently picks them out.

An *autorickshaw* hauls us and our heavy backpacks through monsoon mud. The road, typical of those in India, is crumbling as the potholes grow. The driver grips the handlebar steering mechanism with white knuckles, his arms taut as he constantly strains to keep the vehicle from sliding around.

Sputtering, the vehicle arrives at Sera Mey, a distance of about two kilometers from Bylakuppe. The *autorickshaw* seems as exhausted and as happy to arrive as we are—the poor driver certainly is. I pity him—he has to ply the mud-soaked roads on his return journey. While Art's paying the fare, the amount we had negotiated, I pull extra rupees from Art's hand, adding ample *baksheesh.* Art, who has always controlled the money, gives me a very dirty look.

Lotar, the same monk to whom I had poured out my enthusiasm about studying Buddhism at Rashi Gempil Ling two years ago, is waiting for us. His face beams as he introduces us to the abbot and all the *rinpoches.* He's learned to speak English, and we're his special charges. After all, we're Geshe Tharchin's students ... all the way from New Jersey.

We climb the stairs outside our room. From the roof of the temple, we're privy to all the sights and sounds of monastery life. Each morning, the monks chant. Each day, they blow long horns, held by a person at each end, and study Buddhist scriptures. And each evening, they debate, jumping high and clapping their hands to punctuate each point. Here, they're free to do everything denied to them in Tibet.

For five wonderful months, Sera Mey is our Buddha Field,[3] our attempt to reach that mysterious phenomenon called *enlightenment.* We "take refuge," teach the young monks English, and study Buddhism. I may be the teacher, but I'm also young and naïve. Little do I perceive that this experience is preparing me in ways I cannot possibly imagine.

In the summer of 1984, Art and I spend a week at Milarepa Center, a Buddhist monastery in the Green Mountains of Vermont. To some, it's rustic and charming. To others, it's inconvenient and uncomfortable. As the Buddha says, "Everything is perception."

An old barn adorns the property, reminiscent of a scene from a Norman Rockwell painting. Bats make their presence felt at night, reminding us that they're the tenants and we're only visitors. They swoop over our heads as we try to sleep, testing our bravery and perseverance, which is a major test for me because I have an irrational fear that a bat might get tangled in my dense, curly hair and never find its way out!

Indoor plumbing hasn't come to the main house yet. Instead, bales of hay act as our privacy walls as we sit on large cans to do our business. The waste is then dumped into a special solution and used to mulch the garden. The *gompa* is small and cozy. It is here that we "take refuge" and study the teachings of the Buddha.

\* \* \*

Right before Columbus Day weekend, unexpectedly, we get a postcard from Peter Baker, director at Milarepa Center: "Hello, Rosalie and Arthur. I'm glad you visited the monastery while you were in Vermont. You are welcome to come again. I hope you learned something while you were here. At least the food is good."

Peter always puts extra effort into the meals. "This way you have no excuse," he tells the meditators. "There's plenty of good food so you can concentrate on your *object of meditation* and not your growling stomach."

Turning the postcard clockwise, scrawled inconspicuously along the left side, in the tiniest of postscripts, we read: "Would you like to join the Milarepa group at Middlebury College in Vermont for an audience with the Dalai Lama?" Can you imagine? An invitation to meet the Dalai is a postscript!

\* \* \*

Throughout our study of Buddhism, the Dalai Lama's name is never far from our ears. He's both the spiritual leader of Buddhist practitioners as well as temporal leader of the Tibetan people, a theocratic responsibility that began with the Great Fifth Dalai Lama in 1653.[4]

> *If you want others to be happy, practice compassion.*
> *If you want to be happy, practice compassion.*
> —His Holiness the 14th Dalai Lama, spiritual and temporal leader of the Tibetan people

Always, we hear people speak of the Dalai Lama with reverence and fondness, a combination that seems paradoxical. Usually awe creates a distance between the object of reverence and those who revere. But the Dalai Lama is loved as a human being. This will be our first opportunity to meet this holy man, and, honestly, we have no idea what to expect.

We're in Middlebury to meet the rest of the group, some from Vermont and a few French-Canadians. Of the eighteen participants, Jacques, a three-year-old from Montreal, is the youngest. His mother is distressed because Jacques is impatient and moody. Expecting that he will embarrass her, she's willing to miss the audience and wait with her son outside. We encourage her to set that notion aside.

"But what if he's disruptive?" she asks. "He'll distract the Dalai Lama during his teachings."

"Why would he be disruptive?" we ask.

"Jacques doesn't speak English."

"Even if he spoke English, he probably doesn't understand Buddhist teachings."

"If he doesn't understand the teachings, why bring him?"

"It's a blessing. Just think, at the age of three, he's meeting the Dalai Lama."

We're led into a small room and look around. There's no elevated throne, the traditional platform for a teacher in the Buddhist tradition to sit upon while giving instructions to those seeking enlightenment. "Where will he sit?" we ask each other. Then we spot it: a small, velvet couch. "That must be it!"

As we race toward the couch, we stumble over each other and end up as a human heap. Everyone wants to sit at the feet of the Dalai Lama. Considering we are about to meet the incarnation of the Buddha, we aren't exactly examples of the Buddhist ideals of patience, compassion, or generosity. Instead, we're demonstrating attachment, greed, and pride, all the *samsaric* qualities that, according to Buddhist tenets, create suffering in the world.

But the Dalai Lama surprises us. He enters the room carrying a small cushion and sits on the floor at the opposite end of the room from the couch. Then the same thing happens. The very *samsaric* qualities that drove us minutes ago overtake us again, and we race across the room and dive at his feet.

Meanwhile, Jacques shows no interest in sitting at the feet of the Dalai Lama. Much to his mother's dismay, he's busy running around the room. But this, in no way, dismays the Dalai Lama. Someone had forethought and brought a basket of fruit, a very traditional offering. His Holiness very calmly takes an orange from the top of the basket and rolls it to Jacques. Jacques rolls it back. The Dalai Lama rolls it to Jacques again. And Jacques rolls it back—on and on for forty minutes. Not the least bit distracted, His Holiness discusses important Buddhist tenets with us as he patiently, graciously, and generously attends to Jacques' three-year-old needs.

After the audience, we gather for a group photo. Jacques, dressed in a white, knitted sweater and hat, stands in front of the Dalai Lama, pressed against His Holiness' maroon robes. The stark contrast makes Jacques the most noticeable member of the group. Jacques would be an adult today. Has his mother saved that photo? Is it displayed in a place of prominence on a coffee table or bookshelf?

Over the years, I've treasured my copy of that photo. Whenever I look at it, I think about my first audience with His Holiness the Dalai Lama. I laugh over the ridiculous behavior of the adults in that group, but another thought is never far from my mind: "What does Jacques feel when he looks at his copy of the photo?"

# Impermanence
## 1992–1999

"Art, please, you must go for help."

"I'll help myself."

We've had this conversation a thousand times already, and so I don't know why I think anything will change this time. Since Art's brother's tragic death four years ago, in 1988, Art has been depressed. He feels he should have been able to help his younger brother, that it was his duty as the oldest in the family. He won't admit that Charlie's problems required more than brotherly love—the help of a professional. Art has been torturing himself over this and, in turn, has been torturing me. I try to bear it as best I can, but on some days, I lose my patience.

"Art, everything was so fine in our lives before Charlie's death." I try not to sound desperate, but my heart is aching. "We returned from India ten years ago, and you went back to school for your master's degree in social work. We went hiking through Scotland for ten weeks, and we both agree it was the best summer holiday we've ever had. It's true that I became restless and left my job at the high school after promising my boss I never would. But I've found another one, and I'm happy with it. We've both changed since teaching at the Buddhist monastery in India. And now you need to change again. Please ... for our marriage!"

"Change in what way?"

"Get rid of your grief and guilt," I answer impatiently.

"I'm doing that. I'm writing a book about it called *The Jewel*," he answers flatly.

"That's good," I reply encouragingly. "It's a way for you to express what you're feeling. But you also need professional help. You need to talk with someone knowledgeable about these kinds of losses. Art, do it for us. Please. Our relationship is tearing apart. It can't last much longer."

"I'll help myself."

"And if you can't?"

"I don't know."

"Well, I know," I retort angrily. "We'll end up divorced. And then you'll finally go for help. That's your way. You can't ever do things like everyone else. You have to do it your own way. That's what I always loved about you, but now it's what I hate about you."

I'm fed up and want to call a lawyer, but I can't bring myself to do it yet. I've got to do something. What?

I've always admired, probably idolized, Mother Teresa. She's a "living saint" who dedicated her life to the "poorest of the poor."

Inspired by her example, I want to go to Calcutta and volunteer during my summer vacation. But, bound by my fears and misconceptions, I'm convinced I can't do it on my own. So, though our relationship has become difficult, I run this idea past Art. "Let's go to Calcutta and volunteer with the Missionaries of Charity," I suggest enthusiastically.

"Can't. I'm busy working on *The Jewel*. It's helping me work through my guilt about Charlie's death."

"The experience will give you fresh ideas for your book."

"Not this book."

"Then do it for me, as my birthday present."

"It's not something I want to do."

"Please."

"If you want to go, then go. I'm not stopping you."

"I can't. I can't go by myself. I want you to go with me."

But he isn't interested, so I don't go.

* * *

My marriage is crumbling. I'm crumbling. The pivot around which my world has circulated for the past eighteen years is no longer able to bear my orbit. Art has emotionally distanced himself from me. I'm being hurled into space. For the first time in my life, I have to face difficulties alone, make my own decisions, and, if I'm to maintain my freedom, travel independently. This is the scariest part. I love to travel, but the thought of traveling alone makes me feel vulnerable.

I need to escape New Jersey. The tension in our home is killing me. All I do is cry and cry and cry. Nothing works anymore. I've hit a dead end and can't figure out how to navigate out of it. I keep bumping into the same brick walls, and, each time, the impact inflicts more damage. I'm in emotional pain and find that only the hours I give to hospice work gives me relief.

My friends are puzzled. "Isn't hospice work depressing? Spending all that time with dying people?" they ask.

> *In order to find yourself, lose yourself in the service of others.*
>
> —Mohandas Gandhi, political leader

"Honestly, it's the only time I feel happy."

Suddenly I get it. "Volunteer work. That's it. That's my

remedy. If I put my efforts into someone else's problems, my own problems will come into perspective." I've always heard that, but now it comes as a revelation.

In January 1993, I frantically start sending letters to various volunteer organizations. I write to American Jewish World Services, Catholic Charities, Tibetan Nuns Project, Missionaries of Charity, and other international charities. I realize that, in my deteriorated mental and physical state, I must be linked to an established organization. This is for my own protection, a buffer against unexpected events, which is what Art has been to me for eighteen years—a buffer.

While I'm waiting for replies—or an enticement so strong that I'll know exactly where I want to go and what I want to do—Art and I go for a holiday to McLeod Ganj (Dharamsala), India, for the month of August, knowing it could be our last trip together.

McLeod Ganj is a hodgepodge, a collection of guesthouses, restaurants, phone shops, and tourist stores piled one above the other, all balancing precariously near the top of a mountain. The Tibetan community immediately captivates me. But what I love the most are the faces: elderly men and women wear red ribbons, threaded through their long grey hair, that accent deep wrinkles carved into their ancient faces; these are in stark contrast to the chapped, red-cheeked, shining countenance of young monks and nuns.

Art and I do touristy things: stay at the Loseling Guest House that's run by monks and overlooks the mountains, walk around the Buddhist Main Temple and the complex that's the residence of His Holiness the Dalai Lama, take basic Buddhism classes at the library. I reconnect with an American friend, Betsy, who lives in Dharamsala, and I realize how much I like hanging around with Tibetan Buddhists. Their demeanor—those faces—inspire gentleness and peace. They appear so self-assured, like they know exactly what to do.

Art is supportive and stands by my side the whole time. For the entire month, it's much like old times. Except, of course, it isn't. We both know that things are changing. A certain air of heaviness, like an ever-present blanket, surrounds us, warm but also woven with fibers of uncertainty about what the future will bring.

When we return to New Jersey, letters in response to my volunteer queries await. Two stand out among all the rest: The Tibetan Nuns Project, based in Dharamsala, needs English teachers. And, typed on her famous old-fashioned typewriter, is an invitation from Mother Teresa. I can barely believe it! I, an ordinary person, am being summoned to Calcutta by a "living saint."

+LDM
30th July, 1993

MISSIONARIES OF CHARITY
54/A, A. J. C. Bose Road,
Calcutta - 700016, India.

Dear Rosalie

Thank you very much for your letter and your desire to share in our works of love for the poorest of the poor.

The work in our Leper Homes is well organised by the Leper patients. So you may not have the chance you have asked. We have somes for the handicapped children and for the physically and mentally disabled. If you are interested to work in these homes - you are most welcome.

Come with heart to love and hands to serve Jesus in the crippled, the abandoned, the sick and dying in anyone of our Centres. I enclose for your information a list of accommodations — they do not make reservations. On arrival you may put up at one of these till you find a more suitable place. You can meet the Sister in Charge of the volunteers between 8.30 - 9.00 a.m. or 5.00 - 6.00 p.m. daily, except Thursday and Sunday

Regarding your visa - you can come on a tourist visa and of course you would be expected to tour.

God loves you. He will reward your generous desire to serve Him in His little ones - the poor.

God Bless you

*M Teresa mc*

So what am I to do? I prayed for an enticement and now I have two. I hold my palms open like pans on a balance scale, each holding an opportunity of equal weight. The Tibetan nuns and the Dalai Lama or Mother Teresa? Mother Teresa or the Dalai Lama?

How can I ever make such a decision? It's impossible. If only Art would help me decide. If only someone could tell me what to do!

I'm going to Dharamsala. My longstanding association with the Tibetans has won me over. But there's a problem: everyone has a different opinion about the outcome. My mother is terrified that a year away from Art will precipitate the death rattle of our marriage. My friends think just the opposite, that after so many years together and without any children, we couldn't bear to be apart. Still others believe that a taste of independence will unleash a part of me that has long been repressed and, once experienced, will never again agree to be unheeded. It's all very confusing.

Like Tevye in *Fiddler on the Roof,* I toss it back and forth from one hand to the other hand. I've made a decision, yet I haven't made a decision. Decisions can be changed, even at the last moment. I've applied for a leave of absence, but even that can be withdrawn. I want to be sure, but short of looking into a crystal ball, the future is anything but crystal clear.

Thinking doesn't help. It's logical that I could make a list of pros and cons, but usually my lists balance each other out. I don't trust my intuition because that might be colored by my desire to escape from a painful situation no matter what the consequences. I slowly lower myself onto the Tibetan carpet in front of our fireplace. I do know one thing: I have to ask for guidance.

"Please, Green Tara, help me. I don't want to hurt Art. I don't want to destroy our marriage. So many things have changed in our lives over the past few years. I know things will never be like they were before. But is going to Dharamsala the right decision? Should I go? Should I go? Should I go?"

I lie peacefully on the Tibetan carpet. Memories of the months at Sera Monastery flood my mind. Art and I took a risk then, but that was ten years ago and we took the risk together. This decision is mine alone and the consequences will be my responsibility alone. I don't know what to do.

"Green Tara, please give me a sign. If I should go to Dharamsala, then give me a sign. Give me a sign. Give me a sign."

Suddenly, I'm disturbed by an unexpected odor. I sit up, more confused than before. The aroma is sweet and, distinctly, that of roses. I rise and go from room to room. I check under the counters in the kitchen for a bottle of air freshener that may have suddenly exploded. I check in the bedrooms to see if the windows are open, allowing outside air to waft in, but I can't find anything. And the aroma is only in the living room!

I sit down on the Tibetan carpet and draw a deep breath. It's sweet. It's good. It's confirming, comforting. Green Tara has given me a sign. I'm going to Dharamsala.

I've taken a one-year leave of absence from my teaching position, starting in January 1994. Art supports me. I'm hoping— and maybe he's hoping—that this year apart will save our marriage, confirming the saying, "Absence makes the heart grow fonder."

But what should I do with the letter from Mother Teresa?

I go upstairs to Art's library with its ceiling-to-floor bookcases that house his thousands of books. I extract a thin volume, *Something Beautiful for God*, about Mother Teresa and slip the letter inside. Then I replace the book among the others.

I step back and take in the tomes that surround me. These books define Art's life as a teacher, writer, and scholar. I have only a small collection because I like to pass books on after reading them, but *Something Beautiful for God* is one that I've kept and treasured. And now it secrets a letter from Mother Teresa inside. Somehow, my personal collection no longer seems meager or insignificant.

\* \* \*

Arriving in Dharamsala in January 1994, the weather is cold, in fact, colder inside the stone buildings than outside when the sun is shining. I've returned to the Loseling Guest House and am teaching at Gaden Choeling Nunnery.

> *In the depths of winter,*
> *I finally learned that within me*
> *lay an invincible summer.*
> —Albert Camus, author, journalist, philosopher

The nunnery is a large complex built on a mountainside. The buildings, sitting on many levels, require that a person have strong legs to ascend and descend numerous outdoor stairways. At first sight, Gaden Choeling seems well-maintained, but, on closer examination, almost all the buildings are in need of repair. Unfortunately, in this patriarchal society, the monasteries—not the nunneries—are given first priority.

The contrasting character of the buildings is reflected in the actions of the residents. While the monks confidently roam around McLeod Ganj, mingling freely with foreigners and often getting gifts and finding sponsors, the nuns cling to each other for security and courage. These young women are dependent and insecure—and I identify with them.

In class, the nuns are reticent. They sit on the floor, leaning against one another, their robes and blouses blending into a maroon-and-yellow patchwork. When I call on someone to answer, she throws the loose end of her robe over her head, muffling her voice.

What will intrigue them?

With chalk, I draw a large circle on the floor and write "USA" inside. I step into the circle and say, "I wish you would come to America and visit my mother. She would really love to see you. But anyone who wants to visit America must talk like an American."

"What does that mean?" comes a whisper from beneath a protective cover.

"That means you must talk loudly and use your hands." Of course, that might be closer to speaking like an Italian, but I don't go into that. "Watch me."

With a great wave of my arm, I point to myself. "*My* name is Rosalie, and I *come* from America." I spread my arms wide and tilt them as if they were wings of an airplane. "I like to *travel*."

The nuns think this is funny and laugh softly, their hands politely covering their mouths.

"Now who will try it?"

Thank goodness there's one brave soul in the room. She's very eager to step inside the circle. She grins broadly and begins, pointing at herself, "*My* name is Ngawang." She brings both of her hands to her heart as though beckoning the others. "I *come* from Tibet." She holds an invisible book. "I like to *study*."

"That's great," I exclaim, even though her rendition is a very tepid version of my own example. "You did great. Now, someone else try."

One by one, the most confident step into the circle and pretend they are in America. There are a few who refuse but that's all right.

"Next time," I tell them.

But the bolder nuns have a different idea. They grab those who haven't taken a turn, pull them up by their robes, and playfully shove them into the circle. The nuns now in the circle try to escape, but their laughing classmates block their path.

Before long, they become a blaze of maroon and gold, and it's impossible to tell the brave ones from the shy ones. Everyone laughs with complete abandon. My English lesson has turned into a party.

Finally, the hysterical heap disentangles and everyone finds a spot on the floor, smiles crossing their broad faces.

"I'm very proud of you. Today, everyone went to America and had a nice chat with my mother. Tomorrow we'll do it again." Then I add teasingly, "Something tells me that you don't come to my class to learn English. I think you come to have a good time."

And having "a good time" is perfectly all right with me, something I wouldn't deny them. Just a few months earlier, these shy Tibetan nuns epitomized strength and bravery. Unable to study Buddhism in their homeland, which has been under Chinese occupation since 1949, they crossed the Himalayan Mountains to freedom.

In doing so, they couldn't risk taking provisions. Carrying a change of clothes or baskets of food would be like waving a red flag, proclaiming, "I am escaping!" So with only a vague idea of their route, they walked for thirty days until they reached Nepal. Along the way, they ate whatever they could find under the snow, their fingers and toes frozen.

Tragically, many were captured and experienced the horrors of rape, imprisonment, and torture. Yet, somehow, they were able to set out again for India. Their physical and emotional scars—injuries from beatings and frostbite as well as the torment of not knowing about reprisals to their families—serve as daily reminders of their perilous journey. But, perhaps, what's most painful is the knowledge that they can never go back, that arrest awaits them if they attempt to return. This is the price they willingly and wholeheartedly pay for religious freedom.

Although the nuns are banned from returning to Tibet, going there is a privilege not denied to me. My friend Lauren, a fellow volunteer who also stays in the Loseling Guest House, is traveling overland from Kathmandu, Nepal, to Lhasa, Tibet's capital, with her mother and brother in May. Afterward, Lauren's mother and brother will return home to San Francisco, and Lauren will remain for ten weeks in Tibet.

"Why don't you join me in Lhasa?" she asks over breakfast.

"Of course," I reply.

As soon as the words come out of my mouth, I regret having said them. Lauren and her family will be traveling with a group, but I'll be going on my own. They'll be safe; I'll be vulnerable. Within minutes, I'm flooded with all the old insecurities and fears that initially prevented me from traveling without Art.

Yes, it's true that I'm in Dharamsala on my own now, but I've gradually become comfortable in India. Tibet is occupied by China, and China is, after all, a "Communist country"—and those are words programmed to induce fear in many Americans who grew up during the Cold War, the Bay of Pigs standoff, and within, supposedly, a missile's arc from Cuba.

"Anything can happen," we were programmed to think then. "Anything can happen," I'm thinking now. Do the people there speak English? Do they respect human rights? Will I get in trouble? Will I be arrested?

India is one thing. Tibet—alone!—is completely different.

Lauren left a week ago and will be waiting for me in Lhasa, so there's no escaping my decision. My anxiety grows day by day. I can't sleep or eat. I'm desperate.

I seek solace from my friend Annette who tries to understand, but, being a world-wide photographer, fear of new places isn't something she experiences.

"Art and I always traveled together. We were very close. We had no children, so our lives were intertwined. I guess you can call it codependency," I explain helplessly.

She laughs lightly, "Yeah, when the relationship works, they call it love. When it doesn't work, they call it codependency."

Naomi, an Israeli woman staying in Dharamsala, is a healer. She's so busy that it's almost impossible to get an appointment with her. It seems everyone needs to be healed. Actually, I've observed that only the Westerners need to be healed. The Tibetans just take some herbal medicine, meditate, and they're fine. But we Westerners, on our spiritual journeys and on our sojourns of personal growth and development, seem to be wrecks! Maybe that's why we've gravitated to India, living in Dharamsala, within the shadow of the Dalai Lama.

Luckily, Annette has an "in" with Naomi and arranges an emergency appointment for me. We pass by people of all ages waiting patiently to see her and step into her room. It's small and bare. Naomi checks me the way she checks people who need to be healed: she spreads out her fingers and runs them along my body to see if I have cold spots, hot spots, energy blockages, and other maladies.

"There's nothing wrong with you, Rosalie. Why are you here?"

"I'm going to Tibet."

"That's why you are here, because you're going to Tibet?" She can't hide her disbelief.

"Yes."

"Then go to Tibet."

"I can't. I'm too anxious."

"You'll be just fine. I promise you. When are you leaving?"

"At the end of next week. Can I see you again next week?"

"That's impossible. I'm too busy. You see all the people waiting."

Suddenly inspired with a random thought, I blurt, "You know, you look just like my great grandmother Bessy."

"Really, where was Bessy from?"

"Vilnius, Lithuania."

"My great grandmother was from Vilnius," she says and becomes pensive, "Okay, come back next week."

I go the following week, and she checks me again. I have no hot spots, no cold spots, no blockages. There's nothing wrong with me. But I'm still filled with fear.

"Rosalie, just go to Tibet."

I have no choice. I go.

> *Feel the fear and do it anyway.*
> —Susan J. Jeffers, author

\* \* \*

My travel plan is simple. I'll take an all-night bus from Dharamsala to Delhi, where I'll get my Chinese visa, then catch a plane to Kathmandu and fly on to Lhasa.

But travelers know they have to join a group in order to get a special stamp for Tibet. Lauren and her family are with a group. They have the stamp for Tibet. I'm not with a group. How will I get the stamp? And if I don't get a stamp, Lauren will be waiting in Lhasa for someone who will never arrive.

Even though I don't have any idea how to make this happen, I make my way to Delhi, check into a spacious room at the YMCA, and, without waiting to enjoy the balcony and flower-laden garden, go directly to the Chinese embassy.

I stand in a long queue, slowly making my way to the counter. I'm also approaching a sign with red letters and a black border hung obtrusively on the wall: "No Independent Travel Allowed In Tibet." I pass under the sign, hoping it won't fall on me.

I try not to shake as I hand over my application form. The official on the other side of the counter skims the form and looks very puzzled. "Where are you going?"

"China."

"Where in China? What is your itinerary?"

"Oh, Xi'an, Beijing, Kunming, Changchun, Yangshuo," I say casually, as my heart pounds inside my chest. People had given me names of different places, but I have no idea where these places are. The agent looks at me very strangely. He keeps questioning me. He didn't question anyone else, only me.

"Why are you going to China?"

"To travel, to see the sights."

"What sights?"

"Oh, the Great Wall of China." I propose weakly.

"Come back in three days," he replies indifferently.

* * *

I'm knackered. This interview was like being hit in the *kishka*. Of course, he saw right through me. Of course, he knew I was trying to go to Tibet without a stamp. Of course, I'll never get there in this lifetime.

I go back to the YMCA and collapse on the bed. When I summon up the courage, I check the guidebook. As I suspected, my stated itinerary makes no sense. It was like saying I'd be going from Boston to San Francisco to New York to Seattle. I'm doomed!

I return in three days. I'm a nervous wreck. Why do I put myself through these things? Why can't I be satisfied to stay in Dharamsala and teach? Or better yet, why can't I be satisfied to stay in New Jersey and teach? Why do I have this restless spirit that's doing nothing for me but drenching my body and mind with anxiety and fear?

The same official I had spoken with previously asks, "What is your profession?"

"Teacher."

"It is May. Why are you not teaching in your country?"

"I took a year off to teach the nuns in Dharamsala." Oh, God. I just mentioned the Tibetans. *How can I be so stupid?* Now, for sure, he knows I want to go to Tibet.

"What do you teach in your homeland?"

"I teach handicapped children to speak."

"How many years have you been doing that?"

"Twenty-one years."

"That is a noble profession." His tone is softening. Yet, surely, he knows that something is fishy.

"Thank you."

He fusses a bit with stuff on his counter and then disappears into an adjoining office. When he returns, he hands me the visa for China.

I have no idea why. It makes no sense. Maybe he was moved by the fact that I teach disabled children. I'm so relieved I could cry.

But getting the visa for China is only the first step. I still need the stamp for Tibet, and I have to consult someone who knows about these things. I go to a Tibetan travel agency in Delhi. "I want to go to Tibet, but I don't want to go in a group. My friend is waiting for me in Lhasa. What should I do?"

"Well, you can join a mock group in Kathmandu. You give them your passport, they get the stamp for Tibet, and you travel with them to Lhasa. Once you arrive, you're on your own."

"How much does it cost to join a mock group?"

"Three hundred dollars."

"Three hundred dollars! That's an awful lot of money."

I'm feeling more and more discouraged, but while at the travel agency, I buy plane tickets for both Kathmandu and Lhasa.

After we finish the transactions, the travel agent hands me a card with a Kathmandu address. "Go to this travel agency. Maybe they can help you." He reaches behind his chair and brings forth a box that looks big and heavy. "And while you are there, could you please deliver this box of business stationery?"

So that's why he wants me to go to the travel agency in Kathmandu. He wants me to be his delivery girl so his box of business stationery can get there and he won't have to pay postage.

"I can't," I protest. "I have hiking boots and clothes and toilet articles and books and tons of stuff. I can't possibly add another thing to my backpack." I'm trying to sound normal, but I hear myself sounding indignant.

And then the Universe gives me one more chance. "I would really appreciate it if you would carry this box of business stationery for me," he persists.

> *At every moment, the Universe is making you an irresistible offer.*
> —Anonymous

Now I feel like an ungrateful lout, so I agree.

I'm weary by the time I reach my hotel in Kathmandu. The flight was short but the worry made it anything but relaxing. I want nothing more than a good meal and a good night's sleep. But first things first. I have to call the travel agency. "Hello. I've just arrived from Delhi, and I have a box of business stationery for you from Tibetan Tours in Delhi."

"Thank you. Can you drop them off?"

"Drop them off? I'm dead tired. I'm starving. Can't someone come and pick them up?"

"There is no one here but me. I cannot leave until the travel agency closes at 9:00 p.m."

"By 9:00, I'll be fast asleep. Can't you come earlier?"

"It is impossible."

"Well, I'm exhausted and your agency is far from my hotel, and I don't think I should have to bring the box over." I'm both defensive and desperate. "But while I have you on the phone, can you help me with a little problem. Tomorrow, I'm flying to Lhasa. How far is the airport from the city?"

"Three hours."

"Three hours? Is there a bus?"

"No, you go with your group in a van."

"But I don't have a group."

"Well, I will tell what I can do for you. We have a group going to Lhasa tomorrow morning. If you meet the van in front of the travel agency, you can give the box to the driver, and he will give you a ride to the airport. He will also give you a letter so that when you arrive in Tibet you can get a ride from Lhasa Gonggar Airport to the city. Is that okay?"

Is that okay? It sounds fantastic. A group, a ride, and papers—and I don't have to pay the 300 dollars. "You've got a deal."

The next morning, I'm standing in front of the travel agency, trying to look inconspicuous. I don't want to let on that I didn't pay for the mock tour. "After all, it's only a ride to the airport," I think.

The driver is expecting me. He takes the box and gives me a letter written in Tibetan. The group and tour guide get into the van. I follow them. At the airport, everyone is shuttled into a waiting area. I don't know what to do, so I just tag along—close, very close.

We're led to the gate. I don't understand why the immigration authorities didn't check our passports for the Tibet stamp. I casually mention this to another traveler in our group. "Why didn't they collect our passports?"

"It was all taken care of when we joined the group."

"Everything?"

"Everything."

Then it dawns on me. They've already surrendered their passports to the authorities. Their passports are already stamped. Mine isn't. And even though I appear to be with this group, my passport won't ever be stamped. I'm truly, truly here illegally. Oh, my God.

Now I stick like glue to the group. I don't dare leave, even to go to the bathroom. We board the plane, and it takes off. I've never been so silent in my life. I can't figure out how all this has happened.

Suddenly, the pilot announces, "Storm over Lhasa. We will land in Chengdu, China."

In Chengdu, everyone, including me, is lodged in a hotel. I share a room with a young German woman. I don't dare tell her the truth. I don't even dare tell myself the truth. I'm that scared of ending up in a Chinese prison. Just because they didn't check passports in Kathmandu, there's no guarantee they won't check them in Lhasa. After all, immigration is immigration.

The Kathmandu travel agency that organized this Tibetan trip gives us lunch and a tour of Chendu. I don't pay. I keep a low profile. I'm with this group, and I'm not leaving their side, walking so close to them that they must think I'm a weirdo.

The next morning, we fly to Lhasa. When we land, the same thing happens. No one checks our passports or looks to see if we have the proper stamp. The group had just flown from Chengdu— on a domestic flight—so the authorities apparently assume we already cleared immigration there. Because everyone believes I'm with the group, I don't even show the driver my letter of introduction. I get into the van, and we start toward the city.

While riding in the van, I see an explosion nearby and, to my shock and horror, a man with his clothes on fire. *"An omen?"* I feel panic-stricken but try to stay calm.

I'm relieved to be on the van, but my relief is tempered by a new worry. I'm supposed to meet Lauren at the Holiday Inn, but the van is taking the group to the Yak Guest House. It's getting later and later.

Banks must be closed, and I don't have any Chinese currency. I don't even have a phrase book to ask, "How do I get to the Holiday Inn?"

And I know that the driver doesn't speak English. Some girls needed to use a bathroom and asked him several times to stop at a toilet, but the driver kept repeating, "No English. No English." Finally, through gestures, he got the idea and stopped so they could pee by the side of the road.

We drive on and on until finally we enter Lhasa. The night is dark, so I can't really form an impression of the city. I'm just happy to be close to my destination. Suddenly, the van swerves into a long, tree-lined driveway and toward an impressive building. I'm surprised that the Yak Guest House is so large and imposing. I was expecting a small, cozy place, but, by now, I'm ready to accept anything. I've made it into Tibet and feel nothing but gratitude and relief. My only remaining question—which might have to wait until morning—is how to find the Holiday Inn … and Lauren.

The van stops in front of the building and, out of the dark, a man steps forward. "Anyone staying here at the Holiday Inn?" he asks, obviously a hotel employee. The others in the group look confused, but nothing can surprise me any longer. With no time to say good-bye to my temporary tour mates, I grab my backpack, leap from the bus, and run through the hotel doors into Lauren's waiting arms. Her relief and my relief are so co-mingled we can't tease them out.

After three weeks in Tibet, I'm back in Dharamsala. The nuns gather tightly around me as if I've carried a bit of Tibet with me.

I speak to them through a translator: "I felt very emotional the whole time I was in Tibet, connected to it in so many ways. Lauren and I visited Sera Mey Monastery, the original one. I taught at Sera

Mey in southern India in 1982. Standing in front of the altar where the monks had prayed before they fled Tibet was deeply moving. We went to the Potala, the Dalai Lama's palace. It's a museum now, not a center of learning, but we tried our best to imagine how it was when His Holiness lived there.

"We took a four-wheel-drive vehicle out of the city and into the countryside. In the cities, it's difficult to tell the Tibetans from the Chinese because they blend together. But in the countryside, we saw the *real* Tibet. The men and women dress in traditional clothes, and they practice Buddhism secretly.

"I had pictures of His Holiness the Dalai Lama hidden in my money belt, and Lauren and I gave them out wherever we went. The people fell on the ground and wept. We also distributed *mani* pills and red protection strings. We had gotten these from the Dalai Lama's monastery here in Dharamsala before we left, and that made them even more precious to the people."

I pause for a minute to let the translator catch up with me.

"We visited a nun who is sequestered on the top of a mountain. She doesn't usually allow visitors, but she invited us into her cave because we made an extra effort to find her. She gave us a special blessing, and I felt like I was in the presence of a holy person.

"We bathed in hot springs that spew out of the mountainside. The roads in Tibet are punishing, full of potholes, so the water was healing.

"On our last evening, we were again back in Lhasa. There was a demonstration by the women who sell things in the marketplace. The cost of renting space had recently tripled, and they were protesting. The police were forcing the women into open trucks and taking them away. Lauren took a picture of the demonstration, and a policeman confiscated her camera. He demanded that she sign a statement that what she'd done was wrong, but she adamantly refused. Eventually, he just exposed her film and gave the camera back. It was unnerving!"

"Will you ever return to Tibet?" a nun asks expectantly, as though my return can somehow replace her own.

"I don't know," I reply. "I was lucky this time. I may not be lucky next time."

Soon, I'm settled again into my routine in Dharamsala, mostly teaching English at the nunnery and studying Buddhism at the library. I'm also writing the life story of each nun in order to get sponsors for their education and living expenses. Even though I love to travel, I also enjoy putting my energy into projects. So when other friends plan a trip to Calcutta, I decide against going with them.

"It's only for a week," they implore. "Join us. It'll be fun."

"I'm just back from Tibet. I don't want to interrupt my routine a second time."

"Don't you want to see another part of India?"

"Of course I do, but it just won't work. I have so many sponsorship interviews to do. If I keep taking holiday, I'll never finish by the time I have to leave for the U.S."

"We're going to visit Mother Teresa's nunnery. Don't you want to see Mother Teresa?"

This really gives me pause. I can't help but remember that I asked Art to accompany me to Calcutta a few years ago, and, because he refused, I didn't go. Do I dare miss another chance?

My friends sense an opening, so they persist. "Just think, she's old now. It might be the last time she greets the public. It would be a missed opportunity."

"You're right. It seems I keep missing the chance to see Mother Teresa even though it's been my dream. But I just got back to Dharamsala and feel guilty leaving again so soon. I think I'll pass."

My friends accept my decision and leave for Calcutta. They meet Mother Teresa who tells them to become nuns. They don't follow her advice, but they're happy to receive her blessing.

"If you have been to a public audience before, please do not come to another," the Dalai Lama's attendants tell the long line of foreigners waiting for clearance. "Give others a chance."

These words echo through my head as I register for the *eighth time*. I try to balance out the bad *karma* of being selfish with the good *karma* of receiving the Dalai Lama's blessing, and the blessing always wins. But this time, I will bring Tenzin, a nine-year-old boy who lives at the Tibetan Children's Village, a kilometer or so up the mountain from McLeod Ganj—one of twenty such facilities that educates 17,000 Tibetan children in India. That makes me feel less greedy.

Tenzin is one of many children lucky enough to escape from Tibet. It couldn't have been easy for his parents to say good-bye to him, knowing that their son probably would never return to his homeland. But they made this huge sacrifice in order for him to grow up in a free country.

I climb the steep hill to his hostel. Tenzin is sitting on the edge of his bed, clutching a picture to his chest. When I ask to look at it, he can barely release it; it's that precious to him. Of course, it's a picture of the Dalai Lama.

"Oh God, what should I do now?" I ask myself because, when you register, you're explicitly told, "Do not bring any pictures with you to be signed. It holds up the line." I decide to let Tenzin take the chance and face the possibility that the picture will be confiscated.

Walking downhill is a lot easier than climbing up, but Tenzin isn't relaxed. His face is serious, clearly reflecting the importance he attributes to the occasion.

Each month, His Holiness patiently stands for hours as, first, Tibetans and then foreigners stream past him, shake his hand, and receive a blessing. He gives each person a red protection string to be worn around the wrist or neck and *mani* pills. There isn't much conversation. Everyone waits expectantly and then leaves quickly, before His Holiness' energy escapes.

When it's our turn, I gently nudge Tenzin forward.

His Holiness is delighted to see us and asks Tenzin, "What is your name?"

Tenzin stands there, speechless, staring wide-eyed.

Again, "What is your name?"

Again, silence.

His Holiness asks me, "Can he speak?"

"His name is Tenzin," I reply. "I think he's a bit nervous."

The Dalai Lama gives a belly laugh and takes the picture. "Hmm, good picture," he jokes and signs it.

Tenzin smiles.

All the way back to the Tibetan Children's Village,

> *My religion is simple.*
> *My religion is kindness.*
> —His Holiness the 14th Dalai Lama,
> spiritual and temporal leader
> of the Tibetan people

Tenzin clutches the picture, now made even more precious by the Dalai Lama's signature. When we get to the hostel, he runs to his room and stands the picture on a small table at foot of his bed. He moves his pillow to the opposite end of the bed so that his head will lie next to the picture. Even at nine years of age, he knows that his feet should never face the picture.

A circular path surrounds Tsuglagkhang complex, which includes the Dalai Lama's official residence, the public Main Temple, other temples, a monastery, *stupas,* bookshops, a café, and a museum.[5]

The path begins at a main gate, descends a steep, potholed public road, then veers off to a pedestrian footpath that's very narrow and rutted in places.

It undulates, mostly downward to a half-way point. Here, people can easily spin dozens of medium-sized prayer wheels. Another prayer wheel, twelve feet high, sits in a small enclosure and is pushed around as a person walks beside it. Below, a hillside is covered with colorful prayer flags that blow in the wind, sending inscribed prayers to all corners of the Earth.

The footpath then rises steeply, widens into a vehicular road, meanders past side entrances to the compound, and returns to the main gate where dozens of vendors wait with Buddhist paraphernalia and Tibetan food. The entire route is about two kilometers and can be walked in approximately thirty minutes at a comfortable pace.

Dozens or hundreds of people walk this path. Some are elderly, dressed in traditional Tibetan garb, moving slowly. Others are younger: monks, nuns, and foreign visitors. Devotees come here daily, circumambulating Tsuglagkhang at least once if not several times. In the West, this spiritual practice is called a walking meditation. In the Buddhist tradition, it's called a *kora.*

The week after our audience with the Dalai Lama, Tenzin and I are doing a *kora.* As tradition dictates, we walk clockwise, our right shoulders always toward Tsuglagkhang.

We finish the *kora* and enter the courtyard of the Main Temple. We glance up and see the Dalai Lama appear at the top of a long set of steps. He spies us, quickly descends, and purposefully walks in our direction.

Again Tenzin is struck silent. But, for me, what is more alarming is that he's standing ram-rod straight and holding some books. I quickly grab the books so he can bow and join his hands in prayer position, the proper form of respect when in the presence of the Dalai Lama.

His Holiness sees this and laughs heartily. "Hello, Tenzin," he says. "It's good to see you again."

Tenzin smiles broadly.

"I have to go," I explain to the nuns on my last day at Gaden Choeling. "My leave of absence from my job in America is finished. My husband is waiting for me. I've been so happy here. I love all of you and will never forget you, but I can't stay any longer. I'm flying next week." The nuns are disappointed, but they understand. People come and go, and they can't expect volunteers to make a life-long commitment.

I'm leaving the Loseling Hotel, my home for the past year, with no idea of what to expect when I return to New Jersey.

The lepers are lining the street to say good-bye. I've given money to them, as have many other Westerners, but what they really appreciate is that I always put the rupees into what is left of their hands, not into the begging cup. I feel it gives them more dignity. The lepers wave their stumps at me and smile warmly.

"I've never seen such a farewell," Allyson, a volunteer who works in the office of the Tibetan Woman's Association, says with appreciation. Monks and nuns are also here to see me off. They put *khatas* around my neck—so many that I'm about to suffocate under them. When I get on the bus to Delhi, people stare because I'm so swathed in white greeting scarves that my head is barely visible.

In the late fall 1994, prior to Thanksgiving, I return home from Dharamsala with high hopes that my year away has saved my marriage. But those hopes quickly fade as my relationship with Art continues to deteriorate. Within months, we separate, and the divorce follows in February 1997.

We decide that I will stay in our house. It has a front porch, which gives it an old-fashioned look and feel. The living room is small and cozy, and Art kept a fire blazing in the fireplace all winter. The hardwood floors add warmth to an, otherwise, stark décor—white walls, white wicker furniture, white cushions. The backyard is large by New Jersey shore standards, and we had worked hard to make it flourish with ivy, shrubs, and colorful flowers.

Art and I always loved this house. How can he walk away without a second glance back? And he doesn't even take his precious library!

I try to make a new life for myself, but it isn't easy. Everything evokes a memory and most of them are terrifying. So many problems plagued us—six deaths in the immediate family in six years from 1987 to 1992. Perhaps it was too much for us to bear.

Gradually, though, I learn to enjoy my freedom. I take trips with my women friends and make my own decisions. I'm comfortable being alone to the extent that I say no when a friend offers to become my housemate.

I'm free. But free to do what? That's been my dilemma for the past few years.

I don't want to squander my freedom, so during Christmas vacation 1998, I consult Robina, a visiting nun at Milarepa Center in Vermont.

"Robina, I don't know what to do with my life. I want it to be meaningful and gratifying, but I can't figure it out."

"Pray on it. Pray to a deity to whom you feel connected and seek assistance," she advises.

I'm very disappointed with her response because I want something more definitive, but I do as she says. The deity, of course, is Green Tara. Every night I ask her, "What should I do with my life?" But I do not get an answer.

Then, in March 1999, before my summer holiday, I'm lying on the bed in the downstairs guestroom, asking myself, very absent-mindedly, "What should I do this summer? What should I do this summer? What should I do this summer?"

That's when the book falls off the shelf. Maybe the book falling off the shelf wasn't an accident. Maybe Green Tara finally answered.

And that's how I conclude telling my life story to the Japanese man sleeping soundly in the seat next to me as the plane carries us from Calcutta to New Jersey in August 1999. Of course, it wasn't for his benefit that I've told my story. I needed to tell it to myself.

# Early Retirement
## Labor Day Weekend 1999–July 23, 2001

After spending the summer of 1999 in India, I'm mentally and physically exhausted.

In June, I had been lucky to find summer tenants for my house, but they haven't moved out yet. It's now Labor Day weekend, and my friend Jane has invited me to stay with her. She's a speech teacher who works with disabled children, so she'll appreciate the progress the boys at Daya Dan made during my time there. She'll also understand when I tell her that I feel my work at Daya Dan isn't finished.

"Jane, these kids didn't even walk when I arrived. Now they walk, feed themselves, some dress themselves. We sing songs. We go to the park on Fridays."

"Who will take over now that you're gone?"

"I guess Sister Innocencia, but it's a big job for her to do alone."

Then Jane says something that shakes me to the core. *"You must retire and return to Calcutta!"*

"Jane, I can't retire now. I'm only fifty-three. I'm too young."

"You can take an early retirement."

"They'll slash my pension. I'll be poor the rest of my life."

"You don't need a lot of money to live in Calcutta."

"I can't live in Calcutta the rest of my life."

"Let's call the New Jersey Pensions Office and make an appointment for you."

"It's Friday afternoon of Labor Day weekend. No one will be there."

"Let's try."

"Jane, you try. I just got off an eighteen-hour flight. I'm exhausted."

So Jane calls Pensions and, by some miracle, someone is there. "My friend Rosalie Giffoniello wants to retire and move to Calcutta," Jane says into the telephone.

I quickly interject, "I don't want to retire and move to Calcutta. *You* want me to retire and move to Calcutta!"

"Shh. Shh. Let me speak." Then into the phone, "And she wants to retire in January 2000 because that's an auspicious date."

I can't believe this conversation. The poor secretary at Pensions probably just wants to go home and start her holiday weekend but, instead, she's listening to Jane's crazy ramblings.

"What do you mean she can't retire in January 2000?" Jane holds the phone away from her mouth to speak to me. "They have no appointments available until the end of November, and it takes three months to process the paperwork. So you can't retire until March."

"Well, that makes no sense. The school year ends in June," I reply.

"What should I do?"

"Take the appointment. I have nothing to lose." Secretly I'm relieved that I don't have to make a decision.

"Okay. She'll take the appointment. Her name is Rosalie Giffoniello." She gives my address and phone number.

When Jane hangs up, I ask, "Where do I go for the appointment? What papers do I bring with me?"

"I don't know," she replies with a shrug.

So I press the re-dial key, and the same woman answers the phone. She says, "Oh, Rosalie Giffoniello. I was just going to call you. As soon as I hung up with your friend, the phone rang. I got a cancellation in September. If you take the September appointment, you could retire in January 2000."

I take the appointment, thank her, and calmly inform Jane, "I'm retiring in January."

\* \* \*

My back is stiff after the long flight, and I'm nervous about the appointment with the woman in Pensions. So right after the first day of school, I go to see a chiropractor.

While being adjusted, I tell her in confidence, "Mary Ellen, don't tell anyone. I'm thinking of taking an early retirement and returning to Calcutta."

"That's great. You should do it," she responds enthusiastically.

"But my house. What about my house? It's my only asset."

"You can rent it out. It's a pretty little house. Someone will take it."

"But what if they wreck it? You hear these kinds of stories all the time."

"So rent it to someone you know. Then you'll have peace of mind."

"I don't know anyone who's moving."

"Someone will turn up. Don't worry."

"Maybe and maybe not," I say defensively. "But if I can't rent my house to someone I know, then I'm not going to Calcutta."

I go food shopping and return home. It feels odd to be back in the house after eight weeks in Calcutta. My new life is juxtaposed onto the old, and they're both vying for attention. I notice the light blinking on the answering machine. I assume it's someone welcoming me back.

The recorded message says, "Hi, Rosalie. It's Lee, Mary Ellen's friend. She called and told me that you're moving to Calcutta. If your house is available, then Kevin and I will rent it. We're getting married next month and need a place to live."

"I guess you aren't letting me off the hook," I reflect, directing the thought to Green Tara, the Buddhist deity who seems to be guiding my life.

> *Once you make a decision, the Universe conspires to make it happen.*
> —Ralph Waldo Emerson, essayist, lecturer, poet

When I tell my friends about this "latest coincidence," they aren't surprised. "It seems the Universe is pushing me toward Calcutta," I conclude.

"The Universe is busier than that," they add affably. "The Universe is packing your bags."

\* \* \*

My greatest fear is that I won't be able to sleep now that I'm back in New Jersey. When Art left our home, I didn't sleep for four months. I'd get into bed, my heart would start pounding, and it wouldn't stop for hours. "Count your breaths," my yoga teacher advised. "Concentrate on the rise and fall of your belly." That never worked. Sometimes, I'd pray that I'd have a heart attack just to end the panic attack.

I had slept fine in Calcutta, but now *that* fear has returned. It's gotten seared into my brain. I get into bed and immediately think, "What if I can't sleep tonight? I'll be exhausted tomorrow. I won't be able to work. I'll never get through the day." It's been three years since Art and I divorced, yet, stupidly, I act as though it were yesterday. I'm fine during the day, but at night I come apart.

I feel like I'm always struggling—struggling to cope, struggling to fulfill everyone's expectation, struggling to fulfill my own expectations. I sometimes wonder why I chose such a challenging path. But most of the time, I don't feel like I've chosen it at all. Rather, forces greater than my own have intervened, and those forces are guiding me.

But then I catch myself. That's such a powerful idea that I'm almost embarrassed to harbor it. I feel undeserving of such potent protection.

Undeserving—perhaps that's the clue. I feel undeserving. Maybe that's why can't I sleep.

And then I lie awake, secretly praying, if, indeed, I'm being led back to Calcutta, that the potent protection won't end.

I'm tired, dog-tired. I'm officially retired as of January 1, 2000, but have no time to enjoy my retirement. I'm trying to empty the house while, at the same time, people are dropping off all kinds of useless stuff for the kids in Calcutta. I'm pissed at myself for saying yes to all these donations and at the donors for not realizing that winter coats are totally inappropriate for a hot, humid climate. But, really, I'm pissed at Art.

His thousands of books need to be taken to the library. Books are heavy—back-breaking heavy. Why isn't he here, hauling them down the stairs? How did I get stuck with *his* job? I'm thinking of just tossing them out the upstairs window, calling him, and letting him see his precious books strewn all over the driveway. Why not? He deserves it. But the more I think about doing that, the guiltier I feel— not about upsetting Art but about damaging the books. Our family grew up respecting books, and I can't bring myself to do otherwise.

Education was always the first priority in our family. Hard times during the Depression forced my parents to drop out of college, and they never went back, so it fell on the shoulders of their children to do that for them. I was the middle child, so I had to do something grand to stand out.

I chose a combination of good grades and rebellious behavior. I graduated high school at sixteen and was accepted into Hunter College, a large, progressive liberal arts college in Manhattan renowned for providing educational opportunities to women and minorities. But I also engaged in all sorts of delinquent behaviors like stealing cars and smoking pot. Luckily, I was never caught.

At home, I was restless, angry, and stubborn; I didn't want anyone to tell me what to do. I went on peace marches and wanted to join the Peace Corps. I felt great empathy for the underdog, and that probably contributed to my decision to become a speech therapist and work with disabled children.

So instead of throwing Art's books out the window, I call Mary, my friend's daughter, and she helps me carry boxes of books down the stairs and into her van. We also bring cartons of *chachkies* to The Salvation Army. I have no feelings about parting with these things. I just feel tired—tired of having one foot in each world.

Then, as if I don't have enough to think about, I decide to put in a new bathroom. The bathroom has had problems for years, but Art would never agree to renovate it.

"You're never satisfied with anything," he'd say in an accusatory tone.

"The bathroom has problems. It needs to be fixed."

"That doesn't mean you have to put in a new one."

"Every plumber who gives us an estimate for a patch job says it's cheaper to put in a new one."

"Of course, they say that. Then the bill will get higher and higher."

"The bathroom looks terrible, and it'll look worse if we get a patch job."

"It's an old fashioned bathroom."

"It looks like a dingy, old bathroom."

"Don't you remember anything Geshe-la taught us about nonattachment?" he would insist.

"Of course I do."

"Well, then, the problem isn't with the bathroom. The problem is that you're a bad Buddhist."

So now, fifteen years after that discussion, I decide that my tenant shouldn't have a problem with the bathroom while I'm halfway around the world.

I'm overwhelmed and nervous. I can't sleep. I keep thinking and thinking and thinking about all I have to finish at the New Jersey end and all I have to do when I arrive in Calcutta. My mind is like the wild monkey Geshe-la talked about when he was giving an example of a faulty meditation. "You can't stay focused on anything; your mind jumps and jumps and jumps." So I guess I'm a bad Buddhist after all.

The plumbers have ripped out the bathroom. I can live without a sink and bathtub, but how can I live without a toilet? Doris, a friend with whom I traveled to Norway and Scotland after my divorce, owns a house nearby. She allows me to stay there until the bathroom is finished while she visits a friend in Massachusetts. It's snowing like hell outside, but I have to leave.

I throw a few odds and ends into my small Volkswagen convertible.

I love this car. It's so sporty with a white body, white top, and white leather seats. It's a fun car and I bought it because I thought it would put fun back into our marriage, but Art hated it from the first day and refused to ride in it for months.

Now I'm driving the Volkswagen very slowly, but it's such a light car that it's skidding all over the road. I keep reassuring myself, "It's only two miles. It's only two miles. Stay calm. I'm almost there, only one more mile to go."

Suddenly, the car is spinning out of control. It isn't going anywhere, just around in circles. It can't hit another car—that isn't the problem—because there isn't another car or person out on a night like this. Just an idiot like me!

I smash into a snow bank. The car won't move. I can't drive forward or backward or sideways or any way. I am stuck. Really, really stuck. The irony isn't lost on me—I'm stuck between two worlds.

\* \* \*

The bathroom is finished, and I'm back in my house. I laugh aloud at the irony that, after waiting fifteen years, I'll use the new bathroom for only two weeks before the tenants move in. There's nothing left in the house except for the bed in the downstairs guest room and a snack table. I'm lying on the bed, and another irony hits me.

I was on this very bed seven months ago when the book fell off the shelf and guided me to Calcutta. At that time, I thought I was absent-mindedly trying to decide what to do during my summer vacation. But, instead, I was sending out an *intention* to the Universe about what to do with my life. Now I've come to realize that nothing in these recent months—or throughout my life—has happened by accident.

So now I'm speaking directly to Green Tara again, beseeching her with all my heart and soul. "Green Tara, if you want me to go to Calcutta, I'll go. You know I'm not afraid of hard work. You know I'm not afraid of challenges, but I can't do this alone. You have to send someone to help me. You have to send someone to help me. You have to send someone to help me."

I begin to cry hysterically.

The phone rings, but I don't pick up the receiver. Instead, I let the call go to the answering machine and listen to the message.

> *When your heart*
> *is in your dreams,*
> *no request is too extreme.*
> —Ned Washington, lyricist
> (from "When You Wish Upon a Star")

"Hello, my name is Janet Grosshandler. You don't know me. You teach with my sister-in-law, Nancy. I'm at Nancy's house right now, and she told me that you're going to Calcutta. I just want you to know that I want to help you."

I stop crying immediately. I look up, as though to deities hovering directly above. I exclaim in wonder and relief, "Green Tara, *that* was quick."

On February 2, 2000, I'm back in Calcutta. I step off the plane in the middle of the night, and Sister Innocencia and Sister Bosco have come to meet me at the airport. I'm struggling with my luggage: two large suitcases filled with nothing but educational materials. Clothes I can buy later.

"I'm here. I'm here," I shout as I emerge from the terminal.

"Bless you," Sister Innocencia says. "You arrived safely."

"Welcome back," Sister Bosco adds.

"The ambulance is waiting. Let us help you."

I'm tired and gladly accept their help.

We arrive at Daya Dan, and everything is dark and quiet. They lead me up the staircase to the top floor. There are guest rooms there, one of which was already occupied.

> *To stand up, to leave everything behind—to say "Yes!"*
>
> —Dag Hammarskjold, diplomat, economist, author, Secretary-General of the United Nations

"Stay here until you are settled in a guesthouse," they generously offer, showing me to a vacant room. "Tomorrow, you will see the boys."

I sleep soundly except for the mosquitoes buzzing around my head, but even the thought of malaria is far from my mind tonight.

I shower and eat breakfast, and it's already 11:00 a.m. when Sister Innocencia comes to get me. "*Chalo, chalo.* Let us go. Everyone is waiting for you."

I go downstairs, and there are the boys, waiting curiously for something to happen. I can't help but think that, perhaps, they'll be disappointed. I stand in the doorway for a few seconds then walk in slowly. It doesn't look like anyone recognizes me. That's okay. I've been away five months. That's a long time in the life of a little boy.

Then, cautiously, Surendra walks forward with his characteristic awkward gait. Then Patrick rushes ahead, nearly knocking Surendra down. Then Peter is suddenly hanging onto my leg, nearly pulling me over. Before long, I'm surrounded by laughing boys.

"We have been practicing that group hug for all the months you have been gone," Sister Innocencia says. "Sister Bosco was your stand-in, so I was a bit worried. I was not sure they would realize the greeting was for you."

"You're a good teacher, Sister Innocencia," I tell her delightedly. "They understand completely."

"We have only smart children at Daya Dan," she announces to all the kids. "I am very proud of you."

* * *

I've shifted to the Gulistan Guest House again.

I really like staying here. It's clean and comfortable, but you would never know it when you first enter the building nor from the view of rubble-covered rooftops on the other side of my single grilled window. The downstairs hall is dark and narrow, and fuse boxes plaster the walls. Outside, tangles of electrical lines hang everywhere in huge hoops and bundles, stringing themselves across streets, against buildings, through alleyways, and often falling onto the footpath. It's part of the landscape, like the beggars on the streets and the babies crawling across railroad tracks. India doesn't hide its blemishes, unlike in America where fuse boxes are in basements, electrical wires are underground, homeless people are in shelters, and babies are in daycare.

The hotel lobby is one flight up from the street. One of the white marble stairs is chipped. The banister near the top is handsome wrought iron topped with dark brown wood.

Mr. Khan, a small man with two wives and children from each of them, is the owner. He sits on a narrow bench and proudly oversees the operation. Every day, he smiles and makes a point to ask me, "Madame, is everything all right? Is everything fine?" I guess he wants the Gulistan to be like a Western-style hotel, and because I'm American, he assumes I'm an expert on these things. Little does he know I always travel with a backpack and stay in youth hostels.

"Yes, everything is fine," I assure him.

"Let me know if there is ever a problem," he implores. "This is your hotel."

After a few weeks, I approach him. "Mr. Khan, there is a problem."

Mr. Khan looks chagrined. "What problem, Madame? Please tell me." He seems practically aghast.

"The walls in the hallway are covered with blood."

"That is not blood, Madame," he says with obvious relief. "I explain you. That is betel juice. The men chew betel and then spit it out after their mouths are overflowing with liquid. It is a stimulant and cannot be swallowed. That would be very dangerous."

"Why do they spit it on the walls?"

"Oh, they spit it everywhere, on the walls, trees, footpath—"

"And sometimes on people's feet if they happen to be in the way," I add, knowing this from experience.

"It happens, but it is not intentional. When the mouth is full, the betel must be spit. Otherwise it drips down the chin and front of the shirt."

"But it makes your hotel look shabby. You must do something about it."

"Do not worry about it, Madame. I will do the needful."

A few weeks later, Mr. Khan is waiting expectantly at the top of the stairs. He has had the hallway painted and very tall plants placed along the walls. It looks fresh and clean.

"Congratulations, Mr. Khan. This makes a big difference."

"Madame," he says respectfully, "I did this for you."

* * *

In April 2000, I write this aerogramme to my friend Barbara in New Jersey:

It's been a very busy transition—back in my old hotel, back in my old room, lots of people remember me from the summer, a friendly group of volunteers. I'm a lot happier here now than I was before—not putting myself under pressure. Have lots of projects going on already and have run into lots of obstacles already but trying to let it go. Everything will get done "eventually"—that's the Indian way. The education program has been a big success. The children love school & I enjoy teaching it. We're having murals painted to brighten up the orphanage (Noah's Ark, ocean). & it's made a big difference. The place is like a dungeon (no air, no light because no windows)—we're trying to solve the problem of dampness before we repaint everything—need a solvent perhaps. The kids are all healthy & seemed to have matured since the summer—more social & independent. So it's easier to work with them. The hot weather is already upon us. Lots of volunteers have left for cooler places. By May, I'm told, it will be unbearable. The monsoon will bring relief but it also brings problems of its own, (flooding, mosquitoes, illness).

Then, in June, I write to her again:

Dear Barbara,

My life is so full and busy at the orphanage—I have so many projects going on at one time. Yet in other respects my life is totally boring. I get back from the orphanage at 2:00, eat lunch, nap, watch the news, check my email (that takes 1-1/2 hrs.), eat dinner, read & go to bed. No variation in my schedule. Once in a while I go to a movie. I went to Sikkim for a week to get out of the heat (115°). I don't know if I'm bored or not. It's a relief to do nothing after the orphanage because I'm always so tired & it's so hot, but a little distraction or fun once in a while would be welcome.

On Thurs, our "free day," I catch up on my aerogrammes. It's an existence so different than the one I'm used to at home. I have to go to Bangkok on July 10 for 1 week to renew my visa. I can't renew it until it expires (July 11). Calcutta in the heat & monsoon is no picnic. The program at the orphanage grows & grows as we add more & more components to it. It is a model program in that other homes & orphanages come to Daya Dan to learn from us. It's amazing how much we've accomplished in 4 short months.

* * *

I haven't spoken to Art since our divorce, now more than three years ago. My decision to remain out of his life was painful. I didn't want to make it, but didn't know how to get out of making it. So, grasping each other at his aunt's house one day, I had blurted out, "I don't want to see you anymore. I can't live a life that's without hope."

He started to cry. "This will be like you're dead, but you aren't dead."

Here in Calcutta, that conversation circles around and around and around in my head. I pray to Green Tara without end, "Please pacify my distorted mental wanderings. Please pacify my distorted mental wanderings. Please pacify my distorted mental wanderings." Unfortunately, my distorted mental wanderings take many forms, with the trivial and the momentous given equal importance. So that conversation with Art is mixed up with an insensitive remark to a volunteer and a missed opportunity to raise some money for the children and an accidental brushing of my teeth with tap water instead of bottled water. Even Green Tara can't sort it out.

I think of Art often and, each time, I have an actual "pinch" in my heart. But since working at Daya Dan, I realize that I've been missing the point. Difficult as it is, I should be grateful for a broken heart, which is far better than having a closed heart. And to make that easier for me to grasp, I clear my conflicted mind for just a second and focus on a sentiment beautifully expressed by mystical scholar Andrew Harvey: "When the heart is broken open, then God can put the whole universe in it."[6]

And then I feel calm.

Sister Innocencia and I are trying desperately to get services for the blind boys. The volunteers are able to manage with the other children using lesson plans and educational materials that I've provided, but the blind boys need specialized services. We decide to go to the National Institute for the Visually Handicapped to seek their advice.

The director is young and charming, very solicitous. We have five children in his office and keep reiterating that these are very complex cases, while he keeps assuring us that the specialists are equipped to handle problems. He calls two men who are teachers of the blind into his office.

"Sirs," Sister says, "I do not want to mislead you about their conditions. These boys are blind and also neurologically impaired. They can neither speak nor follow directions."

"We are trained to work with a wide variety of cases. Please rest assured," says one teacher confidently.

"Are you sure?" Sister continues. "These boys are not easy to understand."

"Madame, it is our duty."

Sister and I are reassured, and we make arrangements for one teacher to come to Daya Dan on Monday at 9:00 a.m. and the other on Wednesday morning at the same time.

On Monday at 8:30 a.m., the children are already sitting in their chairs. I don't want to waste precious time collecting them after the teacher arrives. Two hours later, the poor boys are still sitting, and the teacher still isn't there. All day, we wait. The teacher doesn't come. More frustrating than waiting is the fact that he didn't call.

On Wednesday, I figure out a new strategy. The children are in the classroom, the chairs are lined up in a row, but the boys aren't sitting in them. We patiently wait, but the second teacher doesn't show either.

On the following Monday, the teacher who is supposed to come at 9:00 a.m. arrives at 10:45. The children, who eat breakfast at 6:00, are used to eating their lunch at 11:00, so by 10:45, they're cranky and tired. The teacher stays only fifteen minutes.

Then, to add insult to injury, the teacher who was supposed to come on Wednesdays at 9:00 shows up at 2:30 in the afternoon—when the boys are taking a nap.

"Let them sleep. Let them sleep," he says airily, as if he really doesn't want to be there.

"They have all the time in the world to sleep," I insist. "We'll surely wake them up. After all, you're here. You've made a long journey and were kind enough to come." That's what I say on the outside. Inside, I'm seething.

We get everyone up and into the chairs. The boys are dazed but cooperative to some extent, so I'm hopeful. But at the end of twenty minutes, the teacher tells me that he doesn't want to come back.

"These children are hopeless," he declares with a harrumph of authority and finality.

"After you've come every single week over a period of six months and worked with the boys diligently, if at that time you tell me they're hopeless, then I'll believe you," I hiss through my teeth. "But now, after you've been here only a few

> *But difficulties are meant to arouse, not discourage.*
> —William Ellery Channing, Unitarian preacher

minutes, I cannot accept your assessment. I don't believe these boys are hopeless."

He leaves. I'm distraught.

Neither he nor the other teacher ever returns.

My 180-day tourist visa is due to expire, so in July 2000, I fly to Thailand for a three-week holiday. There, I obtain another visa and return to Daya Dan. This is but one more step in my commitment to remain in Calcutta. And I'm beginning to feel more and more at home on Sudder Street.

Sudder Street is like any other street in Calcutta—a jumble of sounds, sights, and shops. And the people are in your face—or at your elbow.

A man sits on the ground selling bananas, blocking the narrow footpath. Next to him, sits the cobbler with his wooden tool box beside him and pieces of leather spread out in front of him. Next to the cobbler, is the bookseller with books in all languages to tempt volunteers from various nations. In front of a restaurant, a man sharpens knives, pressing blades against a portable grinding wheel that he spins with a foot treadle, sparks flying in all directions.

It's impossible to look upward at the sky or the architecture while walking. Walking requires alertness, always looking downward for potential obstacles, such as broken sidewalks or repaired sidewalks that never get fully repaired. Many sidewalks have a trench, fifteen to eighteen inches wide, to lay a measly four-inch drainage tube. The trench is roughly filled in with dirt and small chunks of brick or broken concrete. Before long, the filler settles, leaving a rutted indentation that could easily twist an ankle.

People aren't the only ones who lay claim to a part of the footpath. Mangy dogs lie about here and there. The males are passive during the day, but, at night, they form packs, flex their muscles, and fight. Many of the females, their milk sacs swollen, seem to be perpetually busy with their pups.

If you're looking for a particular store, you have to stop to read the myriad of abutting signs. Small shops sell everything you want or need. You can't enter most shops because there's no doorway; instead, a counter separates you from the shopkeeper across which all business is transacted. It's possible to buy individual cigarettes, and the stores that sell them also offer a jute rope, hung from the exterior wall, its sizzling end producing an ember from which both customers and other puffers can get a light.

Two men, one young and one older, repair and shine shoes. They're not partners but competitors, and they sit so close to one another that it's embarrassing to choose one over the other.

"Authentic restaurants" welcome you, but, with their doors flung open, you're forced to listen to incessant *horning* while eating or conversing with friends.

Even more "out in the open" are the cookeries that crowd or block sidewalks throughout the Sudder Street neighborhood. These consist of nothing more than a cooking counter, a fire pot fueled with lumps of coal, a pot for water, a pot for rice, and maybe one or two other pans. These stalls serve *chai* and the Indian version of fast food: barbecued mutton kabobs hand-pressed onto wooden sticks, deep-fried chicken pieces, hand-flattened *chapattis* cooked on a skillet over a coal fire, freshly made potato chips in large woks of boiling oil. When the stalls are not busy, it's possible to walk past them single file, but when customers are present, you have to walk around—into the street and the traffic.

The laundry *dhobis* with their ironing tables and the fruit vendors and vegetable vendors with their old-fashioned balance scales occupy about the same amount of space as the cookeries, but their customers don't linger and block the sidewalks as much.

*Rickshaw* drivers call out, "Mother House, Mother House," even at 10:00 p.m., far past visiting hours there. Taxi drivers annoyingly stop in front of you and block your passage as you try to cross an intersection as if you don't know how to flag a taxi if you need one.

Beggars follow close behind, touching your elbow for attention if you don't immediately drop a coin into their outstretched palms. It doesn't take long to grasp their universal signal of hand extended, palm up as if to form a bowl, then fingers touching the lips—back and forth, back and forth. "Give me money so I can eat. Give me money so I can eat. Give me money so I can eat." Yet, often, they and ignore the fruit vendors and point to potato chips and chocolate bars for sale in many shops.

A Fire Brigade station marks the east end of Sudder Street, its tall overhead doors open in the daytime to reveal bright red fire engines and firefighters standing around inside. Nearby, a handful of drug addicts shoot up. I walk past them often, never feeling threatened. Sometimes, they extend a hand for money. Mostly, they sleep or sit quietly, sharing a needle. Among them is the boy, now a teenager, who helped me find a room at the Gulistan when I first arrived in Calcutta in the summer of 1999 and who cheated me over buying powdered milk supposedly for his sister.

Toward the Fire Brigade end of Sudder Street, Hindu women congregate with their children hoping for generosity from foreigners but find it gradually decreasing as guide books warn against scams and schemes. I never give *baksheesh*, but sometimes I buy food, which costs far more. Otherwise, I give them a warm greeting and handshake. But they're clever, these street women. They sidle up next to me, stroke my arm, and kiss my hand. They're so ingratiating and such good actresses they should each win an Academy Award.

Muslim families live in a sidewalk community at the other end of Sudder Street near the Indian Museum. They do not beg—men join their wives and children after working during the day at menial jobs. At night, they cook with kerosene-fueled woks and sleep in make-shift tents or under tarps or on blankets in the open.

Then, as if the flexible flow of tightly packed humanity weren't enough, a seven-foot tall concrete pedestal and clay bust of Rabindranath Tagore, the world's first non-Western Nobel Laureate in Literature, who hailed from Bengal in the late 1800s,[7] stands stationary at one corner. It further blocks a sidewalk already teeming with too many people crowded into too little space.

In the middle of all this is Curd Corner, a tiny eatery with a limited menu of tea, coffee, and yogurt. It's popular with volunteers who like to congregate there although even a small group eventually spills onto the street, eating and drinking while being elbowed by passers-by. Perhaps that's the reason I've avoided Curd Corner. Or because it looks a bit dirtier than most other places. But no one has complained about getting sick, so I take a chance and eat there one day.

Sonny, the owner, is always smiling, which makes the place seem bigger and brighter than it really is. On one wall, he has proudly displayed a picture of himself and Westerners on a trek. I settle on the tiny bench and order a sweet *lassi*, a tasty yogurt drink flavored with cardamom and rose water. It's hot and humid, I'm thirsty, and the drink goes down easily.

I notice that there's a bucket at the edge of the shop. A crow alights on it, bobbing its head, drinking the water eagerly. Then a dog, dirty and bleeding from a recent fight, walks over and laps the water in huge gulps.

"Sonny," I say, "you're really nice to think of the animals on this hot, humid day. Usually they're neglected." Sonny nods and continues his work. A few minutes later, Sonny gathers a tower of glasses, balancing them with ease as he makes his way out of the shop. He goes to the bucket and starts washing the glasses in the water—the same water in the same bucket just visited by the bird and the dog. My stomach becomes a knot.

* * *

My head itches. During the day, it isn't so noticeable, and I just scratch unconsciously while doing other things. But at night, it's maddening! I can't sleep. I also can't ignore it any longer. The problem is lice, and they won't go away by themselves. I try several different shampoos, including one brought by a volunteer from Italy. Nothing helps, so I seek advice from experts: the street women.

So off I go to Sudder Street to be de-liced. The women there de-lice each other all the time so they know what they're doing.

"Sit down, Aunty. Here, on this piece of newspaper. Take the baby, Aunty. Put him on your lap."

The baby has a brown cord around his waist but no diaper, not even a rag as a pseudo-diaper. The cord has a talisman attached to it, intended, the women tell me, as protection from the dreaded Evil Eye.[8] But what if he has to pee? What or who will protect me? I keep staring at his little pecker. If it moves even slightly, I'll jump up. I was once sitting on a long distance bus next to a father holding a diaper-less child on his lap. Suddenly the baby started to pee. The father very calmly held the baby out the window.

Three women surround me. Sumatra takes the left side, Seema takes the top and back, and Laxmi takes the right side. For them, moving their hands through my curly locks that descend to below my shoulders is like embarking on a journey into wild, foreign territory and must be assessed very critically. Unlike Indian hair, which is straight and shiny and luxurious, my hair resembles a complicated tangle akin to overgrown vines or, as the Indians like to say, "Maggie Noodles," a popular easy-to-fix food with tight curly noodles in a broth. Therefore, my hair requires their consideration and consultation—and much ado. But, finally, they begin. They separate my mane down to the scalp, and they search. Laxmi has immediate success.

"Here is one, Aunty. Look."

I look, and, indeed, she has a tiny, biting creature in her hand. Then she squashes it between her thumb and index finger and flicks it away.

"Look, Aunty," says Seema.

Again I look and again a tiny creature is squashed with great delight for my entertainment. They beckon my attention to each and every one, the treasures extracted from the depths of my scalp. Finally, they're done, a look of triumph on each face.

"Are they all gone?" I ask hopefully.

"Come back next week for a check-up," the experts advise.

* * *

In the narrow entrance of the Gulistan Guest House, chock-a-block crowded with fuse boxes, wires, and mail boxes, Raj, a handsome young man with a will to succeed in business, has figured out a way to install six computers and opened a cyber café.

Eva, a German banker in her early 30s who has come to Calcutta to be trained as a Missionaries of Charity nurse, and I like to sit here and send emails to each other, which is like texting someone sitting next to you at the dining room table. It costs only ten rupees an hour, so we aren't losing much.

I write to her: "Hi, Eva."

"What happened?" she replies.

"I walked into my room today and my pillow was brown, completely brown. The window was open, so I thought the pillow was covered with dust. But when I checked more carefully, I realized it was covered with ants."

"Oh, gross. What did you do?" she writes back.

"I called the guys at the desk and told them to spray."

"I thought you took a Buddhist vow not to kill."

"I did, but I figured the guys are killing them."

"That's really lame."

"I know, but in the end it didn't matter anyway. The Universe saved me from getting a lifetime of bad *karma*."

"How?"

"I left for a couple of hours because the spray is so toxic I didn't want to breathe it in. I told the guys to wear kerchiefs across their faces. I don't know if they did or not, but it didn't matter anyway."

"Why not? Why not? Get to the point."

"Hey, this chat is costing us only ten rupees an hour, so I can take as long as I want."

"You're an asshole. Do you know that?"

"Did I teach you that word in our weekly English classes or did you learn it on your own in Germany?"

"Everyone around the world knows asshole!"

I explain, "Do you know that in Mexico if you give them the A-OK sign, the index finger and thumb forming a circle, they become enraged. It means asshole."

"I'd punch you out if you gave me the asshole sign."

"I'll try it someday in front of a cop."

"I'll punch out the cop."

"*Oy vey!* That's Yiddish."

"That's close to German so I know what *oy vey* means."

"So, back to the ants," I continue.

"Yes, finally, back to the ants."

"I came back to the room after a couple of hours, and I gingerly opened the door. Do you know the word 'gingerly'?"

"I know ginger. It's what you put in your tea every morning."

"This is a different ginger. It means cautiously or carefully."

"Okay, you gingerly opened the door."

"I gingerly opened the door and smelled something very familiar. Something very sweet."

"Which was?"

"I didn't know, so I went to find the guys."

"And you found them."

"Yeah, I found them cleaning an upstairs room."

"And they said?"

"They didn't say anything. They showed me the can."

"The can of toxic bug spray."

"No, a can of room freshener."

"Room freshener? Are you kidding?"

"No, I'm not kidding. So instead of dead ants, I have sweet-smelling ants. And I think I'll keep them. This way—no bad *karma*!"

The question of *karma* persistently nags at me. For example, there's a young man from Mexico volunteering at Daya Dan for a few days. He's on a business trip throughout Asia, selling inflatable balls the size of soccer balls. They're wonderful balls, each with an odor that corresponds to the color: yellow smells like lemon, red smells like strawberry, green like lime. He's wonderful with the kids, lifting them high in the air, hugging them, laughing with them. At the end of the three days, he feels so terrible about leaving that he decides to make a gift of the balls to the orphanage. He takes out a small hand pump and inflates forty-three balls, one for each child, upstairs and down. He places one in each crib. Even the children upstairs, who are immobile, smile and respond to the lovely colors and odors.

I ask him, "How will you complete your business trip without the balls?"

"I won't complete it. I'll go home."

"But what will you tell your boss?"

"I'll tell them the balls were all stolen."

So the question is this: Does he get bad *karma* for lying to his boss or good *karma* for donating the balls to Daya Dan? I wonder what the Dalai Lama would say.

\* \* \*

Mithu and I sit on a cement ledge that surrounds a tree. He wants me to listen to his idea.

Mithu is a good-looking thirty-one-year-old who could easily fill his time in other ways. Yet, he chooses to volunteer at Daya Dan, and he's a good role model for the boys. Because there are very few Indian volunteers with the Missionaries of Charity, I've grown to appreciate him—and his ideas.

But the traffic noise is deafening. *Horning. Horning. Horning.* Why do they blow the horns incessantly? *Horning* long ago stopped being a warning that a vehicle is approaching. Now, it's an intrusion. Like surround sound in a movie theater, it comes from every direction and is impossible to filter out. Mithu is Indian so the noise doesn't bother him.

I shout over the din, "Mithu, why do you want to start a home for boys?"

"Because my father would be proud of me," he shouts back.

"How would we choose the boys?"

"*Arre!* There are millions of homeless children on the streets of Calcutta."

"How would we support the home?"

"We can find donors. You are American. Americans are rich."

"Where would we house them?"

"I will get a flat."

"Who will take care of them?"

"My mother."

"Do you think we can really do it?"

"An easy piece of cake."

An easy piece of cake. What's so easy about opening an orphanage? It's a pipe dream in which Mithu and I indulge ourselves. We've had the same conversation dozens of times, and it always ends on his optimistic note: "An easy piece of cake."

I've also had a dream that, somehow, I would do more for children in Calcutta than be a volunteer at Daya Dan. But what? How? Trying to mold this dream—this pipe dream— into a plan is no easy piece of cake. As I've often done, I pray to Green Tara. I don't receive an answer, so maybe she wants me to figure it out myself.

> *You gotta have a dream. If you don't have a dream, how you gonna make a dream come true?*
> —Oscar Hammerstein, librettist, theatre producer, director
> (from *South Pacific*)

When I leave again, this time for New Jersey on March 23, 2001, Calcutta's name has been changed back to its original Kolkata, which might have been the name of a nearby village or a tribute to the goddess Kali or a description of the floodplain of the Hooghly River.[9] Regardless, when Britain's East India Company claimed this territory in 1772 and made this city the capital,[10] they decided they liked the sound of Calcutta better. Now emancipated from British rule since 1947, Indians have finally reversed the name back to Kolkata. The same is true of Mumbai, the Hindi name for the city Westerners know as Bombay.[11]

Back in the States, I attempt to be up-to-date and tell people I work in Kolkata, but they either nod as if to say "that's nice," indicating that they don't yet associate the new name with India's third largest city, or they respond with "I thought you were in Calcutta." Then I have to explain and that detracts from what I really want people to know about my work with the children there. While I think that change is good, this is one change that creates a dilemma, so I find myself going back and forth. Calcutta or Kolkata? Kolkata or Calcutta?

In New Jersey, my house is rented, so I stay in Doris' house, just as I did when I had my bathroom replaced for my first renters.

Through ongoing meetings with Janet Grosshandler, I learn directly to what extent she has become a diligent partner in supporting my efforts in Kolkata. Although she has no desire to go to India, she works unflaggingly from New Jersey. Together for the next four months, we raise money to buy equipment and services for the boys at Daya Dan.

"I think we should expand our activities," she says one day. "There must be other children who need help in Calcutta, I mean Kolkata—I'll have to get used to the new name."

"Of course. There are thousands of children living on the streets and in terrible slums—probably tens of thousands. Actually, they're far more vulnerable than the children living at the orphanage."

"Exactly. That's why we'll create Empower The Children. Do you like the name? I thought of it while I was jogging. I get a lot of brilliant ideas at 5:00 in the morning."

I groan because I'm totally comatose any time before 8:00 a.m. and only feel awake after two cups of strong, ginger tea.

"Empower The Children," she continues. "That's what we'll call it."

"Call it?" I ask. "What is *it?*"

"Our nonprofit. Our organization dedicated to helping poor children."

"A nonprofit? Do you mean a 501(c)3? Do you think we're ready for that?" I ask weakly.

"Of course, we're ready," replies Janet. She was widowed at an early age with three young boys to raise and is unperturbed by challenges. Now she enthusiastically embraces the idea of starting our own programs in Kolkata in addition to our work with the Missionaries of Charity.

"Empower The Children," I reply. "It rolls off the tongue easily, that's for sure."

"It isn't the tongue that counts. It's about children. With a registered nonprofit, we can get more donations and help more children."

"That's true, but who will help us? I mean, more fundraising and helping more children means more work." More responsibility. More logistics. More headaches. Will we enlist our own group of volunteers? Just what does this mean?

"Everyone will help us," she replies. "Just give them a chance."

So Janet and I give birth to Empower The Children, which we formally establish on June 8, 2001, and I can't help but recognize another irony. I never wanted children because I didn't want to be tied down. Now, in what are the "grandmother years," I'll be tethered to Kolkata for a long, long time, helping who knows how many children.

Janet, with her wisdom of financial and organizational matters, is right about fundraising. It is easier, and we get more donations because people are more comfortable giving to a registered charity. We

> *The moment one definitely commits oneself,*
> *then Providence moves too.*
> —William Hutchinson Murray,
> mountaineer, writer

hold a Bollywood event and one hundred people attend. Of course, people think we've misspelled Hollywood, and I have to explain that Bollywood is the name of India's international movie industry.

I give interviews that are published in local newspapers. I even appear on New Jersey News, a local television channel, but I'm so nervous that, even though I can normally expound at great length, I barely utter a word. Thank goodness the interviewer knows both the questions and answers because she's forced to supply both!

But all this extra fanfare convinces me that we've made the right decision. I can *feel* a difference—a difference *within* me. It's about commitment. By creating Empower The Children, we are committed to continuing our work in Kolkata. My being there isn't just a whim or fancy or escape from whatever may have been troubling me in New Jersey for nearly a decade. It's no longer my personal journey. Empower The Children makes this work a collective journey—for my life and the lives of Janet, our board members, future donors, and all the children we will *empower*. I love the change. It elevates the whole idea!

On July 23, 2001, just six weeks after Janet signed the papers to incorporate Empower The Children, I return to Kolkata with renewed passion—and with extra money for the boys at Daya Dan and to help Mithu start a small orphanage, and … .

Who else? What other children? Where to begin? Who do I tell about Empower The Children? How? When? So many questions.

Green Tara, I need you.

# Empowered
## July 23, 2001–July 23, 2002

Jane had a wonderful idea while I was in New Jersey—her second wonderful idea since she first insisted I retire and move to Kolkata nearly two years ago. But this second wonderful idea helps the more disabled boys and girls who live upstairs at Daya Dan.

I had told Jane that, to my surprise, I enjoy teaching these children as much as the less disabled boys downstairs. But, unfortunately, many of them can't sit up. Sister Maria Santa and I had tried everything. We surrounded and propped them with pillows, even wooden supports with belts, but their bodies are so limp that they still slumped.

"Buy feeder seats," Jane suggested, which is exactly what I did. Of course, they were expensive, but, at least, the shipping was greatly discounted thanks to Airlines Ambassadors International, a network of airline employees who use their pass privileges to deliver humanitarian aid items around the world.

Actually, a feeder seat is quite simple. The child fits into an indentation in the seat like a piece into a jigsaw puzzle. Straps crisscross the body, and the child looks like a pilot strapped into a jet. Children who never sat before are now upright and, for the first time, looking at something other than the ceiling. They're making eye contact with other children, eating normally, and are even able to attend our small in-house school.

I wonder if they're shocked by what they now observe. Sometimes their expressions remind me of an old cartoon in *The New York Times* of a chick coming out of an egg: It looks

> *I am not afraid of storms, for I am learning how to sail my ship.*
> —Louisa May Alcott, novelist

to the left, to the right, to the left again, and goes back inside!

I mention to Sister Innocencia that Janet had ordered one feeder seat in an adult size, too big for our kids.

"I will take it to Shishu Bhavan," she replies.

"Shishu Bhavan? The children there are younger yet or infants waiting for adoption."

"There is Sabeena. She is thirty-three. She has been at Shishu Bhavan her entire life."

"Can she use the feeder seat? Will it help her?"

"She cannot move at all. She has a curved spine and cannot sit up. She is totally helpless."

"Why wasn't she shifted to another home as she got older like everyone else?"

"They love her too much."

A couple of days later, Sister Innocencia is beaming, even more than usual. "I have just come from Shishu Bhavan," she says excitedly.

"Oh, I forgot all about the adult feeder seat. Did you deliver it?"

"I did."

"And?"

"God bless you, Rosalie. Sabeena sat up for the first time in her life. She never stopped laughing."

* * *

"Sister, Sister, they're coming." I'm so excited I can't contain myself.

"Where are they?" She's bursting with excitement too.

"They're coming from San Francisco. I don't know the route, but they're en route."

"Thanks be to God."

The ambulance takes Sister Innocencia, Sister Bosco, and I to the airport to meet them. It seems like we're crawling through traffic even though the siren is on and the driver daringly crosses the center line to the wrong side of the road and is, at times, on the footpath. I remember the first time I rode in this ambulance and the young driver did the same thing. Then, I thought I was going to die in Kolkata! Now I realize that this type of driving is *normal*. And today, I don't care; I just want us to get to the airport before they arrive.

Security officers won't let us into the terminal. There are no benches outside, but that doesn't matter; we pace and pace, too excited to sit. We don't dare drink anything because then we might have to pee and the bathrooms are inside. When people exit or enter and the automatic doors are open for a few seconds, we strain our necks to spot them. We don't see them. The sisters pray the rosary. I pray in my own way.

Then, they suddenly appear, balanced on an airport luggage cart. Our relief and joy are so intermixed we can't discern which is greater.

But the carts are too small to hold the large boxes, and only with great effort are the volunteers who traveled with them able to push them.

"Don't fall off and crash onto the unforgiving pavement; you're too valuable!" I pray, beseeching the last bit of safety for twenty brand-new, shiny, spiffy, child-size wheelchairs.

Pam and Jodie are the volunteers from Airline Ambassadors; it's their first time in India. Exhausted and overwhelmed from their flight and making multiple trips in and out of the airport with the large boxes, they throw themselves into our arms, their mission to deliver the wheelchairs accomplished. Now, they can spend the rest of the week enjoying the children.

Then they break the bad news. Due to red tape at the American end, Pam and Jodie were forced to pay a duty on the chairs of 1,000 dollars.

The sisters look at each other dubiously. "You know that Mother House does not give the homes any money," Sister Bosco says apologetically. "It could take months to get the request processed, and you will be gone by then. What to do?"

"Maybe we could hold a fundraiser," suggests Pam weakly.

It's been months since Airline Ambassadors took the initiative to acquire the wheelchairs, make arrangements, obtain permissions, and finally get the wheelchairs to Kolkata. We should be *kvelling* in their success. And that's the mood I want. "I'll repay you out of my pension. I'll give you a check when we get to the guesthouse," I offer spontaneously, hoping they feel reassured. "I'll take it as a tax write-off," I add cheerfully, knowing full well no one here in India will give me a tax receipt.

The wheelchairs fill the ambulance to overflowing, so we take a taxi. "Straight to Daya Dan," Jodie and Pam suggest, ignoring their exhaustion and desire for a shower.

The excitement at the orphanage can't be contained. Everyone agrees: the wheelchairs are like little, two-toned, red-and-black Ferrari sports cars. Everyone, even adults, vies for a turn to take one for a spin. For those who can walk, the wheelchairs are a source of fun. But for the children who can't walk, they're a ticket to independence.

"Rosalie, let's go to Mother House to show the wheelchairs to Sister Nirmala," suggests Sister Bosco.

"Would she care?"

"Of course she would. But first take rest and after tea, we discuss."

Jodie and Pam are too excited to rest, so we all pile into the ambulance with two of our more sociable children, Madhur and Sujit. Madhur, who is charming and intelligent, has spina bifida so he can't use his legs. And although Sujit has cerebral palsy and can't walk, even with a walker, he has a winning smile and everyone loves him.

The wheelchairs, now unpacked from their shipping cartons and assembled, take up so much room in the ambulance that we feel like they're the honored guests and we're mere add-ons. The boys sit on the floor, so surrounded that only their heads show, faces beaming, reminding me of the smiley-face stickers I give my students after each lesson.

There's plenty of space at Mother House and plenty of admiring spectators, so Madhur and Sujit scoot around the courtyard, showing off their driving skills and capturing everyone's hearts. Sister Nirmala watches from an upper level balcony and waves at them enthusiastically. Then, she signals for them to join her upstairs.

Sister Nirmala is old, slow-moving, and well-protected. She doesn't engage the public the way Mother Teresa did, and I'm sure most people don't know that she's Mother Teresa's successor. I've only seen her once before, at the performance at Daya Dan last March on the day before I was leaving for New Jersey. On that day, we didn't have a chance to speak.

The boys grow more and more excited. They understand the importance of being invited upstairs. Perhaps out of respect, perhaps to receive a blessing for this auspicious occasion, they spontaneously push their wheelchairs, arms pumping, to Mother Teresa's tomb, bend forward and kiss it. The nuns at Mother House are captivated.

Sister Innocencia and Sister Maria Santa carry Madhur and Sujit upstairs in triumph. Rarely in India have I seen disabled persons so honored and appreciated. It swells my heart to see attitudes changing, even if in only one corner of Kolkata.

Sister Nirmala welcomes the children and suddenly, with complete confidence, they begin to sing. She stands in disbelief. "Did you teach them to sing these songs?"

"Yes," I reply, not sure how to read her face.

She laughs heartily. "They sound like Americans!"

All the nuns burst into laughter. Sister Nirmala makes the sign of the cross over the boys' heads.

Humbled, we prepare to leave. As we're waving good-bye, the nuns' daily practice of Adoration to the Eucharist begins. These holy sisters lift their voices in song, and we lift up our hearts with gratitude and

> *My humanity is bound up in yours, for we can only be human together.*
> —Archbishop Desmond Tutu, social rights activist

wonder at the beauty, the voices, the love, the devotion, and the unexpected blessings the boys and their new wheelchairs have received.

*  *  *

The children love music. Each day, we sit in a circle and sing songs. Their favorite is:

*I am a musician.*
*And I live in Daya Dan.*
*I know how to play ...*
*The guitar, the guitar, the guitar, guitar.*
*The drum, the drum, the drum, the drum.*
*The piano, the piano, the piano, the piano.*

The singing is complemented by hand gestures. We sing for as long as volunteers can come up with different instruments.

I suggest to Sister Innocencia that we make instruments.

"How can we make a guitar? That would be too difficult."

"But we can make drums. That should be easier."

To make the drums, I punch holes along the perimeter of paper plates and instruct the children to sew two plates together with yarn.

I demonstrate: "Put the thread through one hole, then pull it through the next hole and then the next hole all along the edge, and eventually the two plates are joined. And you have a drum." I hold up the joined plates. "Now I'll add a long loop at the top so the drum will hang around my neck." I put the drum around my neck and bang on it a few times with a pair of chopsticks.

No one seems confused, so I tell the volunteers to start. Some of the boys can't thread the yarn even though the holes are quite large. Suresh understands what to do, but because he's blind, he misses some holes. Francis, even though he isn't blind, misses some holes. Surendra laces the plates from one side to the opposite side, using a lot of yarn to create an interlacing pattern. Peter playfully throws his plate, more interested in making a volunteer chase after it than making a drum. Paul chews on his plate. Only Madhur's drum is strung perfectly. The volunteers struggle to straighten out as many "expressions of creativity" as possible, and then we are done.

Sister Innocencia is very impressed. "Let us line them up for a parade," she insists. "We will march through the orphanage." So with a drum hanging around each child's neck and chop sticks for drum sticks, we snake through the orphanage singing:

*Oh, when the saints go marching in.*
*Oh, when the saints go marching in.*
*Lord, how I want to be in that number*
*When the saints go marching in.*

I'm at the head of the parade of—well, maybe not saints but certainly angels—beating my drum so enthusiastically that I leave small dents, like little paw prints, in it. I wonder, "How did a Jewish/Buddhist woman come

> *Choose a job you love, and you will never have to work a day in your life.*
> —Confucius, teacher, politician, editor, philosopher

to lead a group of Hindu kids in the singing of a Christian gospel hymn?" But at the moment, an answer doesn't seem important.

When I was in New Jersey early last summer, my friend and board member Rumu had told me to find Reena Das who lives in Kolkata. "Reena works as a receptionist in an architect's office, but her heart is with the poor children. She wants to open a school for them. Maybe the two of you can collaborate," Rumu had said.

"I'm very busy at Daya Dan so I don't know about collaborating," I had replied. But being curious to see what Reena was doing, I added, "Perhaps, I can give her some suggestions."

Rumu had told me that Reena's office is on Middletown Row, conveniently near the Gulistan Guest House. So, I go in search. It's a challenge. Street names aren't posted on municipal signs at intersections, but I pick up some clues by reading addresses on the façade or signs of the few businesses that provide this detail. When I ask for directions, the answers seem to conflict because the street names have been changed from the British version to an Indian version. For example, Free School Street is now Mirza Galib Street.

Then, after finding Middleton Row, I'm confronted with a tangle of office buildings with no numbers. The building I want is actually in a second row of buildings set behind a first row of buildings, accessible through an arch.

I walk into this chasm of relatively modern architecture where electrical lines and window air conditioners are the most predominant feature. Reena's building is seven stories tall. The entryway is marked by large signs on the outside for some businesses and small signs in the foyer for other businesses. "10C Middleton Row," says one of the large signs. An earlier building was marked "10A Middleton Row." So there must be a 10B. Is there also a 10D? A 10E? How far into the depths of confusion does this address maze continue?

When I finally find Reena, she emotes an open friendliness that characterizes people from West Bengal, the Indian state in which Kolkata is located. She welcomes me warmly and with a great smile even though I'm a complete stranger. Sensing her enveloping love, I like her immediately. "Rumu told me you love the poor kids."

"I love all the children, but the poor ones need our help."

"What about disabled kids?"

"Oh, I love them; their hearts are so innocent."

"Yes, I agree," thinking of my special needs students in New Jersey. "They don't know greed or competition. It's true, sometimes they get angry, but that's out of frustration because they can't express their needs."

"Someday, I would like to help the disabled children," Reena concludes with both an air of whimsy and finality.

"Rumu told me you started a small program right here on the steps of this building."

She laughs with the glee of accomplishment. "Yes, on my lunch break. The boys and girls sit on the steps, and we practice the English and Bengali alphabets. We sing songs and recite nursery rhymes. Then I give them a small snack. I take my *tiffin,* my lunch, when I go back to the office."

"Is anyone helping you?"

"Not yet, but I can manage."

"Do you think the kids are learning?"

"I do not know," she openly admits. "I am not a teacher. Mainly, I want the children to feel loved."

"Can I meet the kids?"

Her voice reveals her thrill. "Oh, please come. School starts at noon."

True to her word, at exactly noon, Reena leaves her office and goes to the building

*Let's put our minds together and see what life we can make for our children.*

—Sitting Bull, holy man, tribal chief

entrance. There, she ushers in the boys and girls who have been waiting for her. She hugs each one and tells them she's happy to see them.

Some people on the street stare in disgust. Hugging dirty children in tattered clothing isn't what they expect from a woman in a pretty *sari*, and the smiles on the children's faces are in stark contrast to the scowls on the faces of people passing by. Reena brings them into the building's foyer and organizes them on the steps of the narrow staircase. There are sixteen boys and girls, and she has them sit with the tallest at the top and the littlest at the bottom.

The children range in age from five to sixteen, but, for all of them, "school" is a new experience. With an encouraging and enthusiastic voice that trills with joy, Reena talks to them in Bengali. Then she takes out a small blackboard and teaches the Bengali alphabet, the symbols of the children's mother tongue. She writes a few letters, and the children repeat them over and over; this is the system of memorization typical of Indian schools. She repeats the same process for the English alphabet. The children don't have slates, so they can't copy the letters and only learn from visual observation and retention.

After the lesson, they sing:

*Johnny, Johnny, yes Papa.*
*Eating sugar, no Papa.*
*Telling lies, no Papa.*
*Open mouth, ha, ha, ha.*

This is their favorite song, and the kids roar with laughter during the last line. After a few more songs, Reena gives each child an egg roll. The children devour them hungrily. "Tell your parents that you are going to school," Reena reminds them. "They will be proud of you."

I love what I see in both Reena and these children—enthusiasm, excitement, opportunity, potential, growth. Hope.

I volunteer my assistance—on Thursdays, my one day off from Daya Dan—and Reena is relieved to have me there.

Reena and I continue on the steps for some weeks and then she seeks permission from the building's landlord to move the classes to the roof. To our relief, he grants permission. We now have more space, and, with more space, more kids come. We name the program Middleton Row School.

Reena's enthusiasm is infectious, so I bring stimulating materials to each class, and the children love it. I also notice that as long as they're engaged, they remain cooperative and attentive, but as soon as the lesson is finished, they become wild! They run along the roof's parapet, jumping onto and off of the boundary wall that towers above the street. I'm faint-hearted and cover my eyes, but Reena *kvells* over their enthusiasm and unrestrained joy.

"These kids are finally off the street. That means a lot to them," she says. "On the streets, they are so vulnerable. Their parents force them to beg, the police beat them, and the girls are lured into prostitution and the boys into stealing. At least for one hour each day, here at Middleton Row School, they have their childhood back."

Eva and I are sitting in what Raj calls his "cyber café" crammed into the entranceway of the Gulistan Guest House. Time can hang heavy in Kolkata. There's plenty to do, but the heat and humidity and pollution-filled, oxygen-depleted air makes everyone lethargic.

"Eva, it's getting late. Will you sleep tonight?"

"I never sleep. My brain won't turn off."

"I have an idea. Why not get rid of your brain? What about an amputation? You're a nurse. Can you manage it on yourself?"

"Ha, ha!"

Suddenly Raj squeezes into the tiny, crowded space between computers.

"Madam. Madam, the World Trade Center has just been hit by a plane."

"Raj, don't joke about something like that. We're bored but not that bored."

"Madam, I am not joking."

Eva quickly Googles an American newspaper. "The paper says something about a plane hitting the World Trade Center, but it's hard for me to read it in English. I'll find a German newspaper." Then, a few minutes later, "Oh, my God, it's true. The World Trade Center has been hit."

We're stunned!

"Let's go to Khawaja Restaurant. They have a TV."

So we hurry around the corner to a Muslim restaurant and watch the news. The same two clips of airplanes blasting into New York City's tallest skyscrapers are played over and over until they're branded into our minds. That night, we *both* can't sleep. We see the planes hitting the buildings again and again even though they hit only once. It's such a disturbing image.

Kolkata is the same but everything seems changed. Most of the volunteers have left their hotels, hostels, and guesthouses and hurried home to their various, respective nations. Because Eva and I have homes in Kolkata, we choose to stay. Every day, she goes to Kalighat, a home for the destitute and dying, and I go to Daya Dan Orphanage. Eva has a few volunteers. I have just one, a red-haired guy from Ireland.

"Eva, this is so crazy! What happened in New York has impacted Kolkata."

"I think they said on TV that almost every country lost someone in the attack. Probably a lot of Indians got killed."

"Yes, but I didn't expect the volunteers to leave."

"They feel safer in their own country."

"But Kolkata is safe! If bin Laden were in Kolkata, probably no one would notice."

"True. And we could advise him, 'It's dangerous in Afghanistan right now. Why don't you stay here? We're short of volunteers.'"

"Eva, what a sick joke!"

We joke not because we're insensitive but because we don't know where else to channel our anger and fear. We feel safe in Kolkata, but all around us there's proof that the world can suddenly collapse, like buildings made of cards or toy plastic blocks—or even concrete and steel. There's impending war, and no one dares to predict the consequences. At the moment, the whole world is standing with the United States, but the buildings of the World Trade Center were also once standing—and not that long ago.

The Buddhists have it right: The physical world is impermanent.

"We should try," Reena begs. "It is Durga Puja. The boys and girls will enjoy themselves. They have never had a chance before."

"But it's a big responsibility. There are thirty kids now and just the two of us."

"We will take only those who obey. The others can go next year."

Durga Puja is Kolkata's most important Hindu holiday. The city becomes transformed as neighborhoods collectively erect thousands of *pandals,* which are temporary shrines to honor Maa Durga or Mother Durga, "goddess of the inaccessible or the invincible," "the one who can redeem situations of utmost distress."[12]

Each *pandal* features a large, stylized image of this famous deity with multiple arms[13] and her entourage of four children: Lakshmi, goddess of wealth and prosperity;[14] Saraswati, goddess of knowledge, music, arts, science, and technology;[15] Ganesha, lord of beginnings and remover of obstacles;[16] and Kartikeya, god of protection and purification of human ills.[17] Consistent with legend, the altar in each *pandal* depicts Maa Durga astride a lion, a slain water buffalo at her feet, and in the process of thrusting her spear into the chest of the demon Mahishasur.

For six days, people go *pandal hopping,* visiting as many temples as they possibly can. Some *pandals* are huge and elaborate, while others are small but imaginative. Collectively, Durga Puja in Kolkata is considered the world's largest outdoor art festival with *pandals* carefully executed by trained artists.[18]

I've gone *pandal hopping* with Mithu and his family. Admittedly, all the *pandals* are impressive but one was particularly memorable. It was made entirely of terra cotta *chai* cups, smaller than a delicate tea cup, cemented together one on top of another like miniature bricks in a masonry wall. From afar, the *chai* cup structure looked solid and imposing, but, as we approached and each tiny cup became visible to the eye, the *pandal* began to appear fragile and whimsical.

I'm aware that the crowds at each pandal push and shove, so I protest warily as Reena and I continue our conversation. "But the lines. Sometimes it takes an hour to get into a *pandal.* The kids will become impatient. They might feel crushed by all those people surrounding them. They might get separated from us and lost."

"We will avoid the big ones. It is less crowded at the smaller ones."

Of course, I give in. Our Middleton Row kids, living on the street, are deprived of food, shelter, and security. Why should they also be deprived of celebrating Durga Puja?

We hire a basic, non-A/C bus, and the kids, ages six to sixteen, eagerly pile in, everyone vying for the window seats. I count heads—twenty of them.

"Look, look," the kids exclaim, pointing at each *pandal* we pass.

"Maybe we shouldn't stop at all," I suggest to Reena, hopefully. "The kids seem excited just to drive past. It would be a lot less risky. No chance of losing one in the crowd."

"No, the kids must pray at the feet of Maa Durga and receive her blessing."

So we stop at a *pandal*, and the boys and girls pile out. I recount heads as they stand beside the bus—twenty, the same as on the bus. But soon they're jostling through the crowd to get to the front. I feel helpless to stop them, and my shouts of "Queue, queue. Line, line" are lost in the confusion of packed humanity. Eventually, they all squeeze to the front of the crowd, directly at the feet of the deities, and Reena and I, amazingly, catch up to them. Then, with hands joined and heads bowed, they begin to pray. The moment is so heartwarming that I forget my concerns and feel grateful that Reena rose above my objections.

Back on the bus, I count heads—still twenty. I sigh with relief.

The traffic is building and the roads are getting increasingly clogged. I'm happy we're headed back.

"We will stop at this one," Reena says.

"Why?" I ask. "They've already gotten the blessing of Maa Durga."

"It is good to get a second blessing. These children are poor, living on the streets. They need many blessings."

I acquiesce to her logic, so we stop again. The children are ecstatic and start running around, happy to enjoy another bit of freedom. We rein them in, then they squeeze their way through the press of the crowd to the altar and pray before the Goddess.

We're back on the bus, and everyone is hungry, so Reena and I discuss dinner. "We will take them to a simple restaurant," she says. "I am thinking of a place on Park Street. Then they will be close to home."

I casually start counting heads, more from habit than from worry. "One, two, three, ..."

The kids think it's funny and begin to giggle.

"... seventeen, eighteen, nineteen." Nineteen? That's impossible. I must have counted wrong.

I count again, this time more urgently. "... seventeen, eighteen, nineteen. Reena, there's one missing!" Panic rises in my voice. "There's a kid missing!"

Reena counts in Bengali and frantically tells the driver to turn around, which, of course, isn't easy in this traffic.

A good five minutes have elapsed since we left the *pandal.* Where is the missing kid? Who is the missing kid?

We return to the *pandal,* and Reena races off the bus. After a few minutes, she returns with a frightened but otherwise unharmed child.

Actually, Reena is more upset than the child. "You cannot imagine!" she exclaims, her voice filled with emotion. "Raju is *a boy,* Everyone wants a boy in India. He could have been kidnapped. He is six years old and fair-skinned. That makes him more attractive. Indians like pale children." Reena is trying to calm herself. "Oh, *baba!* Thank God we found him."

Even though nineteen plus one equals twenty, I count heads one more time just to be sure. Everyone is there, so we begin to relax. But the traffic has now built to a point of gridlock. The bus sits for twenty-five minutes without moving while everyone's impatience and hunger grow. Reena tries to engage the children by singing Bollywood songs. This works temporarily, but soon their restlessness overtakes their distraction. Because the vehicles simply aren't moving, Reena suddenly orders the bus driver to open the door and jumps off the bus.

"Is she leaving us?" asks one small girl. "Is she mad at us?"

"No, of course not," I reply, but, in truth, I don't know what's going on.

I walk to the front of the bus and glance at the driver. He's suppressing a chuckle as he looks out the front window. I'm still confused, so the driver points. There are so many cars that the intersection has virtually disappeared, but I can make out a smear of color and a hand waving about. Reena's multi-colored *sari* is the patch of color, as her hand urgently directs traffic. Commanding some drivers to stop and others to go, she's unsnarling the knot of vehicles. We inch forward.

Finally, we reach the intersection, the driver opens the door, and Reena climbs in. It may have been funny to the driver at first, but he thanks her profusely. The kids cheer. I hug her. And she basks in her moment of triumph as the bus passes through the intersection and on to the restaurant.

"It is not possible, just not possible," the owner of the restaurant tells us. "So many children." The restaurant is near Middleton Row, so he recognizes the kids—street urchins—not the type of clientele he serves.

"There are many empty tables, and we will watch over them. You have nothing to worry about," Reena reasons in a friendly, charming way.

"No, no. Those tables are reserved. They are not free," he insists.

"Then we will wait. We will go inside and wait."

"No, it is not possible. The restaurant will be too crowded with so many children waiting."

"Then seat us and the restaurant will be less crowded."

"No, it is not possible," he repeats.

"I work for a lawyer," Reena says, covering her lie with resolve. "There are laws in Kolkata. These children have rights. They are human beings. They are clean and well behaved and have the right to eat like any other customer."

The man weakens and orders his staff to put tables together to accommodate our group. He isn't happy. "Do not be too long."

We order chow mein, rice with vegetables, and cold drinks. The owner is impressed, and I can almost hear his mental cash register ring. He becomes more and more gracious. "Anything else? What about dessert?"

"No, we will take them for ice cream at the parlor," Reena replies.

He's disappointed, but it doesn't stop him from trying again. "What about a take-away, so they have something for tomorrow?"

"It will be soggy by tomorrow," I reply, viewing these kids as too good to eat soggy food.

But then his prayers are answered as a cluster of kids gather at the door. These are children who live on Park Street but who, for one reason or another, haven't joined the school. They're waving at their friends seated inside and shouting to them. We don't want a disturbance, so we quickly order egg rolls for those on the outside, and a waiter disperses them as quickly as possible. Those kids busily shove the egg rolls into their mouths as they walk away.

"Come again any time," the owner calls after us as we leave the restaurant. "Pleasure to have you."

After a quick stop at the ice cream parlor, our tired but very happy group disbands amidst a chorus of good-byes.

"See you tomorrow in school, Aunty."

"Yes, see you tomorrow. Do not be late. We need everyone's voice for our morning song."

"Okay, Aunty. Good night. Sweet your dreams."

"Good night. Sweet your dreams, too," I mimic.

There's no need for us to see them home. Their home is the pavement, sometimes under a tarp, sometimes in a doorway, other times just stretched out on a mat, arms wrapped around each other for protection. Today they got a taste of what it's like to be a *normal child*, not a beggar, not a thief, not a street kid. That's what we want to instill in them at Middletown Row School—that they have options, that they can make choices, that they can experience the richness of their religion and culture.

That's what I want for them.

Meanwhile, I have problems. The sisters at Mother House are becoming more and more resistant to my educational programs. I envision the curriculum I've introduced as a stepping stone to enrollment in a school so the children can get out of the orphanage and into the real world. The sisters at Mother House see their role as caregivers—suppliers of food, clothing, shelter, and medicine.

People have told me, in frustration, that the Missionaries of Charity are 50 years behind Western countries in their attitude toward education. This is surprising because Mother Teresa was from Albania, raised in a middle class family, received an education, and was, in fact, a teacher. But I believe I can change this outdated attitude and prove to Mother House that fostering independence through education is the greatest gift a caregiver can bestow.

The sisters I've come to know and love at Daya Dan are supportive, but they have no power in this matter. The power of policymaking, along with control of money, rests in Mother House, and the sisters at the various homes are afraid of offending the superiors there.

"I can be transferred. I can find myself in Russia if I do something against the wishes of Mother House," one of the sisters laments. "Please forgive me."

She is doing her best, so, of course, I forgive her. Yet, I can feel my own frustration growing. What to do?

Sister Maria Santa and I are particularly empathetic toward Madhur. He's so sweet and sociable and "normal" except that he sits in a wheelchair. Sister Maria Santa suggests we take him to a local Catholic school—to see if they will let him enroll there. "I know the nun in charge," she tells me.

We go secretly. Until we know the outcome, there's no reason to upset the superiors at Mother House. Sister Maria Santa chats with the headmistress for a while, catching up on nun-news. Then she asks timidly, "Will you enroll Madhur in your school? He is very bright and very friendly and learns quickly. He knows all the songs. Madhur, sing some songs."

Madhur smiles like the sunshine and starts to sing. The sister in charge appears touched.

"Please take him," Sister Maria Santa entreats. "He deserves to have a normal life," she whispers.

The Sister in charge is very sympathetic, but she replies, "I cannot take him."

"Why not?"

"It is just not possible."

"Why not?"

"What will I say to the mothers of the other children?"

I'm letting Sister Maria Santa handle this, so I wait for her response. There is no response. I wait a bit longer, but still no response comes. So I say, my voice tinged with resentment, "Say that he's a child of God."

We have no luck with Madhur, but that doesn't stop us from trying with Suresh. There are schools for the blind, and he's blind, so that's a good match. Once the decision is made that Suresh will attend the Lighthouse For The Blind, we are eager to get an application and start the process. We have Sister Bosco's approval, so she makes the ambulance available to us. Sister Innocencia, Sister Maria Santa, and I agree that Suresh should come along as well even though it's only a preliminary step. We want him to know that something important is happening in his life.

The school is quite far and, as usual, the ambulance driver drives recklessly, but our spirits are so high that we don't seem to mind. The Sisters aren't saying the rosary and I'm not complaining. We have our minds on our goal and, for the moment, that seems enough. We arrive at the school and the sisters slowly climb out, mindful of their blue and white *saris*. Suresh and I are ready to jump out when suddenly, for no apparent reason, the driver puts the ambulance in reverse and, to our horror, knocks down a woman standing behind it. With the door still flung open, the driver rams the shifter into a forward gear, steps on the accelerator, and speeds away. He doesn't stop at red lights. He swerves around pedestrians and animals on the road. He's making an escape!

I grip Suresh tightly, fearful that he might fly out of the open door. "*Aste, aste*," I beseech. "Go back. Slow down." But my pleas are for naught. He doesn't understand English. But the frantic tone of my voice should be signal enough.

We drive so far from the school that I no longer recognize the neighborhood. Then we cross the Howrah Bridge, which spans the Hooghly River, and are no longer in Kolkata. When he finally stops the ambulance, I beg him to go back, but after a long while, I realize he has no intention of doing that. Clutching Suresh, I exit the ambulance, hail a taxi, and we make our way back to the school. It's a long ride. Yet, the sisters are standing at the curb, anxiously waiting for us. They look as relieved to see us as I am to see them.

"Sister Innocencia, the ambulance driver took off as soon as he hit the woman." I don't mean to shout, but my emotions overwhelm me and take control of my voice.

"Good for him. Otherwise, the people on the street would have beat him to death."

"But if the woman was hurt, then an ambulance is the best means of getting her to a hospital."

"He could not take a chance. He had to run."

Beginning to calm down, we pick up the application, then take a taxi back to Daya Dan, and I go home. All evening, I have a gnawing feeling that even though Sister Innocencia believes her logic is sound and that the ambulance driver had the right to protect himself, I believe he also had the responsibility to protect the woman he injured.

The following day, the atmosphere at Daya Dan is glum. The family of the injured woman immediately reported the incident to the police. The Missionaries of Charity ambulances are clearly marked, so the police had only to contact Mother House, and it didn't take long for them to figure out that our ambulance was there at the time of the accident. The superiors at Mother House were furious. Sister Innocencia and Sister Maria Santa rushed to the hospital to apologize to the injured woman and, perhaps, offer to pay for her expenses. The ambulance driver was reprimanded but, to my shock, wasn't fired.

I am left with the notion that something very wrong has occurred. Or maybe that's only my Western perception. Maybe, in India, this is normal.

As if trying to change the subject, the sisters quickly fill out and submit Suresh's application. Sister Innocencia makes an appointment for an intake interview at the Lighthouse For The Blind. If Suresh is accepted, it'll be his first taste of independence. He'll spend most of his day away from Daya Dan, so his primary identity will be as a *student,* not an orphan. That's life-altering.

I'm filled with both pride and anxiety. He can't miss this opportunity. He must pass the interview. So, as a teacher, my immediate response is *preparation*: a mock interview.

"What is your name?"

"My name is Suresh."

"How old are you?"

"I am seven years old."

"Where do you live?"

"I live in Daya Dan."

"Are you a good boy?"

"I am a good boy. I listen to my teacher. I do pee pee in the toilet."

We practice every day for two weeks. I mix up the questions, and still he knows the answers. I add new questions.

"What do you want?"

"I want to go to school."

"Who is your teacher?"

"My teacher is Rosalie."

Suresh knows the answers by the end of the fourth day, but I force him to keep practicing so that I can control *my anxiety.*

> ***Intellectual growth should commence at birth and cease only at death.***
> —Albert Einstein, theoretical physicist

Finally, the interview day is here. Sister Innocencia and I feel like parents, like we are on the hot seat, like Suresh's success is a reflection of our own success—or failure.

Suresh is innocent, of course, but we recognize the importance of what is happening. Sister Innocencia had informed the superiors at Mother House and impressed them enough with Suresh's potential, plus our inability to teach Braille, that they granted their permission. With Mother House's backing, the pressure is even greater. If we succeed with Suresh, then possibly they'll agree to back the next child too.

We climb into the ambulance and head for Lighthouse For The Blind. Despite the recent mishap, Suresh loves riding in the ambulance. He can't see the passing scenes, so he must be enthralled with the movement, a sense of freedom and adventure. He starts to sing. The sisters start the rosary. I'm numb.

We arrive on time but have to wait. There are other applicants ahead of us. No one is chatting. Mothers, sitting with their children, look as obviously nervous as we feel. Sister Innocencia and I watch as they enter the interview room and watch as they leave. We don't ask any questions. We have no idea what to expect. But now it's our turn.

We go into the conference room. Ten people sit around a table. Observing the way they hold their heads, not specifically looking in our direction, we realize that all the interviewers are blind. They introduce themselves one at a time, and then we introduce ourselves.

Sister Innocencia says, "My name is Sister Innocencia. I am the

Sister in Charge of the downstairs children at Daya Dan Orphanage."

I say, "My name is Rosalie Giffoniello. I am the teacher at Daya Dan."

Suresh is sitting on my lap, and he pipes up, in a noticeably squeaky voice, "My name is Suresh. I am seven years old. I live at Daya Dan. I am a good boy. I listen to my teacher. I do pee pee in the toilet."

There's a moment of silence and then a round of broad smiles and appreciative nods, "He seems like a nice boy. We will take him."

So Suresh becomes one of the students accepted that day. Sister Innocencia and I are elated. It was easier than we had expected. May the next child also be accepted so easily.

* * *

"Freshly ironed school uniform?"

"Yes."

"White handkerchief?"

"Yes."

"Soap?"

"Yes."

"Red water bottle?"

Lighthouse For The Blind gave us a list, just like the lists camp directors used to give our parents when we were kids going off to summer camp. But Suresh isn't going to camp. He's starting school today, and we're all so proud. I'm taking loads of photos of him at Daya Dan. I wonder if this "first day of school" picture-taking is an American thing or do people all over the world do it.

There's a lot of excitement but an equal amount of uncertainty. We don't want anything to go wrong. Suresh's success at school will impact his life and possibly the lives of other children at Daya Dan who might follow him. So we decided that I will take him to school the first day and then a *maisie* will take him on later days. Luckily, the ambulance is available to drop us at the Metro (subway); otherwise we'd have a fifteen-minute walk.

It's rush hour as we board the Metro at Girish Park, and poor Suresh is crushed between the legs of tall men, their briefcases pressed against his face. I manage to maneuver him to a seating area. No one relinquishes a seat, but one man puts Suresh on his lap. Suresh covers his ears. The roar of the train is new to him, and he has always found loud sounds to be disturbing. Ten stops later, we're at Kalighat station and take the escalator up to the street. I've noticed, in the past, that many Indians are timid about stepping onto an escalator. Suresh doesn't seem to mind.

We arrive at the school early and have time to visit a toilet. With funds from Empower The Children, we'd recently had toilets installed at Daya Dan. At the orphanage, the boys sit in a row on a raised cement platform over holes into which their waste drops. The toilets aren't exactly "modern" by Western standards, but, at least, we got rid of the plastic baby potties—far too small and totally inappropriate for our big boys— that, previously, were placed on the floor for their use several times a day.

I taught Suresh how to pee standing up, including how to "shake it" when he's finished. When I had asked one of the male volunteers to teach this very male function to Suresh, he told me, "This is a mother's job."

At the school for the blind, my confidence is suddenly drained when I see Indian-style squat toilets. I never prepared Suresh for this, but he very obligingly squats and pees—all over his new school shoes! Suresh is oblivious to his "misdirection," but I'm worried. I presume there are only squat toilets at the school, and I don't want the staff to realize Suresh is unfamiliar with this form of toiletry. So I sort out the problem by discreetly washing his hands and shoes at the same time.

At 10:00 a.m., all the children are brought to the lunchroom for their *tiffin*. The first-day-of-school list had included a plate, curry bowl, and metal cup, but Suresh is also carrying a spoon and fork. As with the toilet, I see a potential problem. Everyone is eating

Indian-style, with their hands. The hours of conscientious American training I poured into this child are all for naught!

Some parents drop their children off at the school. Others, who have come from a far distance, remain until dismissal. The headmaster asks those parents who are waiting for their children to go to the waiting room. Everyone complies willingly, but I'm too curious. So, instead, I move to the stoop outside the lunchroom. After about fifteen minutes, I can't resist the urge to roam, explore—oh, to be honest, to check on Suresh and see how he's doing.

I glance around to see if I'm being watched and then very nonchalantly sneak a peek into the lunchroom. Suresh is managing. But my relief is tempered by red streaks across his freshly pressed, clean white shirt. And I know from experience that curry stains!

The children get ready for prayer so there's not enough time for me wash the shirt. The head teacher, aware that it's Suresh's first day, leads him into a long, long hall where he queues up amidst a sea of students, all older and taller than he. The only sign of him that I can now see is an occasional glimpse of the red water bottle strapped to his belt at his hip.

After prayer, the queue of other children pushes him up a flight of stairs. I wait at the bottom, craning my neck until I see the red water bottle completely disappear.

Then, finally, I go into the waiting room. Other parents are chatting with each other to pass the time. I can't relax and start pacing. The parents stare at me with what appears to be a mixture of curiosity and humor. Perhaps they think I am a neurotic foreigner. Or perhaps, when their child started school, they felt the same emotions. Maybe that's empathy in their eyes.

The steps that Suresh ascended, not that long ago, are quite close to the waiting room, so I decide to sneak up to the classrooms, just to have a "little look." There's no harm in that, I figure. I tiptoe upstairs—and I mean tiptoe—because I know that blind people have very keen hearing, but, of course, I'm caught straight away—

by the headmaster, no less, whom I recognize as the person who conducted Suresh's interview.

"Where are you going?" he inquires politely.

Being quick on my feet, I cleverly reply, "I'm a teacher from America, and I thought I'd visit a school in Kolkata to see how it differs from ours."

The headmaster is very obliging and takes me back down the stairs to see the classrooms. He explains the curriculum and how it's been adapted for blind children. It's all very interesting, but I really can't concentrate. I thank him warmly and start up the stairs, but before I reach even the third step, he says, quite patiently, "He is fine."

I'm back in the waiting room when, quite unexpectedly, Sister Innocencia and Sister Bosco come in. They'd spent the morning at Daya Dan, but their curiosity and anxiety overtook them, so they rushed to the school before dismissal. I show them the problematic toilet, equally problematic lunchroom, prayer hall, and forbidden stairway. As if reading our minds, the headmaster suddenly reappears and, this time, reproaches me quite firmly, "He is our responsibility now."

At 1:40, Suresh emerges from the school, and the three of us lunge at him, hugging him and kissing him and stuffing him with sweets, the sugary Indian reward for a job well done. We assume he's tired, so we carry him to the Metro and he arrives back at Daya Dan in triumph.

We dress the boys in their Sunday best and bring them upstairs to the chapel at Daya Dan for Mass. It's a small room, filled to overflowing with nuns, volunteers, visitors, and children, with a few plastic chairs in the back for those unable to sit on the floor. In front is an altar with various religious paraphernalia on it. I vaguely recognize the items from the few times I attended a Catholic church for a wedding or funeral.

I like Father Pasquale, the celebrant. He has a grey-speckled moustache and beard, and he wears brown robes tied with a cord. He looks like a village priest out of an Italian movie from the 1940s.

The Mass is primarily for the nuns, but I get the feeling that Father is doing it for the children. He plays the guitar and sings simple songs. The children sit attentively, always responsive to music.

After Mass, he blesses each child individually. He knows their names and walks among them unhurriedly, unlike other priests who maintain some distance as if the disabled children have a contagious disease. "May God be with you, Debashis," Father Pasquale says as he places his hand on a bent head. Debashis, unable to speak, answers with his eyes.

There are no classes after Mass, so I go to Daya Dan's *godown,* the storage area where we keep educational materials. Sister Aurora follows me in. She belongs to the Sisters of Mercy order, which is much less strict than the Missionaries of Charity. She wears normal clothes, goes back to Spain to visit her family once a year, and moves around Kolkata unescorted, whereas the Missionaries of Charity sisters wear their signature blue-and-white *saris*, go home only once every ten years, and must always move about in pairs when outside the convent.

Sister Aurora lives with other nuns of her order in a lovely home in the Sudder Street area. She's a trained teacher of the deaf and has a special feeling for disabled children. For this reason, she volunteers at Daya Dan once a week, teaching the blind children.

"May I speak with you?" she asks, with only the slightest hint of a Spanish accent.

"Of course," I reply.

"I got news from a school in Spain that they plan to raise some money. I wonder if they might give it to you directly, rather than to Mother House. Through your Empower The Children, you can help the boys here at Daya Dan and other places. I know you will use it wisely for many children."

"Sure. That would be great."

"They will have a fundraiser before Christmas."

"Good, that gives us a chance to decide how to use it. I can talk this over with Sister Innocencia and see what she needs here." It's getting hotter and hotter in the windowless, airless *godown,* and streams of sweat are rolling down my face. I can't wait to get out of here. "Sister, how much money are you talking about?"

"Ten thousand dollars," she replies.

"Ten thousand dollars?" *Now I really begin to sweat*! Ten thousand dollars! That much money will go a long way in India. Oh, my god!

Then my mind races to those ongoing conversations with Mithu and his summations that opening an orphanage would be "an easy piece of cake." To Sister Aurora, I say, "You know Mithu. He volunteers here at Daya Dan and is really committed to the children. He's already rented a small flat and taken in five orphaned boys. His mother shifted from her home to take care of them, seeing to all of their needs. Mithu doesn't live at the orphanage but goes every day, so the children have both motherly love and fatherly love. Now he wants to find a building and open a real orphanage, a nice place, a place with a garden." I'm babbling on like a madwoman, but I can't think straight. I'm so hot that I feel like I might faint, which wouldn't make a very good impression.

> *I have learned to use the word "impossible" with the greatest caution.*
>
> —Wernher von Braun, rocket scientist, aerospace engineer

But Sister Aurora isn't fazed by either the heat or the proposal. "The kids in Spain will love the idea," she concludes.

So that's how we will get our orphanage. Mithu *was* right—"an easy piece of cake." Sister Aurora will get the money from the students in Spain. Empower The Children will cover the cost of school fees. A friend of Mithu's from Japan will pay for rent, electricity, and food. And additional money will come from Antonio, a Spanish man who is looking to fund a special project.

Without delay, Mithu starts to search for land. But buying land proves to be nearly impossible. Much of the land in Kolkata is *occupied,* which means people are living on it without proper papers of ownership or lease.

India's Independence from Great Britain in 1947 led to the Partition. The British Viceroy of India, Lord Mountbatten, with permission of the Indian National Congress, Sikhs, and Muslims, divided this one nation into two: the Union of India and the Dominion of Pakistan.[19] Pakistan consisted of two parts—East Pakistan on the Bay of Bengal and West Pakistan on the Arabian Sea—with more than 1,000 miles of India in between.[20] Later, in 1971, due to political discord, economic woes, and ethnic discrimination, Pakistan's eastern part would fight for independence. That conflict, the Bangladesh Liberation War, created the country now known as Bangladesh.[21]

The Partition created nationwide upheaval that uprooted people from their familial villages and forced them to resettle in areas that, they believed, offered safety and security within agreed-upon religious districts. The people, cast into a new locale, grabbed whatever land and lodging was available. Details, such as ownership papers and back taxes, were largely overlooked or ignored.

So when Mithu attempts to buy land or a building, he's repeatedly told, "Sorry, no papers," or, "We can make up fake papers," or, "I will sell it to you for eighteen *lakh*, but give me a receipt for only ten *lakh* so I don't pay taxes."

That thinking may work for private transactions between

Indians, but a nonprofit organization, based in the United States with a board of directors and volunteers and financial contributors, must account for every rupee. So how can we make such a deal? It's nothing less than a nightmare.

And the pressure on Mithu is enormous. Now he has the money but can't figure out where to use it. For months, he continually searches without success.

Daily, I ask, "Did you find anything?"

Daily, Sister Aurora asks, "Did you find anything?"

Daily, Antonio asks, "Did you find anything?"

The answer is always the same: "No papers."

Adding to the spiritual ironies in my life, I find comfort in the Catholic Mass. Each Sunday, we walk with or carry all of the children—the more-abled ones from the ground floor and the more disabled ones from the second floor—to Daya Dan's small chapel, located on the third floor, the same level where the nuns sleep and eat. The more active children sit on the floor toward the front of the chapel, the sisters kneel or stand in the middle, volunteers are generally behind them, and the children who have no comprehension of the ceremony are placed in special chairs or on the floor in the back.

One Sunday, I approach the altar as Father Pasquale is carefully wrapping the chalice in soft cotton cloth. "Father, it's obvious you love the boys. You treat them with respect and heart-felt compassion."

"They are God's blessings on this Earth."

"I feel the same way, but in a world that equates disability with inability, it's rare to find a person who can see the inner beauty of a handicapped child."

"They may be handicapped in the temporal world, but, in God's eyes, they are perfect."

"Father, you inspire me to make a suggestion. Why not groom two children from Daya Dan to be altar boys? Then they will be part of the service and add their special qualities to the Mass."

For a long moment, Father says nothing, and I don't know what to expect. If he disagrees, should I push my point with time-honored arguments about the rights of the disabled or just

> *Good instincts usually tell you what to do long before your head has figured it out.*
> —Michael Burke, author

let the idea slip away like the smoke wafting up from the still-burning incense?

"I think that is a good idea. You can start immediately to train them."

"Me? Father, I'm Jewish. I know nothing about Catholic rituals."

"Your surname is Giffoniello," he says, pronouncing it correctly as only an Italian can do.

"That's my ex-husband's name, and he was a lapsed Catholic. We never went to church."

"You are a teacher."

"You are a priest."

"But I do not know how to teach the children."

"And I don't know anything about the Mass."

"Sister Innocencia will help you."

* * *

"The boys should sit in the back until it is time for them to assist," Sister begins. "Otherwise, if they become restless, they will distract from the service."

"That sounds reasonable," I reply.

"One boy must carry the tray with the lavabo bowl to the front and the other must carry the small linen towel. The priest uses these to symbolically wash his fingers prior to the Eucharist."

"That doesn't sound so difficult."

"Luckily, the lavabo bowl will be empty. Father will tell them what to do once they are at the altar, but we must practice with them or else they will become confused."

"If you practice with me, then I'll practice with them."

So Sister and I go through the ceremony several times, and I, in turn, practice with the boys. We've chosen Surendra and Francis as the most likely to succeed although their short attention span and distractibility are definitely not in their favor. Each object on the altar is a source of wonderment to them, and, when prompted, they're reluctant to relinquish the items they're carrying.

"Give me the bowl, Surendra," I suggest, but he examines it instead. "Give me the bowl, Surendra," I implore, but he hands it to Francis who also examines it. "Give me the bowl," I demand, and Surendra laughs.

After several days, I say to Sister Innocencia, "Sister, I think Surendra and Francis are ready. We have to give them a chance and then we can perfect it afterward."

"Perfection is only in Heaven. On Earth, we can't expect perfection."

"Thank God for that," I say with relief. "But they'll need robes, right?"

"You mean cassocks. White satin cassocks, trimmed in red."

"Okay, let's take the boys to the tailor and have the cassocks made. Maybe that will make them realize the importance of the occasion," I add hopefully.

"Or maybe it will be another distraction," Sister offers as a warning.

* * *

The Mass is ready to begin. Daya Dan's small chapel, it seems, is more crowded than usual. Did Sister Innocencia invite nuns from the Mother House to bear witness to Daya Dan's first altar boys? I glance toward the back of the room. Although everyone else is sitting on the floor, Surendra and Francis are in small plastic chairs because we don't want their new cassocks to get wrinkled. Francis keeps lifting his as if he's uncomfortable. Unfortunately, his exposed underpants don't add dignity to his newly acquired role as assistant to the celebrant.

A few minutes into the Mass, Father Pasquale signals us, and Sister nudges Surendra and Francis into standing positions. She lovingly smoothes their robes and flattens their hair. She hands Surendra the tray with the lavabo bowl and Francis the small linen towel. With a single word of her encouragement, they begin to walk down the narrow aisle between the seated children and nuns.

Our new altar boys smile and laugh. The tray is tilted at a dangerous angle. The bowl slips to one side, poised over the heads of the congregants. "Thank God it's empty," is all I can think. But no one is noticing the bowl. Everyone is looking at the boys. Their satin cassocks reflect sunlight filtering through the windows. Several nuns are wiping tears. Each step brings Surendra and Francis closer to the altar, closer to partaking in a religious ceremony, closer to being normal. Suddenly, I feel a powerful rush of emotion. Maybe perfection is on Earth after all, on this ordinary Sunday morning.

My back is not good these days. I can't lift my left leg when I dress in the morning. The pain shoots down from my butt and my foot tingles.

"Come with us," Mithu implores. "You will feel better." Mithu is trying to convince me to join his family for a weekend in Digha, a seaside town at the northern end of the Bay of Bengal, about 180 kilometers from Kolkata.

"What if I feel worse?" I counter.

"You will not feel worse. The boys from my orphanage are all excited. My mother, brother, and niece are going. It will be fun."

"But what about the long bus ride? I can't sit for four minutes, much less four hours."

"Look out the window at the scenery. You will forget your pain. Please say yes, otherwise the boys will be disappointed."

I know that Mithu will also be disappointed. He needs a break from caring for the five boys while continuing to search for a building for the new orphanage. Also, we need to repair our relationship, which has been damaged due to the strain he feels about trying to find property. So I agree.

We're on a long distance bus that stops in every town. With each stop, the bus attendant blows his whistle once to indicate passengers are departing and twice to announce all new riders are aboard. The attendant drops the fares into a large leather purse as he makes his way up and down the often-crowded aisle. The seats are straight-backed, and the cushions are worn out and uncomfortable. With no air conditioning, the windows are perpetually open, allowing in a rush of air when the bus is moving and pollution whether it's moving or standing still. Of course, the four-hour ride becomes six hours.

In Digha, nine of us crowd onto what Indians call "a bicycle van," a small, flat, open cart similar to those that carry goods to little shops and markets. Of course, there are no seats. I suggest that we take two carts, but Mithu won't hear of it. He wants to save money, but I feel sorry for the driver who has to strain to pedal the cart with so many people onboard. The ride is bumpy, but that's more the fault of the road than the vehicle.

The hotel is plain but clean. Mithu's mother, niece, and I share one bed. Surprisingly, I sleep soundly.

The food is spicy. I ask Mithu if the food will be spicy for the next few days and he tells me, "Same, same but different." So I eat only eggs and rice.

In the evening, everyone wants to climb a stairway to the roof to see the stars, but each step upward is painful, and I'm exhausted by the time we reach the top. The stars are brilliant, a sight we don't see in light- and air-polluted cities such as Kolkata or New York. But it hurts to stand and look at them, and my leg feels like it's on fire. I'm really worried. I can't wait to get back to Kolkata to see a doctor.

Yet, there is much to enjoy about Digha. The weather this late in the fall is beautiful, and the boys are swimming and splashing and tasting the water, experiencing a freedom they don't have in the city. To them, the sandy beach, tropical trees, open spaces, and fresh air must seem like a great adventure in paradise. I enjoy watching them, especially when I consider that they've never been out of Kolkata, except to their villages. In their young minds, they must feel like they've gone abroad!

Mithu's niece is too shy go into the water. She's very quiet, almost withdrawn, until she begins to sing. Then she comes to life. I've heard her sing in front of audiences without any reservations, as she does for me whenever I visit her home.

The bus back to Kolkata leaves in the evening. It's crowded, and everyone is sleeping. I can't sleep while sitting up, so I just look out the window.

Suddenly, I realize that the bus is careening all over the road. The driver is mostly on the wrong side and, at the last second, swerves out of the way of an approaching vehicle. I'm not faint-hearted, and I've been on many Indian buses before, but today I really feel dread.

In spite of my sore back, I cautiously make my way to the driver and give him a biscuit. He accepts it graciously and, for a few seconds, seems to slow down a bit and steer a straighter course. I give him another biscuit. Again, he seems to slow down and drive more carefully. I don't dare leave his side. I ply him with biscuits until the package is empty. Then, I go back to my seat, hoping that he's sated and awake—and in a more peaceful frame of mind. But, within minutes the ride from hell resumes. I'm ready to say good-bye to this world.

I compose a letter to Art in my head.

>Dear Art,

>I am on a bus coming from Digha. The driver is either drunk or suicidal, so I think it's time to contact you. It's been five long years.

> *In the middle of every difficulty lies an opportunity.*
> —Albert Einstein, theoretical physicist

>I think you know from friends that I now live in Kolkata. It has been a good experience for me. I am engaging in *karma* yoga, selfless service to others, and I feel that my life has found a focus and direction.

>I am grateful to you for preparing me for this experience. Although you wouldn't have known it at the time, you were instrumental in 'toughing me up.' You always insisted that we do things 'the hardest way possible,' whether hitchhiking on the back of a truck in Greece or sleeping on tables in Hampi. I have to admit that I resented it at the time, although I didn't have the confidence to complain as often as I wanted to.

>But here's the beautiful part: I can now endure hardships. I can face obstacles. I can hang on even when things seem grim.

>I am often asked, "How can you live in Kolkata? How can you persevere day after day?" And I always give you the credit. "Art made me strong."

>I hope everything is good in your life. Let's meet after I return to New Jersey in March.

>Lots of love, Rosalie

We survive the bus ride from Digha, and I write the letter as soon as I get back to the Gulistan. I mail it the next day.

* * *

I'm still working at Daya Dan even though I'm in a lot of pain. The doctor says there's something wrong with my disc, a diagnosis confirmed by an MRI and x-rays that he orders in early November. He fits me with a belt, gives me pain pills, and prescribes something to reduce the inflammation. But there's still no relief.

Because of my teaching, I do a lot of lifting. By now, there are a lot more children at Daya Dan. Those with severe orthopedic problems can't climb stairs and have to be carried to the upstairs classroom. Also, they have to be lifted into the high chairs that serve as desks. Then, they have to be taken out of the chairs at the end of the lesson and carried downstairs.

The doctor isn't happy with my lack of improvement and suggests traction—immediately. So, for six weeks in November and December, I lie on a wooden platform, being stretched from head to toe. I try to accept this awkward position and unpleasant confinement graciously, but mostly I'm worried that the traction won't work and six weeks will have been wasted. Luckily, I'm in my hotel room at the Gulistan and can ring for help when I need to be disconnected to go to the bathroom. Also, the staff brings food and water.

The staff at the Gulistan rush into my room excitedly and announce that an ambulance is parked in the small lane outside the building. Kindly, they help the kids from Daya Dan upstairs to my room on the first floor for a visit. Sister Innocencia is full of Daya Dan news, which I devour hungrily, and I'm aware that being in traction is not only painful but very, very isolating.

The boys, on the other hand, don't spend much time in my room. They're fascinated with the flush toilet and keep peeing in it just to watch it work. Even Peter, hardly worthy of being called toilet-trained, pees straight into the bowl. It's all a very welcome distraction.

The volunteers visit me from time to time, but mostly I'm alone. Prasanta, the physical therapist, comes once a day to socialize and smoke. He's very high-strung and burdened by family responsibilities. His arm is mangled where his pet monkey tore the muscles and ligaments in an unexpected, frenzied attack. I've become very dependent upon Prasanta, and one day, when he fails to come, I'm sure he's been knocked off his motorcycle and killed. I cry all night.

Sometimes I wonder if it would be better to leave and get treatment in the United States, but I realize that, in New Jersey, there's no one to take care of me, no one to bring me food and water or unhook my traction when I need to use the bathroom. I would feel more lonely and vulnerable in New Jersey even though my friends and family are there and I continue to refer to it as home. For this reason, I stay in Kolkata.

* * *

After six weeks in traction, I'm finally back to work at Daya Dan. And then I get the news.

"Sister Bosco is leaving. We didn't want to tell you while you were recovering," says Judicaille, a long-term volunteer from France.

"Leaving?" I'm trying to understand the implications of this. As Mother Superior at Daya Dan, Sister Bosco never interfered with my progressive ideas. That was her way of supporting me.

"Leaving?" I repeat. "Why? I hope not to Siberia," I add, remembering the sisters' fear of disobeying Mother House.

"No, no, to someplace in India. They transfer sisters every three years so they don't form attachments with people at any one place."

"When is she leaving?"

"By Christmas."

"That soon? That's not good news."

"Yes, and more bad news. The boys who are attending Manovikas are being withdrawn—orders of Mother House."

I am absolutely shocked! Several of the boys had been accepted at Manovikas Kendra Rehabilitation and Research Institute, a multi-dimensional service provider for children with special needs. The facility offers speech therapy, occupational therapy, physical therapy, and even aqua therapy in their large swimming pool. It's an impressive building with a large campus located near the eastern bypass, quite far from Daya Dan.

From the beginning, Sister Bosco was cooperative and made the ambulance available every day to drop them off and pick them up. The boys look so smart in their school uniforms that everyone bursts with pride each morning as they wave good-bye through the ambulance windows.

"Who will be taking her place? Do you know?" I ask half-heartedly.

"Sister Tara."

I suddenly brighten up. "Wow, that's great!"

"Do you know Sister Tara?"

"No, but I pray to Green Tara every night. With both of them having the same name, how bad can this change be?"

* * *

It's bad! Sister Tara is exactly the opposite of Sister Bosco. She interferes in everything.

* * *

Ratna, an Indian woman who lives in New Jersey, has joined Daya Dan. She's a professor of economics at Rutgers State University in New Jersey and, during holidays, she returns to Kolkata to visit her aged parents. We're the same age and think alike.

I try to explain to her what's going on. "Sister Tara wants to get rid of the volunteers. She thinks she can manage better without them."

"I'm not surprised. I was working over at Shanti Dan, a Missionaries of Charity home for mentally challenged women, and those in charge feel the same way. I kept going back despite their overt disapproval of my modern methods of care, like using rubber gloves or needles only one time. Finally, they kicked me out."

"I don't think you'll be any happier here."

"I heard Sister Tara doesn't like Indian volunteers."

"She doesn't like *any* volunteers but is especially spiteful toward Indians."

Ratna and I find solace in each other's company and wait anxiously for the inevitable.

We don't have to wait long. Sister Tara is getting more and more aggressive. It blows my mind every time I say her name. I pray to Green Tara every morning and every night, and I connect her with support and guidance. I find it almost impossible to associate that name to both this human form and that deity.

The *maisies* have warned me. Sister Tara is ready to explode. I try to remain composed, but my insides are churning. I gather the children together for class, but before I can get them upstairs and into their chairs, I'm in the middle of a storm.

"Leave those children alone. You are not their teacher. You continue to disobey me, so now I am telling you to go."

"Sister Tara, these children need stimulation and instruction."

"They will get what I say they will get."

"Sister Tara, the volunteers aren't equipped to teach them. They have no background in special education."

"They will teach them if I tell them to."

"But will they succeed?"

"They will succeed, or they will also go."

"Sister Tara, you aren't being reasonable. These kids deserve a chance at normalcy."

"That is not your problem. Now get out!"

*Problems are guidelines, not stop signs.*
—Robert H. Schuller, televangelist, speaker, author

I feel angry but also deflated. I run for Ratna. She's furious, but we both understand the futility of fighting back. The Sister-In-Charge has the power.

We go into the *godown* and start collecting educational materials that I know will go unused. A quick look around tells the rest of the story: blankets, clothing, toys, dolls, potties, medicine—everything collecting dust. These generous donations from people in many, many countries have not been distributed to the children.

Clearly, poverty is the image that Sister Tara—and presumably her superiors at Mother House—wants to project in order to elicit sympathy and donations. Normalcy is not as powerful a symbol as neediness.

"Mitali is getting married," Mithu announces proudly. "Our family did the search, and a good husband has been found."

"Congratulations." I know that Mithu's sister is approaching thirty, so, by Indian standards, she's almost an old maid.

"Of course, you are invited to the wedding."

"You know I go to weddings only for the food," I tease. "Will it be spicy?"

"No. And spoons and forks will be provided, but only to the foreigners," he adds with a wink.

After the wedding, Mitali moves into her husband's home, which is a typical joint-family arrangement. She lives with her mother-in-law and sister-in-law in a house that is quite spacious for only four people.

"She is a teacher, but her husband will not allow her to work outside the home," Mithu complains. This is also typical of Indian marriages in which the husband restricts his wife's freedom of movement and choice. Mithu finds this practice backward and an obstacle to India's advancement into the modern world.

"It must be boring for her to be home all day," I surmise.

"It is a big house, and she feels lonely. Our house is small and cramped, with many family members, but she misses being with us."

"If the house is large, maybe she can open a tutorial center for girls," I suggest hopefully. "The students can come after school to study and do their homework."

"If it is in the house, her husband might agree."

Before we have an opportunity for any more discussion about salary, supplies, and student population—and how Empower The Children might choose to help—Mithu is on the phone with Mitali and her husband. Unable to mask his excitement, he's grinning throughout the conversation, so I know he's hearing good news.

"Mitali has agreed and, because it will be in their house, her husband has no objections," he reports.

"Did it take a lot of convincing?"

"Not *atall*. She wants to start immediately with twenty-five girls."

"Twenty-five? That's an awfully big class. Can she manage alone?"

"She has a friend who is also a teacher. So they can teach together." Then he adds, "But if the girls come after school, they will be hungry. I think we should give them a snack."

"How much will that cost?" I ask warily.

"Three rupees per girl."

I do the calculation in my head. Three rupees times twenty-five girls times five days a week times four weeks a month. "That's 1,500 rupees, about thirty dollars. I think Empower The Children can manage that."

Mitali starts immediately. Her husband, a sweet-natured man despite his attitude about women working outside the home, makes the trip to the market to buy a blackboard, notebooks, and a globe. Word

> *If you educate a boy,*
> *you educate an individual.*
> *If you educate a girl,*
> *you educate a community.*
> —African proverb

spreads throughout the neighborhood and, almost instantly, Mitali's front room is full of girls studying each evening.

Mithu calls to give me all this good news. I offer my congratulations and ask him to extend my good wishes to Mitali and her husband and the girls. We are about to break the telephone connection when I suddenly think of something important.

"Wait. Wait," I shout into the phone. "What did she name the school?"

"Mitali's Girls' Coaching Centre."

"Coaching Centre? It sounds like she'll be teaching sports," I object mildly. "But if that's what she wants, then that's what we'll call it."*

* *In 2004, an Indian businessman assumed full support of Mitali's Girls' Coaching Centre.*

* * *

Mitali's Girls' Coaching Centre is the good news in Mithu's life. The bad news is that he's having a nervous breakdown. For months, since Sister Aurora's offer, he's been looking but can't find land, and he's buckling under from the pressure. He's taking it out on everyone, particularly me. We go for a meal in Zurich restaurant on Sudder Street, and he's belligerent. "You are raising money for the orphanage, and you are not giving it to me."

"I don't raise money for any particular program. I raise money for Empower The Children."

"*Arre!* You Americans are rich. You get plenty from them, and you are not giving it to me."

"I give you what your kids need. Empower The Children pays the school fees, uniforms, books, school supplies. The rest is paid by Antonio now that your Japanese friend has stopped paying."

"Antonio is also cheating me."

"Doesn't he pay the rent, electricity, and food?"

"Yes."

"Then how can he be cheating you?"

"*Baba!* He collects thousands from Spain and gives me a drop."

"He gives you what the boys need."

"Bullshit!"

Now he's shouting, and everyone is looking at him, which is exactly what he wants. Very dramatically, he stands up, his meal unfinished. "You are collecting money from America and keeping it for yourself. Very nicely, you are keeping it for yourself," and he pantomimes dropping something into his shirt pocket. Then he storms out.

This scene is repeated over and over, only the language becomes more and more abusive. I try to calm him but to no avail. He's frustrated and angry. He feels like a failure, emasculated, and, for a young, handsome Indian male, this is very tough.

I haven't seen Art in more than five years, such a long time. I'm excited and curious. How will I feel? How soothingly or violently will his first words tumble through me?

Am I even physically up to this? I've been on a plane for eighteen hours from Kolkata to Newark and another hour by car to Doris' house. I'm lying on the floor of her home because it's the only place where my back doesn't scream with pain.

With all the places I've visited and all the activities I've engaged in—on my own—in the last five years, Art was occasionally on my mind, but he wasn't the focus of my existence as he had been when we were married and traveled together. Yet, in retrospect, I have to admit that his presence was always with me in some way, whether I realized it or not. In truth, these past five years were really about my ability to stand alone, apart from Art. These past five years were the litmus test of my life.

A couple of months ago, my friend Nancy emailed, saying that she was on a New Jersey beach at a memorial service. The weather was cold and windy, and everyone was huddled together. Suddenly, a figure emerged from the fog wearing only shorts and a t-shirt. She recognized Art immediately. He had asked her for my email address, and, after obtaining my permission, she had given it to him.

He contacted me immediately, and we've been writing on and off since. Our messages have been friendly but nothing personal. Maybe there's nothing personal left between us, just discussions about the weather and politics. Art could go on for hours about politics. His disgust with the United States government is visceral. He keeps threatening to move to Canada, but I don't think that will happen.

The fact is that we're old hippies at heart—of the "make love not war" generation. And we've never let go of that ideal. It was ever-constant in Art's zeal for knowledge. It was ever-constant in my desire to know myself, even when I didn't know that I wanted to know myself.

My friends say in jest, "You went to Kolkata because you never went into the Peace Corps after college. You're making up for it in your old age." That's probably true. Maybe my life is one of old ideals held in abeyance, then lived out twenty-five years later with more experience and, hopefully, more wisdom. Maybe I'm trying to demonstrate never give up, never forget, and never say it's too late.

It's getting closer to the time when Art will knock on the door, and my anxiety is rising. Art always had that effect on me, so I guess nothing much has changed. I'm curious to see how I react to his first words. Will they be an expression of caring, apology, nonchalance? In just a few minutes, I'll know.

The bell rings. Suddenly I feel insecure. I did nothing to make myself look attractive. The pain in my back has been constant, and pain drains the life

> *Every day is an opportunity to make a new happy ending.*
> —Anonymous

out of me. I roll onto my side and rise up carefully. I walk awkwardly to the door and open it.

In front of me, I see a man I barely recognize. Has it been only five years? He's greyer, smaller, less imposing. We stare at each other for several seconds.

"What's he thinking?" I wonder. "That I'm an old lady? Over the hill?"

I can utter only, "Hi."

Finally, after five years that has seemed like a century, I hear his voice. "Not a grey hair on your head." He smiles approvingly.

I feel so relieved I could cry. I think we have the basis for a friendship.

# What Now, Green Tara?
## July 23, 2002–summer/fall 2003

"The homeless are different here than at home," I explain to a volunteer. "In Kolkata, whole families live on the street. They come from the villages, expecting to find a better life and, instead, find thousands and thousands of people seeking the same better life. So they end up as 'street people' when just months ago they were a normal rural family, living among other normal rural families they know."

"Do they have any kind of a chance here?"

"Well, perhaps more of a chance than the homeless in the United States who might be truly indigent or have drug or alcohol addictions or mental problems. The street people in Kolkata carry on their lives as best they can, given the circumstances. They establish routines and try to find menial work. Sometimes they resort to begging, but not always. They have pride.

"Many men choose to sleep near their workplace. The *dhobi* will sleep on his ironing platform, the *rickshaw wallah* on his *rickshaw*, and even the taxi driver on the hood of his car. Some of those men you see sleeping in the streets have jobs during the daytime. They may have no place to sleep at night, or maybe they do but in a tiny room with eight or ten other men. For them, it's cooler and quieter on the street."

"What about government help?"

"There's none that I'm aware of. That's the main problem. When the global economy crashed in the late 1990s and early 2000s, the lives of many people in the West came apart. But, at least theoretically, they were caught in safety nets such as social services and unemployment insurance. Here, the safety net is full of gaping holes or rips. The people are poor and illiterate, and there are too many of them. It's an enormous problem."

"But they don't seem angry or resentful. They always wave and say hello. It isn't scary walking down the street among them."

"You're right. The people are very friendly. And they live in communities, not alone, so they have a kind of security. Five or six families stay together and help each other. The mothers cook food and wash clothes, the kids play, and the fathers bathe at water pumps then go to work. It's outdoor communal living, like camping out every day on concrete with traffic just a few feet away."

"Yes," the volunteer agrees. "When I walk down the street, I feel like I'm walking through someone's living room. It's a very weird feeling."

* * *

In late October 2002, I transfer to Shishu Bhavan, the Missionaries of Charity orphanage for young, abandoned children, located quite close to Mother House. Many of the boys and girls are mentally challenged, and I feel fulfilled teaching them. Things go well there, although I miss the Daya Dan children to whom I'd formed a great attachment. After all, they were the impetus that motivated me to take an early retirement in New Jersey and move to Kolkata.

"Sister, let's take the children on an outing. It will do them good. In fact, it will be good for all of us," I offer enthusiastically to the Sister-in-Charge.

She likes the idea. "I know exactly where we should go."

"Where?"

"To the leper colony."

"The leper colony?" I say in disbelief. "Is Kolkata so bad that the leper colony is an attraction?"

Sister only laughs.

We're at Howrah Railway Station, one of four intercity train stations in greater Kolkata. It's one of the largest railway terminals in the world with twenty-nine passenger platforms. Each day, one million passengers cram into or push their way out of 600 trains,[22] and then rush through the perpetually crowded station.

In fact, Indian train stations are mini-cities, containing most aspects of urban life. Porters carry luggage on their heads, vendors sell food and tea to weary travelers, and children, some very young and naked below the waist, beg for rupees. People squat to chat or rest while others sleep despite the noise and activity.

We're seated in the train's ladies-only compartment and, because the boys are children, they're allowed to be there. The local trains aren't air-conditioned, but this isn't a particularly hot day. We're early so everyone gets a seat.

We settle the boys and girls near the windows and, through the bars, they can see the lovely scenery. Outside the city, the landscape becomes green and plush and inviting. The villages are reminiscent of pre-industrial India, but that's rapidly changing. The population of Kolkata and its primary suburbs is approaching 16 million and growing at an alarming rate.[23] The population density is nearly 25,000 residents per square kilometer—amazing![24] Villages are becoming towns, and towns, in turn, are expanding into cities. The entire area is becoming one huge, sprawling mega-metropolis.

As the train nears our destination, it slows to a crawl but doesn't actually stop, allowing only so many people to board or detrain. Because our children have no experience jumping from a slow moving train, we quickly hand them off to adults on the platform. Everyone else thinks this is funny. I think it's dangerous! My mood is not good as we count heads and sort out the heap of arms and legs.

The leper colony is a twenty-minute walk from the station— along the railroad tracks. The volunteers are wearing comfortable shoes, but the kids have totally impractical footwear: sandals and flip-flops. Before long, one sandal is broken and a flip-flop is in pieces. And then another and another. More and more kids have to be carried. My mood is getting worse.

And now we're walking in a narrow place between a wall and the outer edge of the tracks. And a train is coming!

"What do we do?" I ask frantically.

"Press the children against the boundary wall and shield them with your body," comes a confident reply.

"Who's going to shield me?" I yell uneasily. No one answers. I press two children against the wall just in time. The train comes rushing by, blowing shirts and hair and nerves to the wind.

"Isn't this a bit dangerous?" I ask.

No one answers. Maybe the sisters are praying their rosaries.

We finally arrive at the leper colony, and, indeed, it's a vast improvement over Kolkata. Flower gardens fringe vegetable gardens and animals roam freely. The lepers are all in treatment so no one is contagious, and I'm surprised when they tell us that children of leper parents are born leprosy-free and don't contract it after birth. We find a shady spot and have a picnic lunch. The boys and girls play with animals, and everyone is relaxed and happy.

"Sister, this was a good idea," I concede, my mood greatly improved by the surroundings and food in my stomach. "The kids are really enjoying the animals. Maybe a few goats and calves would liven up the orphanage," I suggest with a half-smile.

"Mine was a good idea. Yours is a bad idea!" Sister replies with a full smile.

On the way back, only half the children and some of the nuns manage to get onto the train as it passes slowly through the station. The rest wait two hours for the next train. The children and nuns who boarded the first train wait two hours for the others at Howrah Station so that everyone can return to the orphanage together.

I'm standing in the doorway of the classroom at Shishu Bhavan, waiting for the Dalai Lama to arrive. I was fortunate to meet him many times during his public audiences in Dharamsala, but I would be made of stone if I didn't try to steal another chance—even though stealing creates bad *karma*.

The children are waiting in the upstairs dormitory, and it just so happens that His Holiness must pass by the classroom to get to the second floor. So, maybe he will grant a handshake.

But this is India, and he's late. I leave my post and hang out with the kids who are dressed in their Sunday best. Being disabled Hindu children, they have no idea who the Dalai Lama is, but they know he's important. For the past couple of days, they've been practicing a few songs and a special dance.

I place a small girl on my lap and idly entertain her. Suddenly, she starts to pee. Alarmed, I jump up. My skirt is dripping with pee! Instinctively, I grab my skirt and start wringing it out—all over my bare feet. Yikes! That was dumb. There's nothing I can do about the skirt, but at least I can wash my hands and feet. I rush toward the bathroom but, at this very moment, I hear the excited announcement, "The Dalai Lama is here! The Dalai Lama is here!"

I race to my previous position by the classroom, put my hands together in the appropriate prayer position for greeting an important lama, and bow reverently. His Holiness is slightly stooped and moves slowly up the stairs with the orphanage's Mother Superior on his arm. They stop for a second so he can catch his breath, and she introduces us. "This is Rosalie. She is our teacher. She specializes in teaching the disabled children," she says.

His Holiness crosses the short distance that separates us, warmly grasps my pee-soaked hand, and says thoughtfully, "Thank you." He momentarily glances away as if collecting his thoughts, turns back again, and looks directly into my eyes. "Thank you for devoting your life to these children." Then he walks on.

I'm moved beyond explanation by his words, a stunning affirmation of the work I've undertaken in Kolkata. Then I have a flash of panic. I want to shout, "Your Holiness, wait, wait! What do

> *Those who dedicate their lives to others ... gladden my heart.*
> —His Holiness the 14th Dalai Lama, spiritual and temporal leader of the Tibetan people

you mean 'devoting your life to these children'? *My whole life*—all of it—or just the rest of my ten-year visa? My whole life is an awfully long time!" But it's too late. I hear the music. He's already watching the children dance.

Then, the unthinkable happens. Sister Tara is transferred to Shishu Bhavan. Her narrow-minded attitudes aren't mitigated by the move, and, here, she openly scorns volunteers. When an Australian doctor offers constructive suggestions, Sister Tara retorts, "Do not show your face here ever again!"

Sister Tara wants me to teach the few children who have normal intelligence. I try to explain, "Sister, my background is in special education. The curriculum that I've brought from the United States is tailored for children who are mentally challenged. The volunteers feel helpless to teach the disabled children without lesson plans and educational materials that I can provide, and they're so happy to have a special educator to guide them. In that respect, it's a waste of my expertise for me to teach the non-disabled children. Many teachers who pass through here are qualified to teach the children without mental challenges. Please let me continue to work with the children I can help the most."

"Teach the non-disabled children or leave," she demands.

I continue to teach the disabled children, and Sister Tara is furious. During one of my lessons, she picks up a doll and smashes it on a table. An arm flies off. One of the *maisies* takes the arm and uses it to keep the beat during singing classes. A Japanese volunteer finds this so macabre that she won't return.

The tension continues to build. I dread going to work.

Then, the ultimate shoe drops.

* * *

I'm sitting in Blue Sky Café, a popular haunt of volunteers on Sudder Street, feeling sorry for myself. I can barely grasp that I've wasted the last three years of my life—from February 2000 to March 2003. The children at Daya Dan and Shishu Bhavan have filled my time. I spent six days a week with them, giving them the culmination of my experience as a special educator. More importantly, I've given them my love.

"The Missionaries of Charity has kicked me out of their orphanages," I tell a group of long-term volunteers who have come to commiserate.

"After all you've done for them," Beck, an Australian, says sympathetically.

"Sister Tara doesn't think I've done anything."

"What about the wheelchairs?" asks Heidi from Finland. "And those feeder seats? They were 350 dollars apiece, and you paid for them out of your pension."

"I left the wheelchairs and feeder seats, but I took the educational materials. I was afraid Sister Tara would dump them."

"Just think, you put in two swimming pools," says Sally, also from Australia, encouragingly.

Her comment prompts me to expound on my disappointment with the pools. "Downstairs, the pool is tiny, just a holding tank, but the boys use it to splash around and cool off in the hot season. It gave me pleasure to watch them enjoy it. Upstairs, the pool is quite large, big enough for swimming," I say with some degree of satisfaction, "but, instead, the *maisies* use it to wash clothes."

"You accomplished a lot," she rejoins. "At least Suresh is going to school."

"But what about Madhur and the others who never got a chance to get out of Daya Dan?" I ask. "What about the few other children who were attending Manovikas Kendra? They were pulled out by Mother House—on Christmas Day. That was a nice Christmas present for them, wasn't it?"

"You tried your best," says Austin. "The sisters are just too narrow-minded."

"They're not the only ones," I reply. "The teachers for the blind said the blind kids are 'hopeless cases,' and the speech therapists said they were 'unique cases,' but no one said they had potential or a right to an education."

"This is India," someone inevitably says.

"Yeah, a convenient excuse for everything," I remind them. "I am so sick of hearing, 'This is India.'"

There's pregnant pause, followed by the germane question: "So what will you do now?"

> *Your practice should be strengthened by the difficult situations, just as a bonfire in a strong wind is not blown out, but blazes even higher.*
>
> —Dilgo Khyentse Rinpoche, master, scholar, poet, teacher

Those words hang in the air for several seconds.

"I don't know. I just don't know."

And what will happen to Empower The Children?

\* \* \*

I'm feeling very shaky today. When things start going wrong in India, I can't cope. I feel too vulnerable. I have friends to turn to and can hear the sounds of many people nearby, but the overwhelming feeling is that I'm alone.

I think many people feel this way. They look at others who are smiling and laughing and think, "Why is everyone happy but me?" They look at couples holding hands and think, "Why am I the only one without a lover?" When I can't sleep, I'm tortured by the thought, "Everyone in the world is sleeping. I'm the only one awake!" So I'm finding it hard to feel hopeful. The outside world is pulsating with life and energy. Kolkata is a cacophony of sounds and smells and sights, but my inner world is barely burning. And now barred from Mother Teresa's homes, I feel I have no purpose.

These are my thoughts as I lie on my bed in my small room at the Gulistan Guest House after the sting of Sister Tara's boot. I need Green Tara's support, but feel guilty for asking. With all the misery in Kolkata, the overwhelming poverty, how can I ask for my own needs to be met?

During twenty years of marriage, I sought affirmation from Art but he wouldn't play into my insecurities. The futility of this never took root, so I just kept trying. I would ask, for example, "Art, should I attend the retreat at Rashi Gempil Ling this summer or not?"

"You decide."

"I can't decide."

"Why not?"

"I'm too conflicted."

"Well, get un-conflicted."

"Just give me an answer, yes or no."

"The answer is 'you decide.'"

"That's not fair. We're married. You should give me help now and again."

"You don't want help. You want confirmation for everything you do."

"It's not confirmation. It's discussion."

"You'll agree with whatever I say. You want me to make the decision for you. That's not discussion."

Art's not here now, so I'm asking for Green Tara's help—again. She's going to get fed up soon. But here goes. "Green Tara, I'm feeling kind of insecure today. Things are a bit rough at the moment. I need some reassurance. I need some kind of a sign that I'm still on the right path, that with perseverance and commitment I will succeed."

My eyes are closed, but after my entreaty, I open them. I watch and wait … but not for long. Through the open window above my head a small, white flower floats down to the bed. Where could that possibly have come from? There are no trees near my room, no potted plants—only the cement landscape of a big city. It *must* have come from Green Tara. I'm awash with relief. I melt.

I receive a telephone call from Ann, an American woman who's visiting Daya Dan while waiting to adopt a blind child. In the past, whenever she was in Kolkata, I would visit her at the Tollygange Club and we would share a meal. I assume she wants to extend another lunch invitation, but I'm really not in a sociable mood.

"Rosalie, I'll be in Kolkata only one week. While I'm there, I want you to meet Neena Singh. In 1992, she opened a small tutorial center for disadvantaged children. A decade later, in 2002, she founded Disha Foundation because, by that time, one hundred children were attending the tutorial center and she saw a need for opening a school. She's a forward-thinking person and has a lot of determination. I think it would be good for the two of you to get acquainted."

My sudden dismissal from Daya Dan and Shishu Bhavan has left a void in my life, so I readily agree.

"Let's plan on Friday at her house for lunch. I'll pick you up."

On Friday morning, Ann calls again. She can barely speak.

"I'm sick, but I want you meet Neena," she says. "I fly tonight, so it's now or never."

"You don't want to fly sick all the way back to the States. Why don't you stay in bed today and rest?"

"I promised myself that you would meet Neena."

"I can meet her the next time you come to Kolkata."

"That will be in the summer, and you are always in the USA in the summer."

"Okay, if you think you can manage. But I totally understand if you can't."

"I'll see you at 1:00," she concludes, forcing her resolve.

She picks me up and we go to Neena's home. It's a large flat, and the interior is decorated to reflect Neena's simple but elegant taste. Neena is an older woman, gracious and dignified with the delicate features of a cameo. I can easily imagine how beautiful she must have been as a younger person. She never married, but I'm sure it wasn't for lack of suitors.

She tells me that she opened Disha to assist underprivileged children. She also operates two other schools in Kolkata: Akshar, which goes up to Level 10, and Divyayan, a Montessori preschool. These are attended by middle class children. With the attitude of a benign Robin Hood, she feels quite comfortable enlisting the assistance of parents from these schools to help the children at Disha, which she runs on a shoe-string budget.

"We charge fees at Disha, but just a small amount, because it's important that the parents have a stake in sending their children to school each day," she explains.

"That makes sense."

"And Disha is a non-formal school, which means we are not accredited like a private school or government school. We give tests, and many of our students are very smart, but our school is not recognized by the government."

I nod my understanding and quietly thank her for defining this term that I had heard many times but which no one had ever explained.

"The youngest students are preschoolers. That awakens in them a curiosity and love for learning."

"What about the older kids?"

"We aim to bring them up to grade level. Then, they can transfer into a formal government school where they can earn a diploma."

"Why wouldn't they go to government school right away instead of going to Disha?"

"Sometimes the boys and girls who enroll are ten or twelve years old. They come to us with no education at all, unable even to write their name."

"Why? What's held them back?"

"They're poor. That's all. There's nothing else wrong with them. They don't have social problems. They just need the opportunity to fulfill their potential."

"So you give them the chance they wouldn't otherwise have."

"A chance that every child deserves."

"What do you pay your teachers? Do you have additional teachers with skills in music and art? Do the students wear school uniforms? Do you give them lunch? How many hours a day is the school in session? How many months a year?" I pepper Neena with endless questions, hungry for this knowledge, and she answers them all patiently.

Then I open my mouth and offer to teach the preschoolers at Disha once a week and introduce them to the curriculum that's now lying unused since I took the lessons

> *Change always comes bearing gifts.*
>
> —Price Pritchett, business advisor, speaker, author

with me from Daya Dan and Shishu Bhavan.

Neena is excited by the idea. She believes the teachers can

benefit from new ideas. Then she laughs and says, "Let's eat lunch before everything gets cold." The table is lavishly spread with food and sweets and cold drinks. Ann can't eat because she's sick, and I don't because the food is spicy. But it's an otherwise perfect day.

I wonder how this good fortune had come to me. "Was it only the work of Green Tara? Perhaps. But the deities don't work alone."

Soon thereafter, I learn that Ann had told Neena I was a special educator from the USA who had worked tirelessly to introduce educational programs at Daya Dan and Shishu Bhavan. The fact that Neena enrolls special needs children in both Akshar and Divyayan, which is certainly not the norm in Kolkata, demonstrates that she also thinks "out of the box." Perhaps Neena recognized the potential for a certain bond between us and was, therefore, happy to answer my questions.

I'm certainly glad she did. In fact, she truly lifted my spirits. With the Missionaries of Charity having burned the bridges between us, Empower The Children needs to find a new direction—perhaps toward opening non-formal schools. Now, thanks to Neena Singh, I have a model, a guide, a potential path to follow.

I communicate all of this to Janet and our board of directors after I return to New Jersey on my annual flight date of March 23. Janet reiterates her belief that Empower The Children should broaden its horizons and help children living in the slums and on the streets. The board concurs. We all see greater opportunity and potential.

So, this summer, I keep an ambitious fundraising schedule, visit with my family and friends, take my mother on holiday, enjoy time with Art, and return to Kolkata on July 23, 2003, wondering, "What now, Green Tara?"

Ratna's parents live in a lovely home in Salt Lake, a wealthy area of Kolkata. Whenever I go there, they make me feel like family. Indians are geniuses at that, a talent that I wish I had.

After lunch and pleasant conversation, Ratna says, "Let's take a little walk. I want to show you something."

Ratna had helped me move my educational materials from Daya Dan and heard what happened after Sister Tara was transferred to Shishu Bhavan, so she knows I have a bit of time on my hands despite my commitment to Neena at Disha School.

As we walk, she starts the conversation gradually, perhaps to entertain or distract me from other thoughts. She tells me that Salt Lake was developed in the late 1950s and early 1960s. It's a planned community unlike so much of Kolkata and India, which are randomly built. Officially, the city is named Bidhannagar in honor of Dr. Bidhan Chandra Roy, the planner and developer, but everyone calls it Salt Lake because it was built on a reclaimed saltwater lake. Popular legend claims the city will sink.

We wander around, passing well-maintained properties, lush gardens surrounded by boundary walls, and cars parked in driveways—all so neat and orderly. The wider, four-lane roads are boulevards with grassy, tree-lined medians, which are impossible for vehicles to cross, thus preventing drivers from driving into traffic in the opposing lane. This means there's less need for *horning*, and drivers generally don't. This alone is a welcome relief from the noise and chaos of Sudder Street and so many other Kolkata roads.

"You're lucky to have grown up here," I comment.

"Oh, my family didn't come from this neighborhood," she corrects. "I bought this house for my parents after I moved to America and started earning money."

Taking care of their families is also something that Indians do very well. They never forget those left behind.

Suddenly, we're facing an aging concrete building with a peeling sign across the front: Prabartak Institute for Epilepsy and

Cerebral Palsy—A Residence for Epileptic, Mentally Retarded and Cerebral Palsied Boys and Girls. It's an impressive building but not necessarily in a positive way. The side wings extend forward to within inches of the sidewalk fence as if to envelope and smother a cylindrical staircase in the center. It's painted exterior might have once simulated bright sunshine and brilliant red but are now weathered to a pale yellow-orange and chalky pink. The windows indicate three floors with very high ceilings.

I hear weird sounds coming from inside and see a few faces peering through an upper level window grill. Most buildings in Kolkata have grills on the windows, but these appear a bit heavier than normal, as if to keep residents in as well as to keep intruders out.

"Let's go inside," Ratna suggests.

We enter through a large, steel, accordion-style security gate, which is unlocked by a young man who appears to be quite mentally challenged.

"He is," Ratna confirms, "and he lives here along with many others with mental and physical disabilities."

As soon as we ascend the large, sunlit staircase to the first floor, we're surrounded by a throng of disabled residents, all teenagers and young adults. They gather very close, a bit too close. They grasp my hand, shake it heartily, and repeat, "Hello, hello, hello." I'm feeling a bit suffocated and look around for Ratna. She's equally squashed between young moving bodies, but she strokes their hair and greets each one by name.

As she speaks to them, I look more carefully and notice something I missed before—every face is radiating love.

We move as a group into a large room. The young people help each other settle on mats along the walls, with boys on one side and girls on the other. The family-like atmosphere isn't dysfunctional as some people might expect from individuals with mental and physical disabilities. Rather, they effortlessly demonstrate respect and affection toward one another.

Two of the bigger boys rush off to find chairs and place them at the far end of the room, near a window, in a sort of front-and-center, guest-of-honor arrangement. They signal that we should sit there. Then, seemingly out of nowhere, a young man places a harmonium, a traditional Indian instrument with a keyboard and bellows, on the floor in the center of the room. A young woman starts to play, and the youths begin to sing.

Ratna whispers in my ear, "This is the poetry of Rabindranath Tagore, India's first Nobel Laureate in Literature. His beautiful and complex spiritual poems have been set to music."

"It's amazing that they know his work."

"It's an accomplishment that they sing his work. And they are honored to do it for us."

They all sing. Even those who can't speak move their mouths and sounds come forth as their eyes gaze upward. It's obvious that they understand the significance of what they're doing.

> *Blessed are those who are so naïve that they do not know what they cannot do.*
> —Alan Cohen

Then I hear a familiar melody: "We Shall Overcome," first in English and then in Bengali and then in Hindi. As I've seen so many times before here in Kolkata and elsewhere on my journey, the irony of this moment is profound. These are disabled orphans, living in one of the poorest cities in the world. But, I wonder, "What do they have to overcome?" They're filled with love, compassion, and innocence. Isn't that what I and many others are aspiring to attain? My eyes fill with tears.

"Ratna," I whisper. "I want to teach here."

"I thought you would."

While in New Jersey the previous summer, I received word that Airline Ambassadors International had arranged for Air India to transport sixty boxes of educational materials and clothing from New Jersey to Empower The Children in Kolkata—for free. I couldn't believe it. But there was one small glitch. In the days of more liberal airline security before September 11, 2001, the boxes could go as cargo, but now they have to be accompanied by a ticketed passenger. Empower The Children can't afford to pay for anyone's ticket so who will do it? For me, there's only one obvious choice: Art.

"Art, have you thought about visiting Kolkata?" I say to him one day.

"I didn't think about it, but also didn't *not* think about it."

"That sounds a bit convoluted."

"Well, you know my mind isn't exactly *normal,*" he joshes.

"That's true. I think that's why I fell in love with you years ago, but I thought maybe you've changed."

"I've changed in a lot of ways but not in that way."

"Well, that's good because

> *Kings and cabbages go back to compost, but good deeds stay green forever.*
> —Rick De Marinis, novelist, short story writer

then you're the perfect person to fly all the way to Kolkata to deliver sixty boxes of things that Empower The Children can use."

"What kind of things?"

"Mostly educational materials. Now that Empower The Children is expanding its activities, I need more lessons. My colleagues in New Jersey have developed a specialized language curriculum that's perfect for both the disabled and slum-dwelling children. Each lesson is in a separate zip-lock bag plus all the props that go with the lessons, things like puppets, marionettes, musical instruments, costumes, and so on.

"There are seventy-eight lessons all together. It's impossible for me to bring them with me when I fly because the boxes will be big and heavy. We'll load them to the max in order to take advantage of this rare opportunity to transport them for free.

"Also, Ratna has collected a lot of clothing that her sister, who lives in Kolkata, will distribute. Before Ratna moved to New Jersey, she lived there, so she'll send things that are useful, not like the winter coats that were dropped off at my house years ago when I first left for Kolkata in February 2000."

"Well—"

"You know we can't pay your fare," I add hastily to avoid misunderstanding.

"Of course not. I would never expect that."

"So ...?"

"I'll do it."

* * *

Initially, I was thrilled about the idea of receiving teaching aids and clothing, but now, having returned to Kolkata, I'm worried about logistics. It's impossible to fix a date for Art's flight with the boxes because there's so much preparation. Airline Ambassadors has to complete complicated paperwork. I have to arrange for pickup, storage, and distribution here in Kolkata. I know I'm in over my head, so I call Ratna's sister, Champa Sarkar, who is associated with Rotary International and the All India Women's Conference, an organization dedicated to the upliftment of women and children.

"Champa, as you know from Ratna, sixty boxes of educational materials and clothing are coming to Kolkata, but I haven't a clue how to manage them when they arrive. Can you and Rotary help with this?"

"We will have to ask them. Come to a meeting on Friday evening."

"What should I tell them?"

"Tell them the curriculum material is for Empower The

Children and the clothing is for distribution by Rotary." She adds, "Everyone is very nice. Do not be nervous."

"I'm not nervous about making the proposal. But what should I wear?"

"Wear a *sari.*"

"I don't have a *sari,*" I reply, mentally scanning my spartan wardrobe.

"Then wear a pretty *salwar* suit."

I wear the nicest *salwar* suit I own, and I'm still out-classed by every other woman in the room, all wearing beautiful silk *saris* and lots of gold jewelry. I definitely feel like the poor relative begging for a handout. I sit through the business of the day, and then it's my turn. Not surprisingly, everyone seems happy with the idea, and the proposal is passed. But there are a few things to be worked out.

First, we need a truck, a driver, and a helper. Then we have to secure a storage area, possibly with a night watchman. Distribution will take several days, so a smaller truck must be available for the drop-offs. All of this will require money. I calculate the cost, compare it to what we would have to pay for sixty boxes of freight to be flown from New Jersey to Kolkata, and come to the logical conclusion: this is a good deal.

* * *

"Art, is everything ready at your end?" I'm calling New Jersey. It's an expensive call, but email isn't good enough. I have to hear his voice.

"Almost," he replies. "We have to figure out how to get all those boxes to the airport. Some are really heavy and bulky."

"I hope someone is helping you."

"Yes, Ratna's son is coming with me to the airport."

"You can't possibly get everything into a car. Will you rent a truck?"

"Yes. I've already reserved one."

"Did you ever drive a truck before?"

"No, but it can't be worse than driving on the wrong side of the road in Ireland. That was a nightmare!"

I laugh at his joke. Obviously, he's feeling confident, but somehow that doesn't quite quell my nervousness.

* * *

Finally, the big day arrives. I'm so hyper I can't think straight. Suddenly, I can't remember which airport terminal to go to. The flight originates in New Jersey, but Art will change planes in Delhi. So does that make it an international flight or a domestic flight?

I run to a travel agent on Sudder Street and find out that he's coming into the international terminal. But now I've wasted time. I'm afraid I'll be late. Can you imagine if I'm not there to greet him? He doesn't know the drivers of the truck. He doesn't know Champa. I pressure the taxi driver to go fast, but, of course, that's useless. The traffic, not my anxiety, determines our progress.

I'm sweating by the time I get to the airport and meet up with Champa and the driver and his helper.

Because the boxes are heavy and bulky, I ask the driver and helper to go with me into the international terminal to give Art a hand. But we run into bad luck. He's arriving on a national holiday—one of so many—so security precautions dictate that only ticketed passengers are allowed inside the terminal. We wait helplessly outside the building.

Here they come. The boxes are balanced precariously one upon the other. Because the airport luggage cart is small, Art has only five boxes with him when he emerges through the terminal's double doors. At this rate, he will have to go back inside twelve times! He makes trip after trip after trip from the luggage carousel, hauling the boxes on the cart and wheeling them outside. He's hot and tired, but he doesn't complain.

But ten boxes are missing. Art goes to a customs office, fills out a form, and "negotiates" with the inspectors who, no doubt, want *baksheesh* to find them. Art refuses to give over any money and patiently waits for them to decide if they're going to help or not. It's a long wait, and, stuck outside, we have no idea what's happening. Eventually, the customs inspectors decide in Art's favor and the boxes are miraculously found. He makes two more trips with the last ten boxes, and we load them onto the truck.

I feel uneasy about not staying with the truck, but, in India, a woman wouldn't squeeze into the cab of a truck with two men, so Art presses himself into the front seat with the driver and his assistant. I bid Champa good-bye and follow in a taxi. The truck is large and powerful, so the driver breaks every possible rule of the road, recklessly overtaking other cars and ignoring red lights. I'm thinking that Art must have nerves of steel or else he's so tired that, by now, he doesn't care.

We arrive at the storage area, which seems far from the airport but perhaps it's close and the traffic had made the ride seem unending. The men start to unload the truck, and, although it's the job of the driver and his assistant, Art helps them. Finally, the sixty boxes are spread out across the floor, thirty marked Empower The Children and thirty marked Rotary Club. Everything is organized.

# Creating Roots
## October 2003–March 23, 2004

For the past three-and-a-half years, I've lived at the Gulistan Guest House in a room with no furniture and all of my belongings stowed under the bed. "I need more space. I've outgrown this small room," I tell myself. "I have to find a flat." So the search begins.

Fortunately, everyone in Kolkata is a realtor: the *dhobi*, the *rickshaw wallahs*, the shopkeepers, the street people. If they hear that someone needs a place to live, they put their ear to the ground and listen. If the noodle vendor, for example, is the lucky matchmaker, then the landlord and tenant give him generous *baksheesh* and close the deal over a bowl of noodles.

It's Ismail, the taxi driver, who hears of a place on Syed Ismail Lane. The flat is on the edge of a *basti,* only a few minutes by foot from the Gulistan, by way of Free School Street, and close to Sudder Street's volunteer community.

If I were still living and traveling only in the United States—if that were my only perspective of the world—I would probably be shocked by the idea of living in a slum. But, in India and Kolkata, I've learned that *basti* can describe many types of communities from tightly packed, make-shift shacks of wood and tin scraps, often adjacent to railroad tracks or canals or even on the banks of the Hooghly River, to a maze of small but fairly well-constructed concrete buildings that are separated by tiny alleys, some too narrow for a motor scooter. Regardless of the structures, the *bastis* are populated by a lot of people.

Ismail leads me past a Muslim mosque that marks one end of Syed Ismail Lane. I can tell immediately that this *basti* is of the well-constructed concrete variety.

It's a village unto itself—in spirit not unlike the Brooklyn neighborhood in which I was raised and played. So it seems, somehow, familiar. Yet, we had amenities in New York that these people lack. Here, they collect water at a hand pump near a concrete bathing slab that's capped with slate-green marble and decorative ivory tile. A communal toilet, with only three walls and no roof, is clearly visible near the pump. A bin of bamboo poles provides a ready supply of temporary scaffolding materials to anyone who wants them.

Men, sitting on a bench made of the same marble and tile materials as the bathing slab, stop their chatter to watch me and Ismail walk by. Women stand near a communal clothesline or tote water in buckets or plastic jugs or carry baskets of food atop their heads. Teens play caroms. Babies are handed from one person's arms to another. And children joyfully scamper about, chattering as they play tag or badminton or spin tops or entertain themselves with no toys at all. "Hello, Aunty," they call gleefully.

As we enter the building, a *dhobi* emerges from a tiny, adjacent doorway to swap a cooling laundry iron for a hotter one that's been warming over a bed of glowing charcoal.

I feel those old embers of guilt warming inside me. This building seems quite nice, and I know that slum dwellers in other *bastis* have often been kicked out of their homes, even small concrete homes like those around us, to make room for nice buildings from which landlords can make much more money. Is that what happened here? By paying rent here, will I be feeding into a system that harms the type of people I want to help?

Qadir, the landlord, is very late, so Ismail tells me to go to the top floor and wait. "His brother, Qayum, lives there," he says. I hope Ismail will accompany me, but he slips away. So, I climb to the third floor, past nine flats, including the one that might become mine, and knock on Qayum's door. I'm greeted with silence and stares by two women, one middle-aged and the other younger—a mother and her grown daughter probably. Yet, they invite me in and gesture toward the sofa. I don't know how long I'll have to wait, so I sit down.

The younger woman sits on the floor chopping vegetables while the older woman sequesters herself in the kitchen. I wait a long time for the landlord, and, not once, do they make conversation.

Finally, Qadir arrives. The women greet him politely, and he tells me to follow him down two flights of stairs to look at the available flat. He uses a pair of keys to unlock two padlocks: one that secures a heavy, steel, accordion-style gate, and the other that holds the hasp of a deadbolt on the door itself.

The empty flat is bright and airy with terrazzo floors throughout. It has a living room, a small kitchen with no room for a stove or refrigerator, which

> *At first, it's unfamiliar,*
> *then it strikes root.*
> —Fernando Pessoa, poet, writer

is fine with me because I don't cook, a bathroom with an Indian-style squat toilet and an overhead, water storage tank, and two very ample bedrooms.

And there are windows! Two in the living room, one in the kitchen, two in one bedroom, and one in the other bedroom. I've never seen such large windows in Kolkata. Somehow, over the years, I'd gotten the idea that Indians don't like windows. I'm delighted. I love windows. And I love the wonderful, richly green tree visible through the living room windows.

But there's a small problem. The windows have no glass. I very politely point this out and remind Qadir to install the glass before I move in.

"No, I will not put glass in the windows," he says.

"What do you mean? You won't put glass in the windows?"

"I will not put glass in the windows."

"You must," I insist vehemently.

"Why?"

"Because during the summer, the heat comes in; during the winter, the cold comes in; during the monsoon, the rain comes in; and all year long, the dirt and insects come in."

"Yes," Qadir agrees reluctantly. "That is why we do not like windows."

We resolve the window problem when I agree to pay half the cost for the glass. While negotiating, I think again about the guilt I felt downstairs when I saw the *dhobi* and the meager way that he and others around here live. It's funny, but I don't feel the guilt anymore. It's disappeared. Is guilt that easy to erase when we get what we want?

We re-ascend the staircase to the roof. The roof is level with a low boundary wall around the perimeter. Qadir says he and other tenants host parties there.

I stand there and look around at what I've already decided will be my new 'hood.

The *basti* is abuzz with activity.

Because there's no running water in the homes, there are also no private toilets or showers or laundry facilities—not as we know them in America.

In the commons area, the *chaupal* they call it, washed sheets, towels, and clothing, including underwear, are hung out to dry here and there on lines of double-braided rope or draped over a steel corrugated wall, even a barbed wire fence.

Men are bathing on the slab by the pump. They expertly wrap their *lungis* around themselves and soap up from head to toe, then rinse off with small buckets of water from the pump. Somehow, they manage to remove the wet *lungi* and replace it with a dry one without ever exposing their private parts.

People are brushing their teeth there too—some with a toothbrush and toothpaste, some with their finger, and some with a stick made out of neem, an Indian pine tree with medicinal properties.

A young woman, wearing a beautiful tangerine-colored *sari*, is scrubbing more laundry. Another, dressed in a glittering green-and-gold *salwar kameez* that would look elegant at a New York City dinner party, scrubs dishes. Toddlers and young children, naked or with only a brown leather string around their waist, sit and splash in the lingering water, cooling themselves.

A young man comes in with a large dark brown bladder, made of a whole goat hide, and fills it with water, occupying the pump for many minutes. Then he slings it, now glistening wet in the sunshine, over his shoulder and leaves.

Everything seems to happen around the pump, the well of life.

"But where do the women wash?" I wonder, and later learn that they bathe in the privacy of their homes while the men wait outside; they also toilet in one of a few communal, closet-size, walled enclosures that provide privacy if not much space.

Some homes have tiny places to cook food, but most women are cooking outside with wisps of smoke rising from their charcoal fires. Someone is using kerosene, and, even from up here, I detect its noxious odor.

From the roof, everything looks very picturesque, even charming with its maze of narrow lanes, too many to count, and its choruses and cacophonies of voices, the epitome of a close-knit community. Even the continuous cawing of dozens of crows conveys a certain allure.

But I know, from my work with children who live in other *bastis,* that slum dwelling is difficult. These people have a life of struggle—mosquitoes that potentially carry malaria, scavenger rats, violence, and alcoholism. Yet, the community offers a sense of protection and security.

So, in November, Qadir and I seal the deal with our word and a handshake—much to the delight of Ismail, the taxi driver, who will receive *baksheesh* from both my new landlord and me. We agree to sign the lease after the glass is installed and I've acquired furniture. This seems backward to the American standards I'm used to, but I trust him. So the deal is done.

Coming down the staircase, I notice that, on two door nameplates, the letters "MD" are attached to the male names. I'm surprised that doctors would move into this neighborhood.

To save time and spare myself running all over Kolkata, I decide to rent furniture. Furniture stores generally have only some of the items I might need—perhaps chairs but not lamps, for example—but a rental shop is likely to have everything. Yet, the search for such a store is also tiring. So when I discover one fairly close to Syed Ismail Lane, I'm elated.

I point expansively around the place. "I'll take that and that and that and that," my finger says, until, I'm suddenly seized, again, with guilt. I've selected only what I need, but, in comparison to what most people living in *bastis* own, it seems I have enough for ten families.

Within a few steps of the building entrance, for example, there are three "dormitories" where eight to twelve men sleep each night on nothing but a sheet of cardboard or a thin blanket or mat. The *dhobi* sleeps on his ironing table while his wife, son, and daughter sleep on the floor in a room less than half the size of my smaller bedroom. I've heard that families of eight to a dozen people sleep in rooms smaller than an American single-car garage. And I've ordered two beds: one for me and one for guests. Yes, I feel guilty.

Cartage *wallahs* load my rented furniture onto a long, flat wagon, and two men strain to pull it through narrow lanes pocked with bumps and ruts. "Be careful. Don't drop anything," I beseech, selfishly concerned about my furniture and not their breaking backs.

The wagon stops in front of my building, and the neighborhood kids gather around to watch. To them, this is entertainment.

Each man deftly wraps a scarf around his head, shaping it like a flat turban, a cushion for the cranium. In this manner, they carry everything up the single flight of stairs, neatly negotiating two landings with one-hundred-eighty-degree turns. In an hour, they have everything positioned nicely. My flat is completely furnished. For that, I'm pleased.

Yet, guilt nags me again. Their hard work for small wages smells of slave labor, but, after years of living in Kolkata, I've also come to understand that poor people are happy to have work. They don't mind what kind of work it is as long as it puts food on their tables and sends their kids to school. They aren't looking for job satisfaction. They're looking for a way to survive in a city that crushes poor people under a yoke of economic oppression. I give the men *baksheesh,* a large amount, a balm for wounds—the workers' wounds sustained by their labor—and my own bruised sensitivities.

When my landlord signs the lease to make my occupancy official, he writes his name as "MD Qadir."

"Oh, I didn't know you're a doctor," I inquire casually.

He looks at me totally puzzled.

"MD," I reply, using my best teacher-tone. "Medical doctor."

"Mohammed," he replies seriously. "Mohammed is part of a Muslim man's name."

"Oh," I answer shaking my head slowly. So there are no doctors living in my building after all.

I'm searching for the place to sign my name when I hear Qadir murmuring something, almost inaudibly.

"Pardon," I say.

"What to say? There's a festival in February, and you will have to move out of your flat," he repeats, just slightly louder.

"What festival?" I ask.

"Eid, a big holiday, when we kill the animals," he replies nonchalantly.

The narrow lanes, angling left and right, and the tiny homes that surround my building don't release their secrets readily, but, once they do, you feel like you belong. My

*Opportunities are never lost; someone will take the one you missed.*
—Anonymous

Norwegian friends, Sissel and Anita, discover that more quickly than I do even though they stay in a guesthouse on Sudder Street.

"We've met your neighbors in the *basti,*" they tell me during dinner one night. "They are so sweet and funny. We really enjoy being with them."

"Being with them?" I ask suspiciously. "Are you already usurping my position as the new foreigner in the slum?" I'm joking of course.

"The family has three teenagers, Shahana, Aatirah, and Mukhtar, who speak very respectable English," says Anita.

"Much better than I do," adds Sissel with her strong accent.

"Each time we go to look for you, your door is locked so they insist we visit their home instead. It's only a single room with—can you imagine?—nine family members sharing that tiny space. But they genuinely love each other. There seems to be no jealousy or possessiveness."

"Where do they all sleep?" I ask.

"In one double bed," says Sissel.

"Except those who sleep on the floor. That would be the older children," adds Anita. "It's a high bed, maybe three feet off the floor, with their cooking cauldrons stored underneath."

"And they're always feeding us even though we suspect there isn't too much food in the house. The father makes buttonholes."

"The mother married when she was thirteen and rarely leaves the house, except to visit her family."

"And they press our arms and legs," says Sissel.

"Press your arms and legs?" I ask. "What does that mean?"

"They give us a massage," she explains.

"It's so relaxing that we fall right off to sleep."

"Imagine going to a stranger's home in Norway and falling off to sleep," says Anita. "They'd never invite us back."

It takes a while longer, but I finally meet the Indian family who has caught Sissel and Anita's heart and fancy. There's the mom, Ruhi; dad, Hasim; four sisters Ruaa, Shahana, Aatirah, and Aisha; and four brothers, Arif, Mukhtar, Sakib, and Aniq. The eldest sister, Ruaa, lives with her husband and small baby but visits every day. So the house is full, and now they've welcomed me as well.

I sit on the platform bed, which is so high, like Sissel and Anita had said, that I need a boost to get on it. The family sits on the concrete floor, looking up at me. I notice something really interesting. They're all leaning against each other with an intimacy and affection that's spontaneous. Fifteen-year-old Mukhtar is stroking the hair of his seventeen-year-old sister, Shahana, and sixteen-year-old Aatirah is holding her mom's hand.

"Tell us about America," requests Mukhtar, who is the most gregarious.

"Well, it's different than India."

"In what way?"

"Well, it's a lot less colorful and exciting," I reply, although what I really want to say is that America is a lot less noisy and chaotic!

"Where would you rather live?" asks Shahana, who is far from shy and not about to allow only Mukhtar to practice his English.

"In India. Don't I live here?"

"But America is so clean. And everyone drives a convertible."

I laugh. While this statement isn't true, I happen to own a convertible, a thirteen-year-old white Volkswagen Cabriolet, but I choose not to mention that. "Not everyone is rich. That's a fantasy that people have," I say convincingly. "People think that if they go to America, they will live on Easy Street."

Only Ruaa, Shahana, Aatirah, and Mukhtar speak English, but the others are listening intently. I feel like I am "holding court," so I measure my words carefully.

"You have something special here in India that we don't have in America," I add.

"What?" they want to know.

"Family closeness. You stay together and help each other and love each other."

"People in America do not love each other?"

"Yes, they do, but they also love their freedom and individuality. Most married children don't live with their parents."

"What about you?"

"I have a mother at home in America," I reply, "and yet I live in India. So what do you think?"

They immediately change the subject, and I wonder if my guilt about not always being there for my mother is visible even though I try to keep it hidden.

The three teenagers are so different. Mukhtar is carefree and never worries about anything, even when he should, like studying for an exam. Aatirah is like Mother Earth, really rooted; at times, her energy can be heavy, but she's not depressingly heavy, just grounded and solid. Shahana is physically heavy, but emotionally she tops Mukhtar; she's a dreamer, but unlike Mukhtar, her dreams are matched to ambitious goals.

\* \* \*

Today, Mukhtar and I are going shopping. He's patiently waiting for me as I make up a list: dishes, mugs, glasses, flatware, sheets, pillowcases, buckets, a broom, dust bins, and so on. To amuse himself, he starts singing hymns at the top of his lungs.

I can't resist asking, "Mukhtar, where did you learn these?"

"I go to Catholic school."

"You're Muslim. How can you sing Christian hymns?" I ask playfully.

He looks at me very seriously and replies, "I pray to both Gods."

On that note, we go off to New Market. New Market is my worst nightmare. It's a maze of tiny shops lined up on both sides of narrow, narrow aisles crowded with stacked goods and shoppers. Often, it's impossible to walk through the aisles shoulder to shoulder with someone else.

I've heard there are more than 2,000 stalls there, but it's impossible to tell. I've been there many times but have never seen it all. And, of course, there's no directory. But there are New Market *wallahs*. These are men who seem to come from nowhere to greet each shopper and quickly say, "Impossible," to the idea of finding a desired object without their help. And, generally, they're right, especially if I'm looking for something I've not purchased before.

Yes, there are sections, sort of: housewares, electrical appliances, fabrics, clothing, flowers, and meats exposed to the air where the stench is overbearing. I know a few food shops and the bakery, Nahoum & Sons Jewish Confectioners, a must-stop destination, but I'm lost when I walk down a new aisle.

"What you want?" The *wallahs* say. "I help you."

I've learned that their job is to lead unwary shoppers to stalls where the owner will pay *baksheesh* to the *wallah* if the customer buys something. If I need a pair of pliers, the *wallah* will take me to a fabric store, an electrical store, a clock store, anything but a hardware store!

"You want this. You want this." Their statements are directives, as though they know my wants more than I do.

Today, the *wallahs* are shouting, "Madame. Madame. Kashmiri shawls, gold earrings, pure gold, Rajasthani handicrafts straight from Rajasthan."

Distracted from my mission so carefully itemized on my list, I quickly look at some silk scarves and find amongst them a few marked cotton. I jump at the chance—actually, a way to fight back at this place that so assaults my senses—and say, rather haughtily, "These are cotton, not silk."

The shopkeeper, equally indignant, replies, "Madame, sometimes cotton can be silk."

With this, I'm ready to quit—and we've barely started—but Mukhtar sweetly assures me, "Don't worry. I am here."

We go from vendor to vendor and, with this able-bodied young Indian at my side, the *wallahs* tend to leave us alone. By the end of the afternoon, we're struggling to carry boxes, bundles, and overflowing bags. We climb into a high-wheeled *rickshaw*. With my purchases piled precariously on our laps and between our legs, it feels a bit tippy as the *wallah* pulls us toward Syed Ismail Lane.

Back at my flat, I check the list and discover that everything is ticked off. Mukhtar calmly informs me that our joint success is *fully* to his credit.

Feigning indignation, I inquire sarcastically, "How do you figure that?"

And he confidently answers, "Because I pray to both Gods."

> *A good beginning makes a good ending.*
> —English proverb

\* \* \*

I have to go to the airport at 1:00 a.m. because Ratna's friend from New Jersey is arriving with two boxes of educational materials for Empower The Children. I'm a bit nervous about leaving my house alone in the middle of the night. Is it safe to walk through the *basti?* What if the taxi isn't waiting for me a couple hundred meters away on Free School Street? And when I return, it'll be even later, and I'll still be alone. How will I manage the heavy boxes?

I have no choice, so I lock my door and then, as quietly as possible, pull the metal gate, which usually closes with a resounding clang. I'm relieved to see that the light in the stairway is on because, sometimes, it isn't and I have to use the thin ribbon of light from my mobile phone to make my way down the steps. I leave my building cautiously, trying to be as invisible as possible. The men who claim the community bench in the *chaupal* and often talk well past midnight have gone home, their loud, sometimes confrontational discussion about religion and politics put to bed for the night.

Suddenly, I hear, "Aunty, where are you going?" I see the outline of a familiar head through the grill of a window. It's the woman who sewed my curtains.

"To the airport," I reply.

"Oh, Aunty, it is late to be going to the airport. Be careful," the voice advises.

"Okay. I will."

Then I hear, "Aunty, where are you going?" There's another face in a different window. It's Ali who invited me to his son's birthday party.

"I'm going to the airport."

"Do you need a taxi, Aunty? I can get a taxi for you."

"I hope my taxi is waiting for me on the road."

"I will come with you in case your taxi is not there."

"Oh, thanks."

I'm only a few steps from the entrance of my building, and already four people, as if out of nowhere, are walking with me to my taxi, chatting as we go. So many people greet me along the way that finally I have to say, "Why isn't anyone sleeping? It's the middle of the night. Everyone should be sleeping!"

Their reply is laughter.

My taxi is waiting. I go to the airport, pick up the boxes, and return to the *basti* two hours later—at 3:00 a.m. Two of the men who accompanied me earlier in the evening are still awake and help me carry the boxes to my flat.

"Thank you so much," I say appreciatively.

"Good night, Aunty," they reply politely. "Sleep well."

\* \* \*

In other ways too, my preconceptions and misconceptions are continually tested. In a casual conversation, my landlord's brother, Qayum, happens to mention, "My good friend was Jewish. He died. I miss him so much." I never expected to hear these words from a Muslim.

I have to admit that I was a bit hesitant about moving into a Muslim neighborhood, given that I am both Jewish and American, a combination I was certain would inspire emotions—none of them good. Since September 11, 2001, when two airplanes struck the World Trade Center in New York City, the American news media has unfairly portrayed Muslims, in general, as terrorists or extremists, but my experience has been just the opposite.

To my surprise, some of the neighborhood children attend the Jewish Girls School, and others go to Catholic schools. I find this hard to reconcile, which proves that the stereotypes I believed about Muslims were just as strong as I had imagined my neighbors' stereotypical beliefs about Jewish Americans would be.

This keeps nagging at me, so when the opportunity arises, I feel compelled to ask Shahana, who attends one of the Loreto Schools, a Roman Catholic facility run by the Sisters of Loreto, "Why do the kids go to the Jewish Girls School and Catholic schools?

"Because we are *modern* Muslims."

* * *

"Kolkata is very dirty. It is best if you get a servant," advises Qadir.

I cringe at that word. It sounds so politically incorrect, but I also realize that someone—many people—out there needs a job, so even though I resist the idea, I change my mind and decide to go along with it.

Qadir arranges everything, a characteristic of living here that started shortly after I moved in and has become very convenient.

Of course, he and my neighbors are dismayed by … . How shall I say it? Me being *a woman alone!* The very idea generates either unveiled awe or unveiled terror.

"But I want to be alone," I insisted then. "I like doing things on my own."

"No, Madame. A woman alone. Very bad."

So everyone has become very protective of me, as if I were their personal responsibility. And apparently part of their responsibility is to find a servant for me. They all ask their "cousin's brother" and "cousin's sister," relationship descriptions that always make me laugh.

"Her name is Pinky," Qadir announces. "She also cleans for me," he adds by way of endorsement.

I'm paying Pinky a good salary, but she doesn't seem to understand the nature of her work. She cleans only in the middle of the floor, not under the bed, not behind the furniture, not even the window sills.

"Pinky, please wipe off the window sills," I request.

"No, Madame."

"No? Why not?"

"It is your fault that the window sills are dirty."

"My fault? Why is it my fault?"

"Because you keep the windows open."

"I like the windows open."

"But if you keep the windows closed, then the dirt will not blow in."

"I like the windows open," I repeat. "I like air and light."

"But it lets the dirt in."

"It's my flat, and if I want to leave the windows open, I certainly will." I answer with annoyance. "Besides," I continue logically, "if I keep the windows closed and the dirt doesn't blow in, then you won't have a job. The open windows are your job security."

She retorts with a scowling face, "You drive me crazy!"

"That's a good way to get fired," I threaten her.

Of course, I don't fire her, but, months later, she still cleans only the middle of the floor and wipes off the window sills only on special occasions.

* * *

I'm so nicely settled that I even have a little routine whenever I leave the house. In the United States, I check the stove before I leave, making sure all the burners are turned off. In Kolkata, I don't have a stove because I eat all my meals on the outside, but I must check the windows. If the windows are accidentally left open, neighborhood cats jump in and, uninvited, make my home their palace. And they don't leave politely. Instead, they run all over the place in total panic, knocking down the Buddha head that Art bought for me in Thailand and the glass birds I carried to Kolkata from Estonia.

Next, I lock my door and my sliding metal security gate. The gate is heavy, and I have to use both arms and one leg to move this stubborn fortification into place. While still on the stairs, I don sunglasses, not to protect my eyes from the sun, which is blocked by layer upon layer of air pollution, but as a defense against the dust created by constant digging and smoke from large wood fires stoked under cauldrons of *biryani,* a stew of mutton or beef, potatoes, onions, chilies, and herbs.

"Aunty. Aunty. Morning song." The boys and girls who were playing outside the buildings are immediately distracted when I emerge from the building.

They surround me, pushing and shoving, vying for my attention. They like it best when I hold each small hand individually and sing: "Good morning, good morning, good morning to you. I hope you are fine and the sun it will shine."

Sometimes, when I'm in a hurry, I sing to the entire group, which brings frowns instead of smiles.

The girls are wearing frilly, sequin-laden dresses that would be reserved for parties, Confirmations, and Bar Mitzvahs in the West. I think it's a prelude to wearing a *sari*. When an Indian woman steps out of her house to go to the market, she looks elegant enough to attend a wedding. Even women who work on the roads, carrying baskets of bricks on their heads, are like tattered tropical birds ready to fly from their tedious task.

"Aunty. Aunty. Stickers. Stickers," the children shout in unison, as though the weight of their joined voices will affect the outcome.

"No more stickers," I reply. "They're all gone."

"Tomorrow, Aunty?"

"Tomorrow." My promise, one hundred times broken, still instills hope in their small breasts.

The kids follow me down narrow Syed Ismail Lane, skirting goats, tripping on broken pavement, and avoiding the gentle rebukes of their parents to "Leave Aunty alone."

I continue down Collin Lane, wide enough for *rickshaws* and motorcycles. The motorcycles have a very high-pitched, piercing horn that shoots pain into my inner ear, so I twist earplugs into place. My friend Nan, while visiting from McLeod Ganj, was working on a crossword puzzle in my house and asked me to give her a couple of pencils and erasers. Later, when we walked out onto the road, the noise was so intrusive that, out of desperation, she stuck the erasers in her ears!

Now I'm walking on Free School Street, the main road, crowded with every kind of conveyance imaginable plus an occasional herd of goats. Yet into that chaotic mess I step because the narrow footpath is blocked by sleeping people, food stalls, fruit vendors, beggars, barbers, ear cleaners, eye cleaners, hawkers, and the rest of humanity not, at the moment, walking in the traffic.

As I'm carried along by this throbbing cacophony, I press on my earplugs to fix them more securely and to further block out the incessant *horning*. I'm convinced that the *horning* is the Indian form of road rage. Drivers *horn* even in situations that are totally useless, like when stopped at a red light. This makes me so frustrated that I shout furiously, "Do you think your *horning* is going to make that light change?" But my words are to no avail. My voice is snuffed out like a used-up piece of incense.

I spy a dog sleeping on a pile of sun-warmed sand in the middle of the road. The dog is further blocking traffic, but no one makes the effort to move it. The traffic just parts and goes around it!

A *rickshaw*, piled precariously high with merchandise, is pulled by human hands. The *rickshaw wallah* bangs his little hand bell, "clang, clang, clang, clang," to declare his presence, although the size of the wooden *rickshaw*, with its high, thin, wooden wheels and thinner rubber tires, is so massive that it's impossible to ignore. But the *rickshaw* bell is a great improvement over the ear-piercing "beep, beep, beep, beep, beep, beep" of *horning*. I always tell volunteers to buy a *rickshaw* bell as a souvenir. Kolkata has the only man-pulled *rickshaws* in India, and someday this occupation, with its distinctive bell, will be a thing of the past.

And then I see it. Oblivious to all the chaos around him, staring calmly ahead, a man is walking through the crowd carrying a sofa on his head. A sofa! "Rosalie," I ask myself incredulously, "Do you realize, *you live here*?"

With Empower The Children receiving increased donations, Janet and I agree that we can start expanding our programs to help more children. Reena and I had worked well together at Middleton Row School, on the roof of Reena's office building, but unfortunately, at that time, we didn't have enough money to make it into a proper school. So, we chose to hand it over to The Calcutta Samaritans, a secular volunteer organization that serves persons in need.[25]

Reena, an innate lover of children, never got over her disappointment and has been aching to open another school. She reminds me of this whenever we get together, which is quite often. One day in 2003, she asks me, "Have you ever heard of Ultadanga?"

"No," I reply.

"It is a *basti* toward Salt Lake."

"Yes?"

"There is a small building there, really just a large room. Men use it as a *chaupal,* a club in the evenings to play cards, smoke, and gossip."

"Do men gossip?" I ask with mock surprise, while Reena modifies her ever-present smile to give me a disapproving look, a clue that she has something serious on her mind. "Okay, okay, tell me about the club."

"The room is empty during the day. We can use it four hours a day as a non-formal school. The children can come to study and, when they are ready, transfer to a government school."

"Is there a need for a non-formal school in Ultadanga? I mean, if it's toward Salt Lake—"

"Oh, ho. There is a need all over the city. There are thousands of kids who do not go to school."

"I hope you aren't planning on enrolling thousands," I scold, half in jest.

"No, just twenty-five to start."

Reena's idea grabs my attention. Her enthusiasm and confidence outshine any imaginary obstacles that come to mind. "Okay, let's start with twenty-five to thirty. We can hire two teachers and give the kids lunch. That's a good beginning."

"We will call it Preyrona," Reena suggests. "That word means 'inspiration.'"

Preyrona School* opens on Republic Day, January 26, 2004. The boys and girls, ages five to fifteen, patiently line up to be added to the register. Some of the children look so

> *Children are always the only future the human race has; teach them well.*
> —Anonymous

small that I suspect they aren't yet five. Reena says they are undernourished. "Soon they will be strong and healthy," she assures me, "because we will give them nutritious lunches at the end of each school day."

We have a flag raising ceremony, and a very thin girl in tattered clothes sings "Jana Gana Mana," the Indian national anthem. Her voice is sweet and melodious, and it carries the message that deprived children can raise their voices for a better future.

*\* Preyrona is spelled Praroyna on some signs and legal documents.*

Recently Mukhtar, Aatirah, and Shahana had a meeting in their house, and Aatirah, now becoming less shy and more assertive, declared to her family, "When Rosalie cannot manage anymore, I will take care of her." This precipitated a vigorous discussion around my eventual debilitation.

They already think I'm a modern miracle. In India, women my age, approaching sixty, are old—*really* old. Women well before that age depend upon a daughter-in-law to run the household.

That's why bearing a son is so important—it eventually leads to a daughter-in-law who moves into her husband's home to care for his parents. So, to everyone's amazement, I'm not only old but still on my feet.

Mukhtar, Shahana, and Aatirah come to my flat almost every evening to study English. They're very fond of colloquialisms, which they call proverbs, such as "He's really on the ball," "Snug as a bug in a rug," and "You can't compare apples and oranges." They use these expressions frequently in order to better remember them, and, often in sentences where they're not a perfect fit. I cringe when Aatirah proudly tells me that she used "It's raining cats and dogs" in her class eleven mid-year exam.

Shahana is very verbal and wants to become a lawyer, but her passion is cooking. "I want to feed the world with my own unique recipes," she declares expansively.

"Maybe you can become a lawyer who only takes on 'kitchen cases,'" I suggest playfully. "That can be your specialty."

"Like what?" she asks, ready to assume a mock courtroom contest.

"Like a person who chokes on a strand of spaghetti and sues the cook."

"Why would it be the cooks fault?" she asks suspiciously.

"That's for you to figure out. You're the lawyer."

Shahana goes to school, but, in every other way, she is sheltered. Like most Muslim women, she doesn't have the freedom to roam around, and her world is quite limited. She is determined never to marry.

"Why not marry?" I ask.

"Because I do not want to be in the yoke of slavery."

Slowly, this Indian family is becoming my family. The kids are giving me grey hair just like all teenagers do, but they also give me so much joy. I can't help but think that Green Tara is taking another step to root me to Kolkata.

\* \* \*

In contrast to the care and concern expressed by this loving family, it has taken months for my upstairs neighbors to warm up to me. When I first came to look at my flat, they gave me a lukewarm reception while I waited for Qadir in their living room, but now Nasima and her daughter, Munni, express their love for me and tell me that they take pride in my work. They tell all their friends and relatives that I'm helping the poor, especially disabled children, and that it's a sacrifice for me because I am used to a different kind of life in America.

Maybe out of love, maybe out of pride, they keep taking me to weddings. I know neither the brides nor grooms, but that doesn't seem to faze anyone. However, as soon as we arrive, they abandon me, running to chat with relatives and friends, and I spend the evening alone. I don't mind. I go to the weddings for the food. Not being a cook myself, I'll go almost anywhere for good food.

"Every time we go to a wedding, you wear the same dress," complains Munni.

"That's the only fancy dress I've got."

"But it makes a bad impression."

"Maybe they'll think I'm poor."

"Oh, *baba!* They will never think an American is poor. They will think you are cheap. And my friends are not cheap!"

"All your friends are not cheap except this one," I tease.

"*Byas.* Enough," she insists.

That seals it. Munni is determined that I wear a *sari* to the next wedding. Because I *am* cheap, I refuse to buy one, but that doesn't deter her. She has a closet full of beautiful, colorful *saris*.

Tonight, we're going to a wedding, and, because I've agreed to wear a *sari,* the wedding has taken on new significance. Munni goes through her closet a dozen times as I stand by helplessly.

"This is a nice one. It suits you," she says finally.

"I don't like green."

"Green is a very good color for you."

"I look like an old witch in green."

But she prevails. I'm wearing the green *sari*. Of course, I have no green shoes, but Munni has several pair, and, unfortunately, they fit. I feel funny wearing someone else's shoes. I can't help but remember my kindergarten teacher warning, "Don't ever wear anyone else's shoes. Don't ever wear anyone else's hat. You'll get toe fungus and head lice."

First, they help me with the petticoat, also Munni's, and a short, tight-fitting blouse, a cover for "my girls" that's more like a sports bra with plenty of midriff showing beneath. Then, I stand like a statue as the first part of nine yards of fabric are tucked into the petticoat and wrapped once around my body. The last bit, the *pallu,* is then draped over my shoulder. And the middle part is folded by hand into a myriad of pleats that are tucked into the front of the petticoat, just below my belly button. There are no buttons, no hooks, no snaps, no pins. How can it possibly not unravel and expose my nearly sixty body?

I see women working on the roads, their arms lifted high, carrying baskets or bowls of rocks on their heads and wearing *saris*. How do *they* do it? I guess *sari*-wrapping is an art passed down from one generation to the other.

Now Munni adds bangles from my wrist to elbow—and even make-up. When she's finished, I have to admit that I look pretty good, so I take pictures to send home to my mother.

The wedding is in a large hall. Yellow and orange garlands, made from marigolds, hang everywhere. It smells delicious, like a botanical garden in full bloom. The bride is surrounded by her family and friends. Each person presents a gift, which is added to a pile in one corner of the room. The women look absolutely gorgeous. There's no one more elegant than an olive-skinned, dark-eyed, ebony-haired Indian woman dressed in a *sari* and adorned with bangles.

As expected, Munni and Nasima leave me and go to gossip with their relatives and friends, so I head toward the buffet—albeit slowly, ever-mindful that the *sari* is held together with a hope and a prayer. I hear something snap. "Oh, shit!" It's the heel on Munni's shoe. I *carefully* bend to pick it up. What should I do with the heel of a shoe? The *sari* not only has no buttons, snaps, hooks, or pins but it also has no pockets. I put the heel in my handbag for the moment and limp to the food tables that line the perimeter of the hall. Up, down, up, down. This is really embarrassing, and I feel like everyone is staring at me.

I take an empty plate, and the waiters stand prepared to heap food on it. I don't eat spicy food, so I accept only what's not swimming in dark red oil. Then I limp back to my seat. Up, down, up, down. "I'm glad I didn't take any oily food," I think, suppressing a laugh. "It would slide from side to side, slosh off the plate, and be all over Munni's green *sari*."

Walking like this isn't so bad once I get the hang of it. I go back to the buffet for another serving and then to the dessert table. I feel pretty confident now, so I walk a bit faster. Up, down, up, down.

An Indian wedding is quite an experience. The most surprising part for me is that there are actually two receptions: the bride makes a reception, and the groom makes a reception, usually a couple of days apart. Yet the same people are invited. So why not have just one joint reception? Also, the number of people far exceeds the number who would be invited to most American weddings.

I once asked Munni, "How many people will be at the wedding?"

And she replied, "Two hundred from our family."

"And from the groom's side?"

"Same, same but different."

At Muslim marriages, a contract is usually signed before the reception, but the couple doesn't sign it together. The woman signs it in her father's house, and the man signs it in the mosque. Sometimes, the contract is signed in the reception hall, but the couple doesn't sign it jointly.

During the reception, the husband sits on a throne in one room and the bride sits on a throne in a different room, as if they've just had a lovers' spat, each greeting guests. Finally, at the end of the reception, around 1:00 in the morning, after most of the guests have left, the new husband and wife meet.

At that time, the husband is led to a room that has a large platform and two throne-like chairs. He wears a tall, white hat that looks, ironically, like an American-type wedding cake. Flowers hang down the front, covering his face, which may block his vision and explain why he is led to the throne. The bride is also led to sit beside him, her face covered with a veil. The groom stares straight ahead and doesn't try to catch a glimpse of his new wife. The girl's father comes on the stage, and she falls at his feet and cries hysterically, "Papa. Papa. Papa." The father hugs her hurriedly and slips away. Then other family members say good-bye to her, and the bride is equally demonstrative with them. Then both the husband and wife are led away, guided by the few remaining family members, to a waiting car and driven to the husband's house.

In a Hindu marriage, the ceremony is performed at the first reception. After quite a long time, the bride, her face hidden, is carried aloft on a chair to where the groom is

> *We should be able to live a graceful life that is full of mutual love and warmth.*
> —Hindu Marriage Prayer

sitting. The groom and bride sit on a mat on the floor with a priest who recites prayers, puts a thumbprint of protective *tilak* on their foreheads, and ties a protective string around their individual wrists.

Gold and yellow marigolds are part of the ceremony, as is incense. A fire is lit in a small pan at the priest's knees, and the bride and groom stand and walk around the flame seven times, holding hands, with her leading. When the couple returns to the mat, she sits in the place where he had been previously, and he in hers. Then, they walk around the flame again, with the man leading this time. He then places a red smear, a sign that she's now married, on the center of her forehead and well up into the midline of her hair. Ceremony assistants bring forth two long garlands of white flowers, accented with red flowers. They place one around the bride's neck and the other around the groom's neck.

When the ceremony is finished, the couple retires to a separate room, where they sit side-by-side on a pair of throne seats, and guests come to greet them, offer presents, and extend congratulations.

What I find most intriguing is that very few people actually watch the ceremony. Parents and siblings may wander in and out. People chat. Waiters roam about, offering food and drink to the guests. Even the man and woman who assist the bride and groom accept phone calls on their mobiles while attempting, with their one remaining free hand, to perform some ceremonial duty.

There's no music or dancing at either a Hindu or Muslim reception in Kolkata, and it's not considered impolite to eat and leave just after greeting the bride or the groom.

At this particular wedding, I search for Munni and Nasima to tell them I'm ready to leave. I know from previous weddings that they'll stay until after midnight, but I have to teach in the morning. Weddings for people of many faiths throughout India are often on weeknights, an "auspicious date" determined by consulting an astrological chart. I find my neighbors with a large clutch of women. I don't mention the heel of the shoe and try to appear as if I'm gliding, doing some fancy ballroom dance maneuver.

Munni looks worried when I tell her I'll walk home alone even though the hall is only a few blocks from the building where we live. She quickly organizes a group of neighbors, also ready to leave, to act as my protectors. So we set off, an entourage of four adults and six children.

I'm gliding along Park Street, chatting away, totally oblivious to anything around me, when suddenly, I hear, "Aunty. Aunty. Your *sari!*" I glance back and notice a long trail of green fabric behind me, like the train on a wedding gown.

"Aunty. Aunty. Your *sari,*" repeats the same boy, this time with more desperation. Then I get it. All the pleats in the middle layer of my *sari* have come undone, and the only part left around my body is the part tucked into the petticoat.

Being helpful, one of the young girls gathers up the long train and places the big bundle in my arms. I feel like I'm cradling an overly swathed baby. Up, down, up, down all the way home.

Early the next morning, before I leave for work, I knock on Munni's door. My face is awash with embarrassment when she opens it. "I'm returning the *sari* and shoes," I tell her. I hand her the broken shoe and the heel rather sheepishly. "It broke off during the wedding, and the *sari* came undone while walking home."

"I know," she replies sympathetically. "I already heard."

It's only 8:30 am and she's already heard. News travels fast through the *basti!*

I had been in denial about the slaughtering festival about which Qadir had warned me, but suddenly it's the first of February, and it's here.

"Eid is an important holiday, Aunty," a small boy tells me. "The animals are killed so the kids are not killed."

That seems reasonable—I guess. But, just to be sure, I ask Mukhtar to tell me about this important holy time, Eid al-Adha, the Festival of Sacrifice.

"God told Abraham to sacrifice the ram instead of his son," he explains. "God is good," he adds, repeating words that are often spoken within this Muslim community

So I do my best to share in the excitement as people prepare and transform the neighborhood. First, the cows come—not exactly two-by-two in Biblical terms but enough to make a herd of forty to fifty. They're lined up and tethered along the narrow, alley-like lane outside my building, blocking my primary way out of the *basti*. Their heads face the walls, their rear ends are toward where people walk, and from time to time they lift their tails to pee or shit or both.

At night I'm aware of the sounds outside my bedroom window—the cries of the cows. Mukhtar says they cry because the mothers are separated from their babies. I could picture their eyes bulging as they look around in vain for their calves. They can't move because they're tethered. I know this must be painful for them so my wish for this holiday to end is for their sake as well as mine.

I've left my flat, walked down the stairs, and am standing near the door of the building, looking at the long line of cows. I'm on my way to work, so I'm dressed in a *salwar kameez* and carrying my lessons for the day in open shopping bags. I'm running late. I hate to be late and don't want to waste time, but from here to the main road, all I can see is a long, linear corral of very large animals standing amidst the stench of urine and feces. So, in complete panic, I shout to no one in particular, "How do I get out of the lane?"

A child's voice yells back as his small hand grasps my arm, pulling me toward what I don't want to face—or smell. "Run, Aunty. Run!"

And that's what I do for two weeks. I run past cows that have now been joined by more than a dozen goats and sheep. I'm beginning to feel imprisoned.

I call Qadir. "When will they slaughter the animals?" I ask bluntly.

"We are waiting for the camel," he replies.

I find out that a camel has been walking for, perhaps, two to three months all the way from Rajasthan, which is on the border with Pakistan, 1,500 kilometers west of Kolkata. A camel is coming all that way—all the way across India—to be slaughtered in front of my door! I have to admit I feel quite relieved when it finally arrives, relief tinged with a fair share of guilt because it's the cutest camel, sitting very peacefully chewing its cud and letting everyone pet it.

But, by now, I'm anxious for all this to be over, so I ask my neighbors, "When will they slaughter the camel? Why are we waiting?"

"I explain you. It has to rest."

"Rest?" I ask in disbelief. "Rest? Once it's dead, it has the rest of its life to rest!"

While we're waiting for the camel to rest so it can be slaughtered, I inquire about the dogs. The dogs in Kolkata are strays, most of them diseased and missing hair from mange. Many limp and have open sores, and they all seem to be about the same size and color. They lie about the streets during the day, forcing people to step over them, and bark and howl and fight all night. So I have a great idea, albeit not a very Buddhist one.

"While you're slaughtering the cows and goats and sheep and camel, why don't you do a 'service' to Kolkata and kill the dogs as well," I suggest to the handful of men sitting on the bench in the *chaupal*.

"*Arre,* Madame," they reply, aghast. "We cannot kill the dogs."

"Why not?" I insist.

"Because they are God's creatures."

* * *

Finally the slaughtering has begun, and the blood is running! With efficiency, professional slaughterers secure each cow's neck and legs with a rope, topple it onto its flanks, and kill the animal with one quick cut to the throat. Butchers remove the head and hooves then, with a hatchet, cleave the meat into cookable chunks.

This all takes place near the water pump in the *chaupal*, so most of the blood washes down the municipal drain, but a residue remains that is soon covered with lye.

The number of cows to be slaughtered depends, in part, upon the economy. Certainly, most people living here can't afford to buy a cow, so only the wealthier people do. A family might contribute one or several. Once butchered, the meat is divided equally among the family who bought the cow, their extended family, and the poor who line Syed Ismail Lane and wait. On the third day of Eid, when the last of the cows are still being slaughtered, Qadir tells me, "The poor have already received their meat."

I don't know into which category I fit, but Qayum, Nasima's husband, presents me with a giant plate of *biryani* that's, thankfully, not spicy, so I eat it eagerly. Later in the day, Nasima comes to collect the plate and asks, with a little mischievous twinkle in her eye, "How did you like the camel?"

"What part of 'No' don't you understand?" I hate that expression, and I can't believe those words just came out of my mouth. But Dr. Chatterjee, an orthopedic surgeon, is trying to convince me to visit Rehabilitation Centres For Children. He seems to be winning the battle, so I make my point stronger than is, perhaps, necessary.

"It's a nice hospital. I've been doing free surgery there for fifteen years," he pursues, undisturbed by my insulting cliché.

"Yes, I'm sure it's a nice hospital and the kids are adorable and the staff is dedicated. That's why I don't want to go there. I'll fall in love with the place and want to teach there, but I have no time."

"You don't have to teach there. Just give them some help."

"I like to teach in places I help. So I know what's going on."

"What's going on is that kids go into the hospital unable to walk because of deformed leg bones or club feet or polio, and they leave the hospital walking."

"But there's a school there. That means I can teach if I want to. Right?"

"Yes, that's right. Jane Webb, who founded RCFC, saw that most of the children didn't attend school, so she provided education and skills training during their rehabilitation months. But teaching there or not is your choice. You can also give the teachers advice on how to upgrade the curriculum and use new teaching methods. They would appreciate that."

"Let me think about it."

"There's nothing to think about. I'll do the needful and pick you up on Tuesday morning at 11:00. Just take a look. You need not make a commitment."

I nod my head in agreement, and, by Tuesday, my mind has already made a shift. I'm looking forward to going to RCFC.

The hospital is in Barisha, a quiet locality outside of Tollygange on Kolkata's southern fringes.

The entrance has a grayish-red gate with the name and other information painted in large white letters. The grounds, I observe as we drive in, are spacious. The buildings, although suffering from "monsoon decay," are fairly large and impressive and appear to be in decent condition.

Walking, we pass gardens of vibrant tropical plants with broad leaves of green, yellow, dark violet, and crimson. The lane is lined with trees of various genus: palm, mango, coconut, litchi, jackfruit, betel nut, jamrul, and eucalyptus.

"We serve the fresh fruit to the children," says Dr. Chatterjee.

I feel peace and tranquility here, as though coming through the entrance gate has taken me down Lewis Carroll's Rabbit Hole into another, different, beautiful world. This feeling is confirmed by a clown painted on a wall: his bulbous feet stand atop the word "WELCOME" while, with a broad smile, green hat, ballooning blue pants, golden vest, and red suspenders, he juggles an impossible number of colorful balls, four of which contain the letters R–C–F–C.

We tour the buildings that fulfill the facility's purpose: the hospital, an operating theater, physical therapy rooms, residential dormitories for children and mothers of the very young, child development classrooms, and areas for crafts and music. The procedural rooms appear sterile, but some of the surgical equipment looks antiquated. And I'm told that the ambulance no longer runs.

Everything here—inside and out—is clean and cheerful. There are even two playgrounds outfitted with large concrete animals, such as elephants, that the children can admire or climb on. But I notice that both playgrounds need repair.

The entire atmosphere seems to embody the intent and spirit of Jane Pamela Webb, the English nurse who founded RCFC in 1974 to provide compassionate, comprehensive treatment for any child regardless of caste or religion. She learned to speak Bengali so she could better serve her patients, was granted Indian citizenship, and died of cancer in India on December 6, 1998.[26]

A poem, which she wrote, is carved in black marble on the side of a modest statue in her honor. It reads:

I HAVE KNOWN
PEOPLE
TOUCHED
CHILDREN
HANDS
STROKED HAIR
TALKED
LAUGHED
DANCED
I HAVE LOVED
FRIENDS
BROTHERS
SISTERS
I HAVE TRIED OFTEN
FAILED
WON MUCH

*To care for anyone else enough to make their problems one's own is the beginning of one's real ethical development.*
—Felix Adler, founder of Ethical Culture

These words touch my heart. Dr. Chatterjee was right. What part of "Yes" am I still afraid to accept?

"Some of the children remain here for up to two years," he explains. "Many come from Bihar, a neighboring state. We run medical camps there, searching for children who might need our help, and we offer it to them at RCFC in Kolkata. Some of the parents say no because they think we want to steal their child's kidney and sell it on the black market. Of course, that is not true, but we have to reassure them."

Having heard of this practice already, I nod appreciatively.

"Most of the people are day laborers,[27] so their income is small," Dr. Chatterjee continues. "If the children are less than three years, the mother will stay with the child, but, of course, that means the mother is separated from her husband and the rest of her family for that entire time."

"That has to be hard on everyone," I interject.

"If the children are three years or above," he continues, "the parents leave them. Unfortunately, they don't have enough money to go back and forth to visit them. So the children undergo the surgery or multiple surgeries on their own.

"After surgeries, there is a recovery period. If needed, the child is fitted with prostheses or orthoses or both, which is followed by physical therapy. Finally, the parents come to get them. It is a long process, and most of the children face it alone."

My mind is reeling. My own experiences and those of most of the people I know in the United States are like minor skin blemishes compared to what these children endure. "In America, if a child has tonsils removed, the parents and grandparents on both sides are there to give support," I say, almost ashamed by the contrast. "How do these kids face repeated surgeries? After the first one, they know it's going to hurt," I ask a nurse standing near one of the beds.

"They're brave and they want to walk. They don't want to be

outcasts any longer because their legs aren't formed like everyone else's."

I meet the kids. In the hospital block, everyone is confined to a bed, but no one seems restless or bored. And no one is crying or complaining. I look more closely, and I'm horrified to see a series of rods through some of the children's legs.

"The rods are tightened every day," the nurse explains. "That stretches the bones and stabilizes them during healing."

"Isn't that painful?" The answer is obvious, but I feel compelled to ask.

"Yes, very painful," she replies.

"Then why isn't anyone looking sad or uncomfortable?"

"I explain you. They know it will help them. They are willing to bear the pain."

I go from bed to bed and shake everyone's hand and wish them luck. They're shy, not used to foreigners—or women with long, curly hair. "What about the school?" I ask the nurse.

"Talk with Kakali Samadder about that. She is our head teacher and has been here two years."

I walk over to the child development center, which greatly contrasts to the hospital. The walls are peeling and, in some places, look quite deteriorated. There are a few benches but most of the children are on the floor. I'm concerned for the children's safety, sitting beneath chunks of plaster that seem ready to detach at any moment. I make a mental note to ask the Empower The Children board to approve money to repair and paint the classrooms.*

* *The Empower The Children board of directors approved my recommendation at our next board meeting and the walls were soon repaired and repainted. Through my network, I then contacted an organization in The Netherlands, HelpIndiaHelpen, which bought a new anesthesia machine and ambulance for RCFC. Indian*

*American Education Foundation also accepted my proposal to repair one of the playgrounds.*

\* \* \*

I like Kakali immediately. She exudes warmth, and it's clear that she loves the children.

"Some do not attend school in Bihar," Kakali tells me, "so they are lucky to get the chance to learn to read and write here. We have only a small school, and the children attend when they are well enough to leave the hospital. But, of course, before long, they are back in the hospital for the next surgery."

"Do they get bored? I mean, staying here for up to two years is a long time to just sit around waiting for bones to heal."

"Not *atall*. The therapy takes up a large part of their day. We have a music program that everyone enjoys. We teach arts and crafts, and the children make beautiful items with cloth and beads that we sell to raise money to buy more vocational materials … things like hand-embroidered hankies, batik or tie-dye bed and table coverings, jute purses or bags, candles. Many things."

"I have an interactive curriculum that's very engaging," I offer. "The kids would love it. Maybe I could come here and teach." My enthusiasm rises in my voice.

"That would be so good for the children," she replies.

"What about Wednesday? I'm free on Wednesdays. Do you think the teachers would mind?"

"The teachers would welcome you. Please start this Wednesday. We will be waiting for you."

As I walk back through the gate at Rehabilitation Centres for Children—back out of the Rabbit Hole and into the rest of the world—I realize that Dr. Chatterjee won the battle. And what a lesson for me: If young children can do this—and do it alone—what else can *I* do?

I've been in Kolkata for another eight consecutive months, with only one short jaunt out of the country because the Indian government limits a tourist visa to 180 days. Shortly, I'll be going to the United States for the next four months.

> *The sun of true happiness starts to shine in your life when you begin to cherish others.*
> —Zopa Rinpoche, Buddhist lama

Everyone at Prabartak Home is crying: The director, Mr. T. Ganguly, whose teacher founded the orphanage, and his wife who is a nurse, the kids, the *maisies*. I'm the only one with dry eyes because I know I'll be back. The others are afraid I won't. Every conversation is basically the same.

"You gave up your comfortable life in America to come here. You will not come back."

"It was comfortable there, but I wasn't happy."

"Your mommy is there and your friends."

"They understand that I need to come back."

"Maybe they will not let you come back."

"That decision is mine."

"Maybe you will not *want* to come back."

I try to cheer them up but to no avail. Then, suddenly I get an idea. "Let's have a going-away party at my flat," I suggest, and their tears are immediately replaced with beaming smiles.

On the day of the party, Mukhtar, Aatirah, and Shahana help me get ready. The girls are in the kitchen preparing thirty plates of snacks and thirty cold drinks. Mukhtar and I are trying to figure out how to comfortably seat that many people. We finally decide that the twenty-five young people can sit on the floor and the five adults can sit on chairs. If ten people are in the living room, ten in my bedroom, and ten in the guest bedroom, it would be cozy but not crowded.

I get a call that the hired bus has arrived at the corner of Free School Street and Collin Lane, which is about five minutes away on foot. Mukhtar and I rush out to meet it. We help the kids, dressed in their holiday clothes, off the bus one by one. This takes a long time because several of them have difficulty walking and others look around in wonderment at a place they've never been before. The bus is partially blocking the road, and traffic is building up behind it. Simultaneously, Indian pedestrians are building up in front of the young people, staring.

I remember when we took the children from Daya Dan to the zoo. They were in the picnic area, eating lunch, and a big circle of people slowly formed around them, layer upon layer. One volunteer became so upset that she shouted to them, "The animals are over there, not here."

However, the residents of Prabartak Home don't mind being observed. They've been raised with love and attention, and their self-esteem isn't easily bruised. The more able-bodied kids take the hands of the less able-bodied and they walk, two by two, down the lane. For those who can't walk, we hire *rickshaws*, and they are jostled across the irregular pavement that includes several speed bumps.

We reach my building, and they ascend the stairs. It's hot, and they're getting tired, but they don't utter a word of complaint. I can't help but think of all the class trips I've made with students in America and their constant grumblings: "Are we there yet? I'm thirsty. I'm hungry. I'm tired." The contrast is apparent, and I can't help but *kvell* over the fortitude of my special needs children in Kolkata.

Everyone loves my flat. It's decorated European-style, so they haven't seen anything like it before. They may be mentally challenged, but that hasn't affected their curiosity. They look at and touch everything, much to my delight but to the dismay of the adults who think that it's bad manners. "It isn't bad manners," I assure them. "It's healthy exploration."

Shahana and Aatirah won't leave the small kitchen. They

haven't been close to disabled individuals before, and they're obviously uncomfortable or, in the case of Aatirah, frightened. So Mukhtar, unfazed by anything, looks to everyone's needs. He settles the group as we had agreed, ten in each room. But slowly, slowly, they all rearrange themselves until everyone is in the living room. Now it's crowded, way past cozy, but it's exactly what they want. So, I accept and let it be.

After everyone has finished eating, Mukhtar puts on some music, full volume of course, and we all get up to dance. It's an unexpectedly joyful scene. No one is inhibited or embarrassed, except Shahana and Aatirah, who are still hiding in the kitchen.

After the party, I follow the Prabartak kids back to the bus, telling them how happy I am that they came, that it was the best going-away party I've ever had, and that I love all of them. I wave vigorously as the last person is seated.

"I'll see you in four months," I shout to all but no one in particular.

"Please come back, Aunty," they beg through the windows, still not sure if I'll fulfill my promise.

Life in Kolkata can be sweet. As Sissel often says, "I have moments of happiness here." Through the noisy confusion and untamed chaos, there's a thread of constancy, albeit an unexpected one. In the morning as I head to the restaurant where I eat my breakfast, the shopkeepers swing open their doors to shout, "Good morning, Aunty." In the heat of the day when I'm en route back to my apartment, the curled, sleepy bundles of street people say, "Have a good rest, Aunty." When I leave in the evening to meet a friend for dinner, I hear, "Have a good time, Aunty." And when I return in the dark, those still awake inquire, "Back already, Aunty?"

There's something very comforting about that. And it's so different than my life in New Jersey where I get into my car, which carries me to large shopping complexes where strangers impersonally assist me.

The simpler life in Kolkata reminds me of growing up in Brooklyn. The girls outside my building jump rope and play hop scotch, the boys shoot marbles and spin tops just like we did. Teens played baseball in Brooklyn's crowded streets; here they play cricket in a small, litter-strewn field that's visible from my window. When comparing India to America, it isn't a matter of here and there as much as it is of then and now. Likewise, I can't even describe the smiles on the kids' faces and the stars in their eyes. They have an innocence that touches my heart.

Often I'm asked, "Why do you work in India and not America?"

And I reply, "When I walk into a classroom in Kolkata, the kids start to cheer. In the United States, kids cheer when the teacher leaves."

Often, I'm the first foreigner these kids have ever seen. In wonderment, a little girl once asked her teacher, "Who is she? She is so beautiful. Did she grow from a flower?" And even when that innocence works against me, I'm touched. For example, when I stepped into a preschool to distribute clothes and toys, the kids set up a loud wail as if they were seeing a ghost. Indeed, that's how my white skin must have appeared to them. As I approached them, my arms laden with attractive gifts, they shrank away until they were pressed against the back wall. Receiving a gift from a ghost is just too risky!

Life in Kolkata can also be depressing, very depressing. The volunteers who come here from a myriad of privileged nations keep up their spirits by telling funny stories. We've learned that it's surprisingly easy to find humor in a situation, especially if it helps keep our sanity.

I *love* to tell my *dhobi* story: "I was staying in the guesthouse at the time and the *dhobi* knocked on my door. He proudly presented me with a stack of clean clothes, or at least they looked clean until I flipped through the items and found a shirt with a big, red stain right in the front. I told him, 'This isn't clean.' And he said, 'Next time clean.' I said, 'What do you mean next time clean? *This* time clean.' He insisted, 'Madame, next time clean.' And I insisted, 'No, this time clean.' We went back and forth until he finally relented and took back the shirt. The following day, he knocked on the door and gave me the shirt. I checked and found it still had the big, red stain right in the front. I said indignantly, 'The shirt is still dirty.' And he said very philosophically, 'Madame, put it out of your mind!'"

"Your story is funny. Mine is humiliating," says Anita from Norway with a twinkle in her huge blue eyes. "I realize I am toweringly tall and my hair is very blond, which isn't unusual in Norway. Yet, when I arrived in a nearby village, I was received with adulation, almost like I was a goddess. A platform was quickly erected in my honor, and men, women, and children sat on the ground surrounding it. The elders guided me up some rickety steps and requested that I say a prayer, something special from Norway.

"Everyone was in prayer position, and all I could see was the bent heads of the revering villagers with their hands clasped tightly together. I felt overwhelmingly embarrassed by all the attention and my mind went *completely blank*. The only thing that came to my mind was what I learned in summer camp when I was a young girl—rules for safe trekking: 'One, always take a shovel. Two, make sure your flashlight has new batteries. Three, bring plenty of water. Four, keep the map in a plastic bag. Five, tell others where you are going. Six, wear sturdy boots. Seven, check the weather before you leave. Eight, always hike in pairs. Nine, pack the food securely. Ten, don't be afraid to admit that you are tired.' When I finished, everyone started to clap. Tears streamed down my face as I scolded myself for being such a fool. But, in a way, it *was* funny!"

Flying to New Jersey on March 23, 2004, my mind is reeling, mentally checking off the people with whom I've connected and our amazing events and accomplishments of the last three years: Reena and Middleton Row School, Mithu and Bulbulir Basa Orphanage, Mitali and her Girls' Coaching Centre, Neena and the pre-schoolers at Disha School, Mr. Ganguly and the residents at Prabartak Home, Dr. Chatterjee and Kakali and the patients at RCFC, Reena and Preyrona School.

Not bad for a formerly insecure retired woman from America who, when booted out of what is probably the world's most renowned and respected

> *Courage is only an accumulation of small steps.*
> —George Konrad, novelist, essayist

religious charity, forlornly told her friends, "I don't know what I'm going to do."

I firmly believe that, thanks to the good fortune that unexpectedly came my way in Kolkata during the past three years, Empower The Children will help more kids in the long run. But how? I need to discuss this with the board. So going home is important to me.

Then, I gaze out the window as our airplane sails through the night sky. "Where is home?"

# Shift Happens
## July 23, 2004–early 2007

After a four month stay in New Jersey, I'm back in Kolkata. There's a knock on the door of my flat. I'm not expecting anyone, and I'm still in my pajamas, so I open the door gingerly. The mailman is standing there with a big smile on his face. "Parcel, Madame." He hands me a heavy package, and I check the return address. It's from a friend in the United States—long-awaited pen pal letters.

"Thank you so much." I nod appreciatively and start to close the door.

"*Baksheesh,* Madame," he implores sheepishly.

"*Baksheesh*? Why *baksheesh*?"

"I brought you the parcel."

"You're a postman. It's your job to bring me the parcel."

"But I walked upstairs. I brought it to your door."

That's true. The postman usually leaves my mail downstairs with the *dhobi* who puts the letters under his ironing mat. By the time I pick up my laundry in the evening, the letters are flat and warm, balanced atop my pile of clothes.

"Okay," I agree and search in my purse for change.

"Twenty, Madame," he insists as I press ten rupees into his hand.

"Twenty rupees? I live on the first floor. You didn't walk up to the top." But I hand him another ten rupees. It's an insurance policy that I'm willing to pay. Often, mail in India goes astray. Maybe this *baksheesh* will help ensure that mine gets delivered.

* * *

I bring the letters to Mitali's Girl's Coaching Centre, and, amidst a flurry of excitement, we distribute them. We explain that they've been written by students in the seventh grade who are twelve years old, approximately the same age as they are. An expression of amazement spreads across the room.

"Aunty, my pen pal is not twelve years old," exclaims Savita.

"Neither is mine. Neither is mine," the others chime in.

I check the pictures attached to the letters and, after living in Kolkata so many years, I have to agree. The students smiling out from the photos are mature, self-confident young adults. The girls look like movie stars with blond highlights in their hair and carefully applied makeup. They're so well-endowed that some of them reveal cleavage. The boys look like body builders, also with blond streaks in their hair and an earring pressed into one ear. These sixth graders in America look like they'll soon go off to college. My children, in contrast, look like they're emerging from the third grade.

"In America, the children are well fed and take vitamins," I explain to the girls. "When you have a family, you'll give your children nutritious food. You're studying science, so you understand about the human body. You'll have the knowledge you need to make sure your children are healthy and well nourished." The girls nod solemnly. Yet, they look doubtful that they can give birth to or raise such hardy, healthy children as those in the photos they hold in their hands.

The letters are all in English, of course, and the children at the coaching center read only Bengali, so I read them aloud while Mitali translates. It's a slow, tedious process.

I begin, "Suniti's pen pal writes that she has three pets: a dog and two cats. The dog's name is Daisy, like the flower."

When Mitali translates the last sentence, the girls look puzzled, and I realize they've never seen daisies. Perhaps they don't even exist in Kolkata. In fact, while there are quite a few trees in this crowded city, flowering plants, usually kept in pots, are less visible. So, I explain that daisies are white flowers with a yellow center.

I continue, "The cats are named Fluffy and Snowflake. One cat is white like snow."

The girls nod appreciatively. They know about snow from looking at pictures of mountains. But the idea of keeping pets, while becoming more common among middle class Indian families, is totally out of the question to slum-dwellers who can barely feed their children. I resist the temptation to mention doggie hotels and obedience schools and grooming salons. Those would be impossible to explain, even to the teachers.

"After school, Suniti's pen pal takes piano lessons and—"

"What is a piano, Aunty?"

"Well, a piano has a keyboard like a harmonium, but it doesn't sit on the floor. It has long legs, like a table, and you sit on a bench to play it." I realize a picture would have been helpful and put that into the back of my mind for next time.

I clear my throat and read on. "Suniti's pen pal goes to the shopping center on the weekends and hangs out at The Gap."

"What is The Gap?"

"The Gap is a clothing store."

"Why is it called The Gap?"

"I don't know," I have to admit.

We tediously translate and explain each letter as best as possible, but the cultural and economic gap between this group of children and their chronological peers in the U.S. is yawning. Yet, not to be deterred, I push on and distribute stationery with a fancy border. The girls admire each sheet approvingly.

"Now, we're ready to answer the letters you've received," I tell them. "Think about what you want to write. Tell your pen pal about your life, where you go, what you do—just like they did in their letters to you."

The girls stare at me with blank expressions.

"Well, you all have big families. Tell them about your brothers and sisters."

They seem comfortable with that.

"I know you've never written a letter before, but we'll help you," I promise. "We'll start with the greeting. Suniti's pen pal's name is John. That's why he closes the letter with 'Sincerely, John.' Look at the end of the letter and find your pen pal's name. It's the last word on the page."

Everyone looks at the last page of their letter.

"You'll begin by writing at the top of your paper the word 'Dear' then your pen pal's name. I'll show you." On the chalkboard, I write "Dear John." I continue, "John is the name of Suniti's pen pal, so this is what she will write. Do you understand?"

No one looks confused, so I continue. "Go ahead and write the greeting."

Everyone is writing so my confidence is growing. After some time, I check the letters. Each and every letter has "Dear John" scrawled across the top! I'm trying to remain calm. It isn't the girls' fault, I tell myself. Don't ruin this by criticizing them.

I ask Mitali, "Do you have a scissors?"

She brings a pair, and I very patiently cut off the tops from all twenty-five sheets of paper. Now, the fancy border is only on the bottom, so I turn the sheets upside down.

"Let's start again," I tell the girls. "This time, we'll give you more help."

The girls struggle through the letters, at a loss as to what to write. Their lives are filled with household chores, caring for younger siblings, and, in some cases, working outside their homes. Going to school is a relief from their monotonous lives, unlike some American children who view school as a "chore" or "job" and extra-curricular activities as their source of distraction.

I feel drained when I leave, yet more determined than ever to educate children, especially girls. Finding inspiration in the African proverb, "If you educate a boy, you educate an individual, but if you educate a girl, you educate a community," I set out into the night.

"Of course, we will participate," I write in an email to David Kenneth Waldman, the founder of To Love Children, who has conceived the idea of a Walk for Education Worldwide in support of the 130 million children who don't attend school.[28] "Empower The Children is happy and proud to do its small part in Kolkata," I conclude.

But I speak a different, more cautious message to myself. "A walk? That sounds more like a march. It sounds like a lot of people. Except for my time at Missionaries of Charity, I haven't been in Kolkata that long. I don't know a lot of people. Where will it start? Where will it end? Who will participate? Do I need permission? What about police security? Should I invite the media? How can our small group help 130 million children in other parts of the world? *Oy vey!* What have I just committed to?"

Reena is busy with her job at the architect's office and Preyrona School, so she doesn't have time for a big undertaking. The residents at Prabartak Home are unable to walk long distances, so a march or a long walk would be too much of a burden for them. Would Neena Singh at Disha School and Kakali Samadder, my favorite teacher at Rehabilitation Centres for Children, lend their support? "Well, I can only ask."

My idea is that we will explain to our students in Kolkata the significance of 130 million children worldwide being unable to attend school. Although they can't help those children directly, their march will be like a protest, expressing their own feelings about the importance of education. Their participation will bring attention to the problem and, in a certain way, insist that adults and leaders in the world take action.

If it's to be a successful march, we will need a lot of signs. So I go to New Market to buy chart paper. I cover my ears and shout, "Chart paper, chart paper," not knowing if these words have more meaning than "stationery store, stationery store."

> *You can break that big plan into small steps and take the first step right away.*
> —Indira Gandhi, politician, Prime Minister of India

I also wonder if some of the *wallahs* can hear because they seem to use a cryptic sign language, even with each other. As expected, the *wallahs* attempt to lead me in and the shopkeepers try to lure me in. Tea, *salwar* suits, *saris*, silver jewelry, fabric, flowers, *paneer*. Everything but chart paper.

I become disoriented, and time becomes interminable. Finally, someone finds a stationery store, Yacoob's, and I secure what I need.

Once outside New Market, where the *wallahs* drop away like sea gulls searching for fresh fish, I figure it took an hour to buy ten pieces of chart paper. And this should have been the easiest part!

"Neena, I'm organizing a Walk for Education Worldwide to raise awareness about the children throughout the world who don't attend school. Would your students like to participate?"

Because Neena and Kakali are my only two walk-related contacts in Kolkata, if Neena says no, then the march is cut by fifty percent.

"I think that would be a valuable lesson for them. They may be living in a poor city, but they have the privilege of going to school. This would be a good way for them to realize that," she replies.

"Can students at both Akshar and Disha participate?" I ask, knowing the preschoolers at Divyayan are too small.

"I can't get the students from both schools together because they are on different schedules. Is it all right if they march separately, on different days?"

"Of course," I reply enthusiastically. "Thanks a million."

I've never organized even one march before, and now we'll have two.

"And what about the students at La Martiniere?" Neena interjects. "That's not my school, but those children are quite wealthy. It would be good for them to be involved too."

"Of course," I reply. And the two marches are growing!

I pose the same question to Kakali at RCFC.

"How can our children march?" she asks. "They cannot walk."

"That's true," I answer. Of course I know they can't walk. That's why they're at an orthopedic hospital. It never even occurred to me. How can I be so stupid?

After a long pause, Kakali proposes, "Do they have to join with the others on the street? They can march around the grounds of the hospital."

"Sure." I react confidently in spite of my insecurity. Oh, God. Now we'll have three marches! On three different days!

I return to New Market to get more chart paper.

* * *

I arrive at Disha School in the afternoon of Thursday, November 25, 2004—the official day of Walk for Education Worldwide—and find that everything has been arranged. The police have been notified, the signs are ready, and the media has been contacted. Neena has taken care of everything.

Two hundred students, some of them carrying signs they made

from the chart paper, slowly and carefully file into the street, which proves not particularly easy because the streets are clogged with the usual volume of cars, taxis, *rickshaws*, *autorickshaws*, trucks, buses, trams, wagons, and a herd of goats.

The police are very helpful, and the kids march under their watchful eyes. After an hour, they complete one pass around Deshpriya Park, a distance of two kilometers, and return to the school. The kids are all complimenting each other. It's their march, so it's their success.

A few days later, I *schlep* another ten pieces of hard-to-handle chart paper to RCFC via the Metro and an *autorickshaw*. I'm tired by the time I arrive, but the effort isn't wasted. The children sit patiently on the floor, some with legs in casts, others with metal screws through their bones, and a few with bent or twisted limbs, awaiting surgery. I distribute the paper, markers, and wooden sticks that will become the handles for the signs.

We tell the children to take their time. Our plan is to make the signs in the morning, eat lunch, and have the march in the afternoon. We encourage them to be creative, so that, although we provided the slogans, each sign will be a product of their originality.

With Kakali's help, the children write the words in Hindi, Bengali, and English:

> *Kids Want To Learn*
> *Education Is A Human Right*
> *Books For Everyone*
> *Literacy = Empowerment*
> *We Care About Kids Everywhere*
> *Education = A Bright Future*
> *Education For All Children*

After their meal and with much fanfare, the march officially begins. With great physical difficulty, the children march around a large grassy area within the boundary wall, a distance that an able-bodied person could walk in five minutes. The children are aided by staff, wheelchairs, walkers, crutches, even a single stick held like a cane. Some carry signs while others bang drums that hang from their necks and blow plastic flutes. The march ends after twenty-five minutes, and the children sit on the grassy area to rest. The staff distributes more instruments so that everyone can play, and the music continues long afterward.

In the evening, I go to Raj's Cyber Café and enthusiastically email David about our *two* marches: at Disha School and Rehabilitation Centres for Children.

He graciously replies: "The children at RCFC are not crippled but only unable to walk."

The children in the third march gather in the courtyard in front of St. Paul's Cathedral, an impressive Anglican structure built by the British in the mid-1800s. Three hundred students from Akshar, La Martiniere, and Mentaid, a school for physically and mentally challenged children, participate. Again, Neena has arranged everything.

The students from Mentaid have written a play about how it feels to be excluded from mainstream society. Victor Banerjee, an Indian actor who has appeared internationally in Hindi, Bengali, and English films and television,[29] joins their performance, assuming a very minor supporting role compared to the students. Their classmates proudly raise large placards: "We are differently-abled!"

The march commences, and all the students, disabled and non-disabled, walk together, accompanied by a police escort. Many officers remark enthusiastically and positively about the march's purpose and the quality of its organization.

The students snake along Cathedral Road, around the cathedral, past the major entertainment center of Rabindra Sadan, the Nehru Children's Museum, and the Birla Planetarium before returning to the cathedral—a triangular-shaped distance of two kilometers along some of Kolkata's major multi-lane inner city roadways. Many people, both on the footpath and in cars, take notice.

This is more than an insignificant march by a few students in a poor city. It *is* a statement!

And it's heartwarming to see such camaraderie. I stay in the background, a facilitator only. So, when I hear a spectator ask, "This is wonderful. Who thought of this?" my lips don't move, but I feel a smile forming in my heart.

My family is putting me under pressure. They want me to be home—in New Jersey, that is—in case of an emergency with my mother in Brooklyn. I can't blame them, but I also can't comply. The tension between us is palpable. I call to wish them a happy new year. Inevitably, we get around to this painful subject.

"I'm sorry. I can't leave my work in Kolkata. It's not possible."

"Why isn't it possible?"

"We've opened our first school in a slum. Without Empower The Children's support, the school will close. That would like giving a wheelchair to a child then taking it away."

"You could support the school from America. You don't have to be in India."

"I have to be in India to make sure the donors' funds are distributed properly ... for the kids' education. I feel a responsibility toward them."

"You're needed at home. You have a responsibility here also."

They're right.

"They are ready. I have full faith that they are ready," says Alok, who translates my lessons to the physically and mentally challenged teens and young adults at Prabartak Home.

Alok is a university professor of economics who, before joining my Saturday classes here, had limited interaction with disabled children. To his surprise, he's discovered something inside of himself that he didn't know existed. When in their presence, he's filled with passion and love for these residents.

I understand what he feels. That's why we call them "kids." Not only because they have the innocence and wonderment of children but because Alok and I feel a parental attachment to them. Every week before we start the lesson, he gently touches each head and whispers a small blessing.

"Ready for what?" I ask casually.

"Ready to perform a drama."

"A drama?" I'm really caught by surprise. "Alok, most of them don't even speak."

"True, but because they cannot speak, they are very expressive. That is their way of connecting to the outside world."

"But what about the script and costumes and a stage? It's a big undertaking."

"I will do the needful. It can all be arranged," he says dismissively. Then he muses, "It has to be a spiritual play because these children are the product of a loving God who has given them simplicity and innocence that the rest of us lack."

Alok speaks in flowery language, and often I think I'm listening to a poem, one that isn't always easy to discern.

I love the idea of course. The old speech teacher in me is jumping up and down with excitement. When I worked in the New Jersey schools, we performed plays annually, some of them as elaborate as Broadway productions. "Alok, I have to admit it's a good idea. Dramas build language skills and self-esteem, and they're so much fun!"

"I know," he says coyly. Then he reveals that he's written a small script entitled, *The Spiritual Journey of Maa Sarada,* which traces this Hindu deity's journey as a teenager from her home in Jayrambati to Dakshineswar where she joins her husband,

Ramakrishna, a nineteenth century mystic of Bengal who founded the Ramakrishna monastic order.[30]

Most of the play is in pantomime, although a few actors and actresses have speaking roles of one or two lines. It's a serious piece, and the children take it seriously. They understand the importance of honoring Maa Sarada's name.

After two months of preparation, we feel the kids know their parts, so we begin to discuss a venue. We consider an auditorium in Salt Lake but nix the idea almost immediately. I'm worried that the venue will be too large and only half-full, and Alok is concerned that the large space will be disorienting after they've practiced in the small classroom.

After some time, Alok proposes, "I think that the perfect place for the drama is on a boat."

"A boat? A boat?" I ask in disbelief. "What kind of boat do you have in mind?"

"A sightseeing launch. One leaves from the dock every few hours. We can hire it for an afternoon cruise on the river, the children can perform, and then we can serve lunch to our guests."

Seeing the practical side to a person I've jokingly called "an absent-minded professor," I acknowledge, "Alok, I'm impressed. You've thought of everything."

"These children give me inspiration. They embody purity and goodness."

A month before the performance, we hire a boat, arrange for costumes and make-up, start to build a set, and order lunches to be served on banana

> *Act as if it were impossible to fail.*
> —Dorothea Brande, writer, editor

leaves. We also contact the local television station because we feel this is an unusual idea and a unique opportunity for viewers to appreciate the talents of disabled individuals.

After weeks of hard work, everything is in place, and I feel jubilant as I leave my flat for the dock. But everything is behind schedule. The kids are late in arriving, and the costume and make-up men are pacing while waiting. The stage set, so easy to assemble in the classroom, turns out to be a nightmare. There's no place on the launch deck to attach anything—everything must be free standing—and it wasn't designed for that.

I'm like a deflated balloon. "This is India," I think. "Nothing is ever done in a timely manner. Why did I think this would be any different?"

But the guests are Indian and accustomed to delays. They mill around the boat and don't seem to mind at all. Coffee and tea is being served with small snacks and everyone seems happy. As usual, it's my own anxiety, not outside circumstances, getting in the way of my enjoyment.

Finally, with ropes and pulleys and all sorts of contraptions, the stage set is standing, albeit a bit wobbly, especially when other vessels pass by, creating small waves on the water. Given the poor motor coordination of the kids, I worry about this but decide there's no other choice but to put it out of my mind.

The guests gather in front of our make-shift stage, and the performance begins.

Nandu, a very high-functioning young lady, plays Maa Sarada. Nandu is confident and self-possessed in the role.

Rajesh's large size and expressive eyes make him a perfect Ramakrishna. He's equally self-assured and has great stage presence.

The forest scene is enchanting with animals scampering everywhere. One of our trees, a girl with very limited comprehension skills, wanders around aimlessly. Akash, our lion, lies quietly in the center of the stage until he suddenly sits up, smiles broadly, and waves to the audience. Everyone starts to clap.

Mahendra, a good-looking young man with a winning smile, is unsure of his lines and looks around for help. He says them weakly, leaves, but then comes back and says them again—with confidence. People nod their encouragement.

And the lesser roles are mostly pantomimed, which comes naturally to these children. Everyone is enjoying themselves.

During the lunch, I mill around and chat with the guests who agree that the performance was a complete success. The TV newsperson promises to show a video clip three times the next day as a segment of the local news.

The kids are ecstatic and too excited to eat. They're hugging each other and anyone nearby. They accept congratulations from the guests, the TV crew, and even the staff on the boat. They are proud of themselves and glad they didn't disappoint anyone. But most importantly, they know that they have honored Maa Sarada.

When I started volunteering at Daya Dan, which seems so long ago, I recall the many conversations with Mithu: his idea for starting an orphanage, the humble beginning of renting a small flat in 2001 and taking in five boys, his mother's loving presence there, his positive fatherly influence on the boys, his dream of having a big building, the gifts of money from Sister Aurora's children in Spain and Empower The Children and Antonio, and then Mithu's frustrating, seemingly endless search for land.

Finally, Mithu has found a building for the new orphanage. It's in Thakurpukur, a suburb of Kolkata, and it's quiet, free of pollution, and surrounded by a lovely garden. Mithu is happy with his accomplishment. He can now provide a better place for the eight boys with room for a lot more.

So today, May 1, 2005, is the day of the opening ceremony, but it's not what we expected. Granted, Antonio, the man gesturing animatedly with the microphone, put in the lion's share of the money, but he didn't do any of the legwork to find and secure this building. Yet, to hear him talk, taking the credit, you'd think he'd done it all.

Because Antonio organized the opening ceremony, he's invited the Spanish volunteers who normally work in the Missionaries of Charity homes. They swarm through the building, taking pictures of the boys who are overwhelmed by the attention. The volunteers speak in Spanish, and the children just smile and nod their heads.

Mithu reluctantly erected a plaque on the boundary wall that acknowledges Antonio's nonprofit organization, but there's no plaque to honor Empower The Children or Sister Aurora's school in Spain. And, except for the children, Mithu and his mother are the only Indians at the opening ceremony. Where are their friends and family to congratulate and help them celebrate?

In 2000, when Mithu just dreamed of opening the orphanage, he told me he'd name it Bulbulir Basa. *Bulbulir* is a small, non-descript, unimportant bird, and *basa* means home. Bulbulir Basa, therefore, symbolizes a safe haven for unwanted children who have become orphaned or abandoned. Bulbulir was also the nickname of Mithu's sister who tragically died at the age of ten after a gas cylinder exploded in the family's home.

Antonio is making speeches. He's speaking in Spanish, yet I can understand some of it. He's thanking various donors. He thanks Sister Aurora for bringing him on board. He thanks the Spanish volunteers for coming to the opening. He thanks … . Am I hearing this right? "*Muchas gracias a British Airways por su donacion de quinientos dolares.*" Many thanks to British Airways for its donation of 500 dollars. British Airways? Five hundred dollars!

What about the 10,000 dollars that Sister Aurora contributed from the school in Spain and the money raised by Empower The Children? What about Mithu and his mother's day-to-day efforts to run the orphanage? Mithu is furious. I'm fuming.

I interrupt Antonio. "Years ago, Mithu had a dream to open an orphanage for the forgotten children in Kolkata. Today, that dream has been realized. The credit goes to Mithu and his mother for their tireless work and commitment to the boys here. They provide a loving home for the children and give them a sense of security and hope for the future."

Antonio is red-faced. He gives me a very dirty look. But he need not worry. The Spanish volunteers are unimpressed. My outrage hasn't been translated, and Antonio's guests don't understand a word I've said. They can only interpret the anger in my voice.

So, today, it's all about Antonio.*

* *Since 2004, an Indian businessman has fully funded Bulbulir Basa Orphanage.*

Reena tells me that her son, Ashit, isn't happy. "All he does is think and think and think."

"What does he think about?"

"He works as a manager for Khadim's, a major shoe company, but he does not like it. They offered him a better position, but he is not sure if he wants to take it. So he thinks and thinks and thinks."

"What does he want to do? If he knows that, it'll be easier for him to make a decision."

"He wants to help the poor. He wants to work with poor children."

"What does he want to do with poor children?"

"He wants to open a school and teach them skills so they can get a job."

"Does he hope to work for Empower The Children? Is that what he's thinking about?"

"He does not know. He hopes you will agree."

"Well, it's difficult, Reena. Because he's your son, hiring him would be nepotism."

"What is nepotism?"

"It means giving a person a job because they have a relative with influence, like someone getting a government job because their uncle or a father works in the office."

"Oh, that happens in India all the time."

"I know. I know. But it doesn't happen in Empower The Children. In America, we believe that nepotism isn't fair. That it's favoritism."

"So Ashit cannot get a job with Empower The Children because he is my son?"

"Yes. I don't think I can justify it to my board of directors."

"Okay. I will tell Ashit. He will understand."

It doesn't sound like Ashit will understand. It doesn't sound like *she* understands.

After another month, Ashit quits his job at Khadim's and begins to work for Empower The Children—but by his own choice, like a volunteer, so he doesn't get paid. He's only twenty-one. I admire his decision, but I wonder if he's made a good one.

I'm back in the States to everyone's delight. I'm everyone's darling and some people's hero, but I don't relish those roles. It's very tiring always being "on," always talking about the work in Kolkata, and never getting a chance to be myself.

In addition, fundraising is on everyone's mind. I'm scheduled to speak in three different states—New Jersey, Pennsylvania, and all the way across the country in California—mostly at churches. Again, there's irony—a Jew/Bu being welcomed into Christian churches but not into a single synagogue or Buddhist temple.

* * *

Our family is enjoying the Passover Seder, and it feels great to be back to what's familiar. I love the Passover Seder, the reading of the Haggadah, and the traditional meal. The singing at the end isn't the same since Dad passed from this life twenty years ago, and, once again, I realize how much I miss him. But Art is by my side, which makes my happiness pretty near perfect.

"It was a beautiful Seder," I say after the meal.

"Thanks. We enjoy making it each year."

"I really appreciate it because Mother is too old to prepare a feast like this, and I don't have a permanent place to live when I'm back."

"So when are you going to retire?" The comment is casual.

"I'm not sure," I reply equally casually. It's a holiday, and I don't want to start an argument.

"You know, if you come back, you can help take care of your mother."

"Yes, that's true," I say sheepishly, wondering if I'm doing the right thing by being in India. Maybe I am reneging on my family responsibilities. Maybe I'm better off staying in New Jersey with Art at my side.

But then I think of the kids at RCFC, Prabartak Home, Preyrona School, the women on Sudder Street, the volunteers from so many nations, everyone in Kolkata I've come to know over the years. They all believe I'm coming back, as do the people in several countries who now donate to Empower The Children. Who's going to do my job if I don't return?

And then I feel tag-teamed by guilt—that awful feeling that no matter where I am, both I and others are going to wish I were someplace else.

"Fingers crossed I can retire in five years," I say, attempting to placate.

"That seems like a long time. ... I mean, it's your choice, isn't it? You can walk out at any time ... if you want to."

"My feet may want to walk, but my heart may not want to follow."

Because it's a Jewish holiday, I feel comfortable giving a gentle reminder. "Don't forget what the rabbis say, '*Tikkun olam*. It is the

> **Tikkun olam**
> —Hebrew phrase that means "repairing the world"

responsibility of every Jewish person to repair the world.'"

Peggy is eighty-three years of age. She's been a volunteer in Kolkata for twenty-five years. She's also a startling presence with coal-black hair, over-sized sunglasses, and a sometimes fierce expression. She eats all of her meals in Khalsa, a Sikh restaurant on a small side street between Sudder Street and New Market. When she's at her home in Virginia, USA, Khalsa's owner keeps in touch with her, and it's through him that we know how she's faring.

Peggy has her own small projects, and she's dedicated to them like a doting grandmother. However, she centers most of her attention on a very special girl, Sultanah. Peggy wants Sultanah to walk. Sultanah has cerebral palsy, and her legs are so spindly, her hips so narrow, and her balance so poor that this isn't realistic. Yet, Peggy still wants her to walk. And this expectation extends to everyone because we all love her so much. Sultanah is like sunshine. She radiates warmth and affection and wins the hearts of everyone she meets. But no matter how hard she tries or how much Peggy desires or how fervently the rest of us pray, she can't do the one thing that everyone wants her to do, which is to walk.

Sultanah and her two sisters and brother have been living with an aunt's family in a small room since their mother died years ago and her father remarried. The aunt chews *paan*, a concoction of betel leaf, areca nut, and tobacco, which stains her tongue, teeth, and lips a bright red. With her head often wrapped in an orange scarf, she appears rather cartoonish. Unfortunately, she's a pathetic figure, bent over from years of worry and burden. She can't care for Sultanah alone, so ever since Sultanah was a small child, she's been taken care of by her oldest cousin, Sabriyah.

These days, the aunt is getting desperate. She wants Sabriyah to get married. After all, she isn't young anymore and the prospects of a good arranged marriage diminish with the passing of time. But, if she does marry, who will take care of Sultanah?

Peggy enrolled Sultanah in the Loreto School near Sealdah Railway Station, and the nuns there have been very accommodating. They allow her wheelchair to be left in the school office while Sultanah is carried to her classroom.

The wheelchair has become the topic of many discussions. The one she has is heavy and clumsy. Sabriyah pushes it through the streets of Kolkata over broken pavement, through chaotic traffic, past dogs and goats, around *rickshaws*, trucks, taxis, cars, motorcycles, and finally into the school parking lot. Only her devotion to her cousin could give Sabriyah the stamina to do that twice a day, especially in Kolkata's heat, humidity, and rain. But it's easy to be devoted to Sultanah.

I like chatting with Peggy in the morning over breakfast, and I like Khalsa because it's a non-smoking establishment. Other eateries are afraid to go non-smoking, afraid of losing business, yet the Sikh restaurant is always full.

\* \* \*

Peggy is back from Pakistan. An earthquake had devastated mountain communities, and Peggy rushed there to give a helping hand. "I arrived the day after Christmas," she reports. "The road to the refugee camp was treacherous. It was icy, and visibility was poor. The driver drove Indian style, fearlessly. I was terrified. I arrived late in the evening and saw tent after tent. It was so cold that I wondered how people could possibly be warm inside those tents. I met the director in charge of humanitarian aid. He asked me what I wanted. I said I wanted to help. I put out my two hands and told him, 'These are all I have.' He told me there were no tents left. All he could offer is an empty tool shed. I said, 'That would be fine.' He put two mattresses on the floor and three blankets on top of the mattresses, and that's where I slept for the next month. Every day, we treated people who were sick. There

> *I am only one, but still I am one.*
> *I cannot do everything,*
> *but still I can do something;*
> *and because I cannot do*
> *everything, I will not refuse*
> *to do something that I can do.*
> —Helen Keller, author,
> political activist, lecturer

was very little medicine, but we did our best. Every day, children were falling ill. Every day, babies were dying." Then Peggy broke down and cried.

Peggy seems changed after that experience. She's lost some strength, some grit. She's gone home to Virginia to recover and has left Sultanah's education in the care of Roisin, a young volunteer from Ireland.

* * *

"Serendipity, that's how I met Roisin," I tell Mukhtar. "I was eating in Khawaja Restaurant, and Roisin was at a nearby table. She nodded to me. Then, just as I was about to leave, she moved to my table and asked, 'Do you know a good doctor?' She was sick, and, when you're a foreigner and sick in a place like Kolkata, you feel very vulnerable.

"I called Eva immediately, and she advised me to send her to Dr. Chakravarty at Apollo Clinic. I gave Roisin both the name of the doctor and my phone number. 'Call me tomorrow and tell me how you're feeling. Don't forget,' I told Roisin. The next day, she called and said she had malaria but started on a course of medication and would be well in a week. She said the doctor was very nice. And she thanked me because she had felt scared and alone." Mukhtar is nodding slowly, absorbing the story piece by piece.

"I met Roisin at Khawaja again after she was feeling better, and we had lunch together," I continue. "I asked her how long she would be in Kolkata, and when she said until the following August—while I would be back in the States—I offered to let her stay in my flat." I pause. "Honestly, Mukhtar, even while speaking, I couldn't believe that I was proposing this to a complete stranger. But she said okay, and now we are friends."

"That is good," he says approvingly. "But what is serendipity?"

Serendipity isn't that easy to explain, but I try. "Well, I just happen to be in Khawaja when Roisin was sick. If it had been two weeks earlier or two weeks later, she wouldn't have approached me. We wouldn't have met. Serendipity means a happy accident."

"Oh, like the way our family met you?"

"Yes, I guess you could call that serendipity."

Then, Mukhtar and I have great fun sharing all the serendipitous events we can think of.

The next day, a long-faced Mukhtar knocks on my door. This demeanor is not Mukhtar, so I'm concerned.

"Mukhtar, what's the matter?"

"Nothing."

"How was your day?"

"It was bad."

"Bad? Why?"

"Because nothing serendipity happened to me today."

\* \* \*

Like a pebble dropped into the pond, I've made some ripples in Kolkata. So when Sissel makes her biennial trip to volunteer at Daya Dan, I look forward to our meetings and the news she brings of the little orphans there who, in truth, I still love.

"Sister Innocencia was transferred back to Africa," she imparts. "I wish her luck."

I nod, feeling the same.

"Madhur and Suresh have both been adopted by families in the eastern part of your country, in what you call New England," she continues.

"Oh, that's great."

"Yes, and their families are friends and live close enough together that the boys meet often."

"And Ann, the American woman who visited Daya Dan while waiting to adopt a child … well, she adopted Ramzia and they are living in Italy."

"That's wonderful. Ann's special. She made sure to introduce me to Neena Singh."

"Father Pasquale returned to Italy and was away for about two years, but he's come back to Kolkata."

"It's hard to stay away. There's something about this place."

We both nod our agreement.

\* \* \*

While these stories make my heart sing, I'm aware that there's also a big risk in helping people in Kolkata. It can make them dependent.

> *No good deed goes unpunished.*
> —Anonymous (frequent reminder by Austin Gibbons, Missionaries of Charity volunteer)

It's easy for foreigners from wealthy countries to come here and think they're doing something good by freely giving money to the poor, but often it turns out otherwise. "It's just a simple act of kindness," they think because they feel for the people here—people who live packed into tiny homes or on the street or neighbors who are struggling to make ends meet.

Then something happens to tip the scales away, and the neighbors you've come to know can no longer make ends meet; it might be a sickness or an accident or a sudden emergency. The heart of the foreigner—and that includes me—is touched, but, coming from a wealthy country, we also feel a fair share of guilt.

With a favorable currency exchange rate and plenty of money to spend on restaurants, taxis, holidays, and an occasional movie, it seems selfish to keep a few rupees from those who need them more. So we give and give and give. And before we know it, we're a running cash machine. Then our neighbor's sudden emergency becomes an ongoing emergency, and every week there's a knock on the door.

"Last time. Last time," they promise, but there's never a last time. There's always an urgent purchase for festival clothes or a sick child who needs medicine or an excuse for an unpaid bill.

"Why isn't Amzad working?" I ask my neighbor Sayyadah when she comes to my flat with her grandson's kindergarten fee book, obviously seeking the payment.

"What to say? We spoiled him when he was a child."

"But he isn't a child anymore; he has a wife and two children."

"I know," she sighs and shakes her head. "I tell him to find work, but he sits all day in front of the TV and watches movies."

When Sayyadah comes again with the fee book, she also has her electric bill, an appeal for the payment forming on her lips. "It is overdue," she informs me. "They will cut off my electricity."

I take a look at it: 600 rupees! "Why is it 600 rupees? My electric bill is only 300 rupees a month."

"What to do? The TV is on all day."

"Why is the TV on all day?"

"Because Amzad likes watching Bollywood movies."

"And why isn't my TV on all day?" I ask pointedly.

"Because you are at work all day."

"Exactly," I add, hoping she'll get my point.

"I come up to the garden at five to imbibe the morning air. I walk barefoot on the grass because my grandfather, a Rajasthani, always said, 'If you walk on dew-moistened grass you will not need specs in your old age.' I do not know if it is true, but I am 45 years and I do not wear specs," says Madhu.

We're sitting in the roof-top garden created by her father-in-law and maintained by her husband, Gautam. When her father-in-law died in 1998, there were 250 potted plants in one small area of the roof. Through Gautam's vision, the roof is now adorned with 5,000 potted plants. In the winter, fruit plants are heavy with mangoes, oranges, lemons, sweet lime, guava, strawberries, custard apple, pomegranate, and star fruit. Huge ferns form a central circle.

A steep ladder leads to an even higher level. Going up there is a bit scary but it's well worth the climb to take in an assortment of *bonsai*. Gautam loves the garden, not just for the numerous awards it has won but because it provides him with relief from the stresses of running his business of making "baby umbrellas" for children. For Madhu, the garden is a heavenly oasis of nature that rises above streetscapes of dirt and dishevel.

From here on the roof, seven floors up, Kolkata, especially the expanse of the Howrah Bridge across the Hooghly River, actually looks pretty. In the evening, as we view it now, darkness and twinkling lights hide the city's underbelly of poverty and congestion.

"The colors here vie for your attention," Madhu continues, bringing my gaze back to the garden. "This group of flowers shouts, 'Look at me,' and that group calls, 'Put your attention in my direction,' and a third group implores, 'Do not remove your eyes from my beauty.' I come to listen to the birds. Whether it is a tiny sparrow or a crow, the sound is beautiful." She pauses reflectively, "All are God-given."

I met Madhu after I hurt my back in 2001. She is an acupressurist recommended to me by the yoga center and, fortuitously, her home is a short walk from Daya Dan. I would go from the orphanage to Madhu's home three times a week to receive her reflexology treatments. Eventually, as our friendship deepened, relief from my back pain became secondary, and we would talk for hours, finding strength in each other's words.

Over those years, she proved to be a textbook of diverse knowledge. Even though a Jain, she led me *pandal hopping* during Durga Puja and explained the numerous tales and legends of the Hindu deities depicted by the artful icons inside. She related the energetic symbolism of *pranāma,* the Bengali practice of touching the feet as a form of greeting or respect. As a Westerner, I had always found it demeaning for the children when they would touch my feet. Madhu said, however, that it's a positive gesture. "When the children touch your big toe, it draws up energy from the Earth; then pressing their fingers to their forehead places the energy in the Third Eye of their chakras."

Though Madhu defers to Gautam regarding the care of the garden, she has her own opinions when it comes to the *bonsais.* "Controlling the growth of a *bonsai* tree is like religious fundamentalists controlling the spiritual growth of their congregations. The *bonsai* hobby is restrictive, unnatural. It does not allow the tree to bloom, and it is natural for trees and plants to bloom and blossom."

Tonight, I'm also learning how much Madhu has valued our friendship, especially as she dealt with problems within her arranged marriage. "When you used to leave," Madhu tells me, "I felt at a loss. There was a void in my life, and I could not fill it. Sometimes I thought I saw you in the market. It was wishful thinking, of course, because I knew you were in America. For years, I suffered whenever you were gone. I waited for the day you would return."

Madhu removes an old notebook from her handbag. She shows me a copy of a letter she had written to me years ago. I remember receiving it, but until now didn't realize just how important it was to her. She was going through a particularly trying time then and wished to share her angst with me. She states that my presence would have comforted her had I been here, but the oceans of miles between us made only correspondence possible. The letter reads:

Dearest Rosalie,

Halo!

With the passage of time God has been hell-bent on putting me to test as I persevere to tread on the right path against all odds. In the turmoil of the activities of the day I seek solace in praying at night to be ready to face the challenge of another "eventful day." I wish you were here to get the feel of it.

The spiritual strength imbibed since childhood lets me not deter from moving forward on the "emotional thorn" laid paths.

I surge forward in spite of the "tsunami emotional water" that tries to engulf and swallow me up. I ebb up as I have yet to meet people whom I love and enjoy life with them. Awaiting your arrival. Good that you spend time with your mother. The root always nourished the stem, the leaves and the flowers.

With love,

Madhu

"Now I have a way to deal with the loss when you leave," Madhu tells me years after this letter was written. "I think of you as a rare, migratory bird that comes at a certain time, in a particular season. You alight in Kolkata, and I can enjoy your company. But like other rare birds, there is a time when you have to leave, fly to other places. You have a rhythm, and I have adjusted to it. Now I am able to let go."

I stare at the stars in order to avoid seeing the tears in her eyes.

"Alok, that's a big transition. Doing a drama on a small boat is one thing. But to perform on a big stage in an auditorium? Are you sure they're ready?"

"They are ready. Their innocence protects them. They do not know the meaning of stage fright."

That's true. The residents at Prabartak Home always enjoy themselves. They have unconditional love for everyone who visits them and approach life as an adventure. But, as a bottom-line realist, I worry they might experience their first sense of failure.

"You cannot protect them even though you want to. That is not your responsibility," Alok counters.

"You're right. Let's do it," I say weakly. I have first-night jitters already, and we haven't even picked the play.

* * *

It's settled. They'll do *Ali Baba and the Forty Thieves*. It's colorful and lends itself to pantomime. Everyone knows the story, so the people watching will be able to follow it easily. Everyone is happy— except Reena.

"Reena, what's the matter?"

She doesn't answer immediately so I pursue. "Are you afraid for the Prabartak kids? That they will fail?" I ask.

"No, not *atall*. I am happy for the Prabartak children, but I feel for my children at Preyrona School. They have never had the chance to perform. Or even enter a theater. I wish they could also be included."

"Why not?" I ask, as an idea takes hold in my mind. "Let's make it an 'inclusion project.'"

"Inclusion project? What is that?"

"It's a practice in America. Disabled kids and non-disabled kids are brought together for a special learning experience with no barriers between them. The Prabartak kids and Preyrona kids can practice together, perform together, and share a meal afterward. Everyone benefits."

Reena looks doubtful. "*Arre!* This is India," she says. "The handicapped are not mixed with the normal members of society. They are stigmatized."

"Our Prabartak kids are normal, in their own way. Actually, they're a lot more normal than I am with all of my hang-ups and anxieties."

Suddenly, Reena's face changes. She's laughing, and her eyes are wide with anticipation. She wraps her arms around me and hugs me tightly. "My Preyrona kids will be in a drama. I am so happy. And all the credit goes to you. Many thanks. Many, many thanks."

* * *

It's the first day of rehearsal, and the Preyrona kids, ages ten to fourteen, are brought to Prabartak Home. They're excited by the bus ride, pointing to tall buildings, other schoolchildren in uniforms, policemen directing traffic, and even cows walking and chewing their cud along the roadway. In a way, they have something in common with the Prabartak kids. Having been sheltered within the confines of their *basti,* they experience everything else as an adventure.

We don't have a plan for today's meeting, just that the kids would get to know each other.

There are more girls at Preyrona School than boys because parents are more likely to send their sons to a government school if they can afford to. And there are more boys at Prabartak Home because boys are more likely to be born with disabilities. So, in terms of the drama, the cast will be a perfect mix of male and female roles. But, in so many other ways, we don't know if it will be a perfect mix or a disaster.

The Preyrona kids approach the Prabartak Home and stand in awe. I remember the first time I saw the front of this building, so this should have been no surprise. Yet, I pause with them, trying to imagine what they might be feeling. Prabartak Home is as tall as some of the buildings in Ultadanga, but, with its rounded entrance and front staircase like the bow of a ship, it is more impressive.

They enter rather sheepishly and, perhaps sensing their caution, the Prabartak kids, who are older, don't tightly surround them and shake their hands vigorously as they usually do with other, even first-time, visitors. Instead, they lead their guests to a room with mats spread neatly on the floor and ask them to sit. The Prabartak residents very politely introduce themselves and then serve tea. So, unexpectedly, we're having a tea party instead of a rehearsal!

After an hour, we tell everyone it's time to leave. Now the Prabartak hosts and hostesses are surrounding their guests and shaking their hands and telling them to come again soon. The Preyrona kids are equally enthusiastic and only reluctantly get into the bus. The Prabartak kids and the Preyrona kids wildly wave good-bye, and everyone is shouting as the bus pulls away.

On the ride back to the school, I ask one little girl through Reena who translates, "So how did it feel to be with handicapped people?" and she replies innocently, "Who says they are handicapped? They are perfect ladies and gentlemen."

\* \* \*

"Lights, camera, action," I say to Eva, who is sitting next to me in the auditorium on the night of the performance.

"It's a play, not a movie," she replies jokingly.

"I'm just trying to quell my nervousness."

I look around. The auditorium is full, which means 450 to 500 people have come to watch our inclusion drama. The children from Prabartak Home who are severely disabled and unable to participate are sitting in the audience. Champa has brought her colleagues from Rotary International. My students from the RCFC children's hospital are here. Alok's peers from the university are here. So are volunteers from various nations, friends, everyone Reena knows, and lots of people we don't recognize.

Perhaps they're curious because this is such a unique idea, or perhaps we did a good job distributing invitation cards. Whatever the reason, everyone has come with high expectations, and I'm sitting in the audience with a severe case of vicarious stage fright. The speeches begin, and only then do I remember that these typically take a long time. How could I forget to tell them to cut down on the speeches? Oh God, what else did I forget?

For twenty minutes, the speakers drone on until we hear, "We hope you enjoy the play." With these words, delivered by Janardan, the master of ceremonies, the final speech is over, the curtain goes up, and the performance begins.

It's everything we had envisioned and hoped for: the stage set is beautiful, the costumes are spectacular, the lights and music are dramatic, the acting is flawless, and the audience's applause immediately crescendos to a loud ovation.

This should have been enough, but, lucky us, we're presented with a bonus, something we had not expected: the inclusion is perfect. It's impossible to tell the Prabartak kids from the Preyrona kids. These two diverse groups performed together and, on stage, became a "whole."

I feel a huge swell of gratitude and pride surge up as these brilliant young performers, amalgamated from two distinctly different institutions, take their final bow. "Can you imagine what they're

> *Snowflakes are one of nature's most fragile things, but just look at what they can do when they stick together.*
> —Vista M. Kelly, children's author

feeling right now?" I whisper to myself. Surely, I can't imagine.

Roisin knocks on my door. She's confused and worried. She has news, both good and bad.

The good news is that Sultanah's cousin Sabriyah is finally getting married. The date has been set for January 2007, a few months from now. Everyone in the family is jubilant. It's the answer to their prayers. In India, a girl unmarried for too long becomes the object of ridicule and scorn. The family suffers as much as the individual because the individual is an indivisible part of the family whole.

The bad news is that Sultanah's cousin is getting married. Sabriyah, Sultanah's primary caretaker, will soon move into her husband's house and become part of his family. She'll be responsible for his family's care, taking the burden off his mother, becoming, in a sense according to Indian tradition, the mother-in-law's retirement annuity.

"Who will take care of Sultanah?" I ask Roisin.

"That's the problem."

"What's the family saying?"

"They're saying to put her in an orphanage."

"An orphanage?" I can't conceal my shock.

"Yes, there's no one to take the responsibility."

"She's not an orphan. She has two sisters and a brother as well as a father."

"But her siblings are in school all day and her father lives with his new family."

"If she has sisters and a brother and a father, then she isn't an orphan," I insist.

"That's what the family is suggesting," Roisin replies with resignation.

"What's Sultanah saying?"

"She's excited about the wedding. She wants to have her hands decorated with henna."

"Does she understand the implications of Sabriyah's marriage?"

"She's a child. How can she understand?"

"Do you understand?"

"I wish I didn't."

"What do you mean?"

"I wish I could be happy for Sabriyah without being sad for Sultanah."

\* \* \*

Mukhtar and Aatirah are also worried about Sultanah. We have a family meeting and "storm our brains," as they say.

"Let's think of a lot of options," I suggest. "Extra is always good."

"Maybe she can go to Prabartak Orphanage. Then you will see her every Saturday when you go there to teach," suggests Mukhtar.

"And her family can go with you in the taxi and visit her on Saturdays," adds Aatirah.

"There's just one little problem with that," I counter.

"What?"

"If her family is visiting, then obviously she isn't an orphan."

"But she does not have anyone to take care of her," Mukhtar reminds us.

"True, but that doesn't make her an orphan."

"Tell them she is an orphan and tell her family they cannot visit her," suggests Aatirah weakly.

"How do you think that will make Sultanah feel?" I pose.

"She will feel terrible. She will miss them," says Shahana.

Aatirah, although it was her suggestion, nods her head in agreement.

"And don't you think they'll miss her?" I continue.

"But they do not want her anymore."

"That isn't true," I protest. "They just can't take care of her anymore."

"There are so many family members. They can take turns helping her." Mukhtar is starting to sound defensive.

"They don't have the time or the energy." I'm trying to defuse the mounting tension. I don't want them to blame the family for something that isn't entirely their fault.

"So what will happen to her?" asks Aatirah despairingly.

"I don't know," I reply.

Now Mukhtar is upset and gets up to leave. "Well, I know something," he insists.

"What do you know?"

"I know that this is really serious. It is not a matter of jokes."

Her name is Subhagya, which means "lucky," and she loves to tell people that she is lucky. That strikes me as odd. She lives under a footbridge with her parents and her younger brother, who is partially sighted and hyperactive. Subhagya comes to Preyrona School every day. She's a big girl, so she doesn't really fit in with the others socially, but she comes because Reena makes her feel valued. "We are all fingers on the same hand," she tells the students when they start to separate into cliquish groups. "Without each other, we are incomplete."

Subhagya brings her brother Kishan with her to school, but he doesn't see well enough to do the work, and he disturbs the other kids with his aggressive behavior.

Reena and I concur that it isn't his fault. "He has no place to put his frustration," I say protectively.

Reena takes Kishan to the West Bengal State Central Library, where the Society for the Visually Handicapped provides educational resources, and they schedule a date to test him. But on that date, Kishan is nowhere to be found. Subhagya and Reena search for him in vain. Subhagya is heartbroken.

"We will reschedule the appointment," Reena says reassuringly.

But each time the appointment is rescheduled, Kishan goes missing.

Subhagya continues coming to school but is increasingly discouraged. Over time, she sees things at home that help her understand the situation. "My parents are the problem," she confides to Reena. "They do not want Kishan to go to the library to be tested. They want to send him out begging."

Today, I'm teaching at Preyrona, and Subhagya is in her usual place on the floor with the older girls. Although it's only a one-room schoolhouse, devoid of desks, a toilet, and adequate lighting and ventilation, Subhagya is happy to have found a safe and secure environment. She knows that Reena will do her best to protect her from the fate faced by many slum girls: prostitution. On some level, she also realizes that I'm part of that shield.

After the lesson, Subhagya jumps up and carries my bag with today's lesson and my backpack to the taxi. She opens the door for me and watches as I settle into the seat. She runs after the taxi as it pulls away, thrusts her hand through the open window, and drops something into my lap. I glance down and see something shining in the sunlight—a gaudy bracelet studded with plastic jewels. "Thank you," she shouts at the taxi. I can barely hear her words as we speed away.

The girl has nothing but has found a way to express her gratitude. I'm at a loss as to how to express my gratitude for the lessons in life these children are teaching me.

"Open your umbrella, Aunty," one of the invited guests from Rotary International suggests.

It's monsoon season, so that seems like a sound idea, but I feel guilty doing so. Drip, drip, drip, drip. Water from the roof finds easy entry into the single classroom at BBD School, a name selected by neighborhood residents to honor three Bengali revolutionaries of the 1930s: Benoy Basu, Badal Gupta, and Dinesh Gupta.[31]

"Do not feel bad," says Champa, who arranged for me to be here. It's one of the schools she oversees and to which Empower The Children donates money for lunches and once-a-year clothing prior to Durga Puja.

But I do feel bad. What about the kids? They don't have the luxury of umbrellas. I look up and around. The roof is just a patchwork of building materials, much of it improperly fixed into place. Judging from the coloring and signs of age, these slabs of slate and sticks of wood have been there a long time. This isn't a temporarily abandoned work in process. This is the way it is.

Between the crevices, the water finds safe passage into the room, dampening kids and books, rusting metal cabinets, and creating the environment for mold. Cobwebs are everywhere, bringing to mind a haunted house at an amusement park, but there's nothing amusing about this place. This is a school, but I feel like I'm the one receiving an education about the way some students are forced, by circumstances beyond their control, to study.

The school sits next to a terrible slum that's nothing more than a collection of plastic-covered hovels. These children don't smile or seem, in any way, excited that they are about to receive new clothes. Rather, they obediently sit on wooden benches and wait patiently, listlessly.

I've been to slum schools before, but the combination of the grim faces and incessantly dripping water here has really moved me.

"Why don't you fix the roof?" I ask Champa.

"*Arre!* That is very costly, beyond what Rotary can afford."

"Why don't the teachers and students clear out the cobwebs?" I feebly suggest, realizing immediately that this isn't going to change the overall situation one bit.

Just to please me, Champa asks the headmistress about the cobwebs. The headmistress gives some explanation in Bengali and Champa translates. "What to say? It's only a temporary school. The government has promised a new building. They are waiting."

"Well, that's encouraging," I reply, brightening up a bit. "When will they get the new school? I hope the kids don't have to go through another monsoon season."

"Still, we do not know. We have been waiting."

"How long has the school been here?"

"Twenty-five years."

Shock apparently registers on my face.

"Do not worry, Rosalie. Everyone here is doing their level best," Champa says encouragingly. "The kids are learning nicely and, thanks to Empower The Children, they are getting a nutritious meal each day and holiday clothes. Things could be worse."

I have to agree that things could be worse, but I feel totally deflated. I hand out the clothes to the kids and pose for a photograph with each one of them.

"*Hashi. Hashi.* You have new clothes," Champa tells them. "Smile!"

But there's no holiday mood in the room. The kids don't open the bags to look at their new clothes. They hug them closely to their chests.

"Do they think we're going to take back the clothes? That this is just a photo shoot?" I ask Champa desperately. "Please tell them that we aren't going to take back the clothes."

"Oh, *baba!* It is nothing like that. They are just overwhelmed and confused. No one has ever been this kind to them. You are really great, Rosalie. We are so grateful for your help."

"I'm not great, Champa. This is a small thing compared to their needs. I feel helpless."

"They are being fed every day, thanks to you. That is not a small thing."

I accept her thanks graciously even though I don't feel deserving of it. I want to give the kids security and optimism. I want to give them hope. The clothes are merely a token. But, apparently, I'm the only one who sees that.

The kids are starting to leave. "Say 'thank you' to Aunty," Champa suggests. "Say, 'come again.'"

The kids say it mechanically. They have bigger problems ahead of them, the least of which is getting their new clothes back home through the downpour outside. Clutching the bags even closer to their

*What are we here for if not to make life less difficult for each other.*

—George Eliot (Mary Anne Evans), novelist, journalist

bodies, they run through ankle-deep water. I want to do so much more, but at the moment, I feel lost, as hopeless as these children appear to me. In my frustration, I can think of only one practical idea: Next year, we'll give the holiday clothes in waterproof book bags!

# More Inspiration
## Early 2007–Early 2009

It's been more than three years since we opened Preyrona School and Reena is looking for more opportunities to educate children. She's spent the afternoon canvassing a slum in Dakhindari and meeting families, trying to decide whether or not to open a school there. Part of the slum is along railroad tracks. The shed-like structures offer scant protection against the elements, and the children play along the tracks because there's no other open space. The railroad tracks are also the drying area for wet clothing and a place for men to play cards and socialize.

"The conditions in the slum are alarming," Reena tells me. "You cannot imagine. The mothers have no feeling for their daughters." She pauses to gather her thoughts. "The mother is the first enemy of the girl."

I nod, so Reena presses on.

"I found Gharam playing on the street in tattered and dirty clothes," she says. "I asked Gharam and her sister Sangeeta if they want to go to school. Sangeeta told me, 'I am from a very poor family. I work as a domestic helper. How can I attend school? How will I support my family?' Sangeeta is only ten years, and Gharam is seven. Their father pulls a *rickshaw*, and their mother is a maid servant. Their parents earn so little that even food and clothing are beyond their capacity. That is why the girls have to work."

Reena is eager for this new school, but I'm reluctant. Preyrona School in the Ultadanga slum has required a lot of our time and energy. I'm afraid of spreading ourselves too thin, the same mistake that other nonprofits have made.

"I want to concentrate on Preyrona School," I tell Reena.

"We can concentrate on Preyrona School and also the new school."

"I can only concentrate on one thing at a time," I counter. "I'm old now. I can't multi-task anymore."

"Preyrona School is running on nicely. The new school will be just as good."

"Yes," I agree. "It's really gratifying to see the kids at Preyrona learning and happy."

"And well-fed. They need that lunch we give them every day. Think of Gharam and Sangeeta. They need a good meal each day too."

"So this new school you want to open … you want to serve the kids lunch?"

"Of course," Reena replies confidently.

"And the money? Where will the money come from?"

"I have faith in God. We will find it."

"Reena, I'm afraid. We can't open a school and then have to close it. That's a very dangerous precedent. It would be devastating to the children, the parents, and the community." I know I'm exaggerating, but I don't know of any other way to break through Reena's enthusiasm, which seems, at the moment, to border on denial of what, to me, is obvious.

"Dangerous?" she asks incredulously. "It is wonderful. That is why we have been put on this Earth—to help the poor children."

"I'll think about it," I answer. Her enthusiasm is too much right now. It's contagious, and I don't want to get infected. I just want to end the conversation.

\* \* \*

"Sonu is thirteen years old, and his little sister Reyhana is eight. They live along the railway line. You know, there are not any barriers along the tracks. The kids cross them freely all day long as if they are walking in a park. Even babies crawl across." Reena is once again promoting the idea of opening a school in Dakhindari.

I'm still unconvinced, afraid our resources will run out and the project will fail. But I listen anyway.

"When Sonu and Reyhana were young, their parents divorced. Their mother, who works as a servant, remarried a day laborer who is forced to sit idle if there is no work. Their stepfather takes his resentment and frustration out on the kids, seeing them only as extra mouths to feed. Their natural father tries to give them food at his roadside stall, but his new wife takes advantage of the situation and makes them work there for every mouthful."

I can see Reena gauging my reaction, and, indeed, I'm starting to weaken.

"Sonu and Reyhana are torn between their mother and their father, craving security, love, and affection but receiving only abuse and rejection," she continues.

"Reena, these stories are sad, very sad," I admit, "but are we the ones to solve these problems? These problems are massive, bigger than we are."

"The problems are big, and we cannot solve them completely. But we can help a little."

"Let's see" I reply. I'm starting to think about it.

\* \* \*

"Sitarah is our saddest case," Reena tells me on another day. "She is nine years old and lives with her family in the tiniest of rooms. She is always cheerful and bursting with energy, but none of the other kids will play with her."

"Why?" I ask.

"Because her parents are ragpickers. That is a lower caste."

"Caste, caste, caste. I'm tired of hearing that word," I complain impatiently.

"It is true," Reena agrees. "The caste system has hurt India. It has made divisions among people who should stick together. That is why we need to educate these children."

"So what about Sitarah?" I ask.

"Her sister is married, but, after she gave birth, the husband's family sent her back. They could not support another child, especially a girl."

"Great," I say. "Another unwanted girl."

"And Sitarah has a brother. He is addicted to drugs."

"How can he afford drugs?" I ask, already anticipating the answer.

"Easy. He steals."

"And Sitarah?" I ask again.

"The family lives in such impoverished conditions. There is no bed in the tiny room, not even the hint of one. They sleep on a pile of rags."

"And Sitarah? Would she be right for our new school?"

"She would be perfect."

"Why?" I inquire, expecting that the weight of the answer will push me over the brink and into the decision Reena wants me to make.

"Do not forget what Preyrona means," Reena replies. "Inspiration. Sitarah is our inspiration for helping the others. Every day, she will remind us of the reason we are doing this work. So that ragpickers' daughters can find a better place in society."

* * *

I'm writing the proposal for Preyrona 2, our *envisioned* new school in Dakhindari, hoping to convince the Empower The Children board of directors that this is the right decision. In some way, I'm still trying to convince myself. Reena has found a single-room building for 500 rupees—twelve dollars—a month. The price is good. But what does it look like? I don't know because, even though I've walked around the slum, I've intentionally steered clear of the building. It's better to leave the negotiations to Reena because, unfortunately, when landlords see foreign backers, the price immediately goes up.

In the proposal, I write: "The Dakhindari area of Kolkata is one of the poorest in the city. The residents live in very crowded conditions, often eight to a small room. The slum has no

> *Give to every other human every right you claim for yourself.*
> —Robert G. Ingersoll,
> political leader, orator

proper drainage system, and stagnant rainwater collects in every small recession, which attracts mosquitoes and increases the risk of malaria. There's one communal toilet for every fifteen residents, which is both an environmental and health hazard. None of the residents have any privacy, which is especially hard on the older girls. The adults are engaged in menial labor, such as servants, day laborers, or *rickshaw wallahs*. While the parents work, the children loiter here and there with no supervision or focus to their lives. Some parents send their children out to beg or to work even though India has laws against child labor. Reena and Ashit, who is now on the Empower The Children payroll, will co-direct the school. We will call it Preyrona 2 School. It will cost 193,800 rupees—approximately 4,500 dollars, depending on the currency exchange rate—for one year, which will pay the salaries of three full-time teachers, three ancillary teachers for art, drama, and vocational training, lunches for thirty-five students, rent, and maintenance. A detailed budget is attached." I haven't included any personal stories.

I also intentionally neglect to mention that it's in a Muslim locality. Some people think that educating Muslim children removes from them the motivation to become terrorists. Others believe that Muslims don't deserve any help after the involvement of a few Muslims in the attack on the World Trade Center in September 2001. As an American, I don't make a judgment. I'm an educator and see only wasted potential and unfulfilled dreams in an uneducated mind regardless of the child's race, religion, or gender.

The Empower The Children board passes the proposal at their next meeting, which I attend via Skype. When I give Reena the good news, she's ecstatic. Winning my support is a personal triumph for her, and now I can't wait to meet the kids she's been telling me about.

\* \* \*

Preyrona 2 opens in May 2007 while I'm on my annual four-month fundraising trip in the U.S. When I return in July, I go to the school for the first time.

> *Education is the most powerful weapon which you can use to change the world.*
> —Nelson Mandela, politician, president of South Africa

Mr. Khan is the taxi driver I use most often because he's agreed to practice my "Golden Rule" of no *horning*. He patiently tries to negotiate the narrow, twisting lanes that lead into Dakhindari. Everything blocks our way: a big garbage truck in front of a bigger mountain of garbage, goats being gently prodded by a stick-wielding child, *rickshaws* unable to move to the left or right because there is no left or right on this road, people on foot trying to maneuver safely to wherever they're going. Today, Mr. Khan has to practically sit on his hands to resist the temptation to *horn*. "True, it is slow going," I comfort him, "but hitting the horn continually makes it both slow *and* noisy."

"Urdu school. Urdu school," Khan yells out the window seeking directions from shopkeepers and pedestrians. His reference is to the language spoken by Muslims. People point this way and that. Amidst all the distractions, we see Ashit standing on the road, waving at us wildly, telling us that we've arrived.

Khan isn't happy—he has no place to park his taxi—although, as always, he keeps his demeanor calm and professional, his smile small and polite beneath serious eyes.

I jump out and follow closely behind Ashit. He leads me down a small road and then a narrow lane through the slum. The people greet me warmly, smiling shyly. They don't have a beaten-like-a-dog expression as I had expected after listening to Reena tell their sad stories. Yes, they're struggling, but I see people with dignity and self-respect.

An old woman offers me *chai*, but I'm afraid to take a chance. If the water hasn't been boiled long enough, I might contract stomach problems. I put my hands together in a prayer position, bow slightly, and say, "Thank you. Not today." She grins and suddenly looks much younger. It's hard to know her age because the slum takes its toll on women more so than men.

After about sixty yards, we come to the dead end of the lane, and Ashit proudly points to an opening—not even a door—on the corner of a brick building with a slate roof. Brick. Slate. Good construction materials, right? You would think so.

But the bricks are three different colors: some natural red at about waist to chest level; lower ones, near the dirt, painted black; and upper ones, near the roof and around the opening, painted aqua blue. The amount of mortar between the bricks seems negligible. Some of the slate tiles are tipped on their side, and the roof has a gentle rise and fall from left to right. My first thought is that someone is going to be severely hurt when that slate starts to slide!

Can this really be the school? It looks nothing like a school, just a room tucked away from the outside world, the kind of place that, if in Brooklyn, would be immediately condemned.

Reena suddenly steps outside with a few small children. She blows a conch shell to announce my arrival, and the smallest girl stretches to place a *tilak,* a dot of dark orange paste, on my forehead. Another girl throws flower petals onto my hair, while the tallest child places a garland around my neck. While the flower and garland part of this greeting ritual is universal and trumpeting a conch is common among many religions and cultures, the *tilak* is actually a Hindu custom, but none of these Muslims seem to mind.

I step into the building, which is the size of a two-car garage in the United States. There are no windows, but a back entrance leads to a large dirt yard surrounded by other hovel-like buildings. On one side of the yard, a man keeps several cows in a corral.

Inside the school, the children sit shoulder to shoulder on mats on the floor. The only air flow comes from an overhead fan hung on a metal hook, tied with twine to the open bamboo rafters. There are several fluorescent lights, but only one is lit. "It's hot and dark in here," I think. But through the dimness, I see a welcome sight: sixty children—not the thirty-five that I had expected—sitting on the floor ready to learn.

> *Although the world is full of suffering, it is full also of the overcoming of it.*
> —Helen Keller, author, political activist, lecturer

Sonu, Reyhana, Sangeeta, Gharam, and Sitarah, the children Reena so exuberantly told me about over the months leading up to this day, are there. I search their faces for anxiety but see only anticipation. Their minds are fresh and unspoiled. The slum hasn't defeated these kids.

\* \* \*

Unfortunately, in the slums, there's a lot of violence against children as well as women. The reasons are complicated but have a lot to do with ignorance about child-rearing. Most slum-dwellers don't understand that beating children only creates angry adults who then beat their own children. It's not a matter of illiteracy. Even educated Indians, such as teachers, still use the stick. Caning is considered an acceptable form of scholastic discipline, and parents support it.

However, in Empower The Children schools, we give the children love. When I interview a prospective teacher, I explain carefully that any form of violence is strictly prohibited and will lead to immediate dismissal. The teachers agree, of course, but I can see that some are a bit confused and perhaps even shaken by this shift in cultural norms.

"If you love the children, then they'll work for you," I reinforce. "They'll want to please you and make you proud. Happy children become smart children, and that's why it's our responsibility to give them the *right kind* of attention."

I realize I'm asking these prospective teachers to do something they're unaccustomed to doing. So, as I say this, I watch them carefully and try to gauge the sincerity of their reactions. Tacit head bobbing seems a bit weak, while an emphatic "of course" seems a bit strong.

Reena tries to reach the parents, counseling them not to hit their children, but often to little avail. Alcoholism sometimes plays a role, and an unfortunate child caught misbehaving by an inebriated father will certainly pay the price. Dilip, eight years old and very small for his age, has the scars, both physical and psychological, to prove it. But, one day, there's a small opening, a crack in the father's way of thinking.

"I was at the school when I saw Dilip's father crossing the lane." Reena tells me. "I was afraid he was angry and would create a scene, but instead he spoke to me very nicely. He said to me, 'Yesterday, I came home from work and Dilip was playing outside instead of doing his chores. He is always doing what he is not supposed to do.' And I told the father, 'But he is a child, only eight years old. He is doing what a child of that age is supposed to do.' The father protested, 'There is no time for play. He has to help his mother with scrubbing the pots and peeling the potatoes. I was tired and angry, so I gave him a tight slap to the side of his head. He started to cry and shout. He never shouted before, so I was surprised and listened carefully. And he was saying: You do not love me. You do not love me. Only Rosalie Aunty loves me.'"

Reena pauses to collect herself, then continues. "I said to him, 'How did that make you feel?' He replied, 'At first, I felt angrier, but then I felt sorry for hitting him. That is why I came to your school today. Please tell Rosalie Aunty I am glad she loves my son.'"

> *In a gentle way,*
> *you can shake the world.*
> —Mohandas Gandhi, political leader

Ashit can't stop working. He matches Reena's enthusiasm but is twenty-five years younger with a lot more energy. He's always running from place to place to buy food, books, educational posters, school supplies, vocational training materials, mats—everything our two Preyrona schools need. He doesn't have personal transportation, so he spends hours each day on foot, buses, and *rickshaws*. But it's in the classroom that he really shines.

"Ashit, sir. Ashit, sir," the children clamor for his attention. "Ashit, sir, look at this. Ashit, sir, help me with my lesson. Ashit, sir, I hurt my foot."

Ashit is Hindu but gently insists that the Muslim children pray during their Islamic *adhan,* the Call to Prayer sung by a *muezzin* five times a day. He places a scarf on each girl's head and bows with the boys on a prayer mat. The other teachers look on in amazement.

> *The best portion of a good*
> *man's life: his little, nameless,*
> *unremembered acts*
> *of kindness and of love.*
> —William Wordsworth, poet

Ashit is getting more and more tired, but he won't take a day off. Six days each week, Ashit and Reena cook the school lunches at 5:30 a.m. By 7:00 a.m., he's at Preyrona 1 School. By 11:00, he's at Preyrona 2. By 3:00 p.m., he starts running all over the city in preparation for the next school day. When he gets home late at night, he begins paperwork. On Sunday, he buys lunch ingredients for the coming week.

Finally, sick with a fever, he's forced to leave school early. The kids don't understand what's going on so the teachers explain, "Ashit, sir, is sick. He needs to go home and rest. He needs medicine. He is very weak. He can't stand up anymore today." The kids are shocked and worried. Spontaneously, the girls cover their heads with scarves, the boys unroll their mats. In their fashion, these Muslim children start to pray for their Hindu teacher.

"It was terrible. I still cannot think about it." Champa is describing a fire that swept through Atmaraksha slum last night. "Atmaraksha means 'defend yourself.' That is what the slum-dwellers are trying to do, become independent. But now … ." She breaks off and starts to cry.

Champa had asked me to support a small preschool in Atmaraksha slum. The teachers were grossly underpaid, and the kids weren't getting any lunch, she had told me. So Empower The Children had voted to support this school and one other pre-school, Nehru Colony, on a trial basis for one year.* Now the slum has burned down to the ground.

"The children are traumatized," Champa continues. "One little girl lost her father, and a boy lost his mother. The other kids are just stunned. We are trying to comfort them, but it is not easy. What do you say to such a tragedy?"

"Are there any medical supplies? Any food? Any tents?" I ask.

"The local community is doing its best, but it was such a big slum. There were thousands and thousands of people there."

"What about the school? Was it damaged?"

"No, the school has been spared but half of the space is being used for other purposes now ... because of the fire. At least the kids still have a place to go every day."

"Is there anything Empower The Children can do?" I ask.

"Just do one thing. We will increase the amount of food so they have something extra. Is that okay?"

"Of course, it's okay," I reply as I calculate the extra cost in my head and determine that I'll have to ask the board for a couple of hundred dollars more. "Do whatever it takes to make the kids feel more secure."

"No one is smiling. All the kids are frightened."

"They'll smile again. Things will return to normal," I suggest weakly.

"It will take years. So much harm has been done."

"They'll get back on their feet again, you'll see."

"Life isn't fair," Champa whispers, almost to herself.

"No, it isn't," I agree.

* *Empower The Children continues to fully finance this preschool in Atmaraksha as well as Nehru Colony and a third preschool, Nivedita.*

Sultanah is looking around cautiously. She obviously doesn't feel free to speak. Finally, she whispers softly, "It is not good here."

Her sister Nasha has come to visit her in Familia, a home where Sultanah's family placed her in March 2007, two months after

Sabriyah's wedding. My neighbor Rosemary, who was Sultanah's tutor, my friend Jannie, founder of the Dutch nonprofit HelpIndiaHelpen, and I have accompanied Nasha. Familia is located in Kanchrapara, fifty-five kilometers north of Kolkata, and we had to take a taxi to the train station, a local train for more than an hour, a *rickshaw* to the bus stand, and then a bus to the orphanage. The positive side of all this travel is that it's in the countryside and is as peaceful and beautiful as Kolkata is noisy and oppressive.

Sultanah has been here several months now, and when she and Nasha saw each other, they fell into each other's arms weeping.

"It is not good here," Sultanah repeats, equally as softly. Then she looks around to see if anyone else might have heard.

"Why not?" I ask. "You have your own bedroom, a big bed. At home, seven family members sleep on one bed. And sometimes you slept on the floor. Remember when we had to get an extra blanket for you because the floor was so cold."

"But I do not like it here. I feel scared to sleep alone. I hear a lot of sounds in the night."

"It's true. You hear sounds in the countryside that you don't hear in the city." As a city girl myself, I appreciate what Sultanah is saying. "But you'll get used to them."

One of the orphans, a girl who speaks fluent English, is pawing through the things we've brought Sultanah: a blouse, a kit to make a belt, sweets, a bracelet. Sultanah is obviously proud that she has Western friends, but she remains quiet and seems nervous by the other girl's presence.

"She takes things from me," Sultanah says after the girl has satisfied her curiosity and left.

"Did you tell the housemother?" asks Jannie. "She seems very nice."

"No, I cannot tell her. The housemother will get mad at me."

"Why would she get mad at you?" I ask. But, of course, the

question is irrelevant. The problem is that Sultanah is hours from home and all alone. She feels vulnerable and doesn't want to start any trouble.

Lunch is served. Before Sultanah can take even one bite, Nasha begins to feed her. She knows Sultanah can feed herself, but this is an act of love.

"You've grown plump," we say in a complimentary manner. "Before, you were painfully thin like Nasha. There is never enough food at your house."

"The food is good here. They give a lot and even give meat and chicken."

"And you can go out into the garden—in your new wheelchair that Jannie bought for you, a *pink* one, your favorite color," I add with feigned enthusiasm because my heart is aching with pain for her.

Sultanah was very pleased with the new wheelchair when she received it a few months earlier, but now, sitting at the orphanage, she doesn't seem to care. "Thank you, Jannie," Sultanah says politely. She forces herself to smile.

"Things will get better," I say encouragingly. "Just give it a chance. In a few months, it will seem like home."

"But I will never be happy here," Sultanah counters. "Never. It is impossible." She starts to cry softly.

"How do you know? Give it a chance. You will change your mind."

"I will never change my mind." Sultanah is now weeping openly. "I want to go to school. I miss Loreto School. I want to study. I don't learn anything here."

"There's no school nearby," I tell her. "There's only the local school for the village kids. It's too far for them to push you in the wheelchair. The path is not paved. It's too difficult."

"Sabriyah pushed me every day to Loreto School. That was far and difficult."

"That's because Sabriyah is your cousin," I reply. I hesitate to say, "and she loves you," but that's implied, and Sultanah understands completely.

"Do not leave me here," Sultanah begs as we prepare to go. "I want to go to school. I want to go to school. I want to learn," she cries hysterically.

> *Wanting something*
> *is not enough.*
> *You must hunger for it.*
> —Les Brown, motivational speaker

There's no consoling her, so we leave as quickly as possible.

Today, a knock on the door brings my three favorite neighborhood kids into my flat. They're nervously milling around, and I perceive that they're ready to spring something on me. Mukhtar looks amused. Aatirah looks worried. And Shahana looks determined. I wait patiently.

"Guess what?" Shahana says casually.

"What?"

"I have good news for you."

"That's nice. I always welcome good news."

"I am getting a passport."

"Really? I know a passport is good for ten years, but why not wait until you've finished school, get a job, have some money, and are ready to travel?" I counsel.

"I need it now," she continues.

"Why on earth would you need it now?"

"Because I am going to Scotland."

"What?" I jump up as if suddenly aware of a hot poker under my butt.

"Yes, I am going to Scotland. I have been selected by Napier University in Edinburgh for their Hospitality Management program."

"What about your studies in Kolkata?"

"I am finishing up my two years at the Institute of Advanced Management in Kolkata. Then I will transfer and complete my last year abroad and get my degree from Napier."

"And how much will this cost?"

"Ten *lakh.*"

I exhale a whistling breath. "That's approximately 25,000 dollars in the U.S. Where will you get that much money?"

"I have faith in God. If he wants me to go to Scotland, then I will go."

I understand what those words really mean ... and that they are directed at me.

* * *

Shahana's *modus operandi* is to wear me down until I give in. She tries every tactic.

"I must go to Scotland. Otherwise, my life will be ruined," is Monday's argument.

"In Scotland, I can earn a lot of money and help my family," she says on Tuesday.

> *Whatever you expect, with confidence, becomes your own self-fulfilling prophecy.*
> —Brian Tracy, self-help author, speaker, business coach

"If I study abroad, my degree will be worth so much more than a degree from Kolkata," she offers on Wednesday.

And on Thursday, "I can put Aatirah through nursing school. I promise, I will earn a lot of money and put her through school."

On and on, day by day, she keeps at it—with persuasion and perseverance.

I'm lying in bed thinking about the day I've had today. It was a day of contradictions.

When I was in New Jersey during the summer, our board had a meeting, and I suggested that we should forgo giving the kids clothes for the holidays this year because of the worldwide economic crisis and difficulty raising money. To my surprise, the board members disagreed. "We've given them clothes every year. Why should this year be different?" they argued. We voted, and mine was the only nay vote—and that rarely happens. I was secretly pleased that the board doesn't just rubberstamp whatever I request.

Today, I went to Preyrona 2 School and found myself sitting in front of a pile of clothes: frocks, shorts, shirts, pants, *salwar* suits. The kids were obediently lined up, their heads moving left and right to get a better look. They reminded me of those bobble head dolls whose heads are on a spring. Each child, in turn, came forward and accepted the clothes.

Inside, I was *kvelling*—not only because the board insisted that we give clothes to the kids, that's the least of it, but because they're also receiving an education and lunch and love and attention. It's almost inexplicable that, just a few months ago, these same children were loitering on the streets.

Back in the taxi, after riding for only twenty minutes, traffic came to a complete halt. "*Bandh,* Madame," Mr. Khan said.

"Strike? They didn't call a strike," I protested.

"Not city-wide. *Bandh* today is district-by-district. Now they are striking in this district."

"In this district? Where we happen to be?"

"Yes."

We sat in the taxi for two hours before the traffic started to inch forward. I was hot and tired and fed up. I hadn't eaten lunch, and my mood was getting worse and worse. I got a call from Bina, project coordinator at Disha School, who was also stuck in traffic but enduring it much more patiently.

"People are lying on the road. That is why the cars cannot go," she reported.

"Why don't they run them over?" I asked, as if this were a reasonable suggestion. Even as I was speaking, I couldn't believe these words were coming out of my mouth.

I finally reached home and stepped into what seemed like, especially in my sour mood, an inch of water on my living room floor with a small tsunami rolling toward the bedrooms.

The woman who Qadir hired to open the water supply lines from the cistern on the roof each day had done so while I was away—and given me way too much. Again. It had overflowed the 40-gallon overhead tank that sits on a platform above my bathroom door and water had poured over the door sill. Again.

Fortunately, the floor throughout the flat is terrazzo because carpet would quickly mold. I got out rags and started swabbing, my resentment rising.

"Tell the woman who fills the tanks to give me just three minutes of water. That's enough," I tell the landlord whenever I see him.

"Definitely," he replies agreeably, but either the message doesn't get delivered or my request gets lost in the translation. Maybe three minutes in Kolkata isn't the same as three minutes in New Jersey.

I was just about ready to collapse, but I forced myself to go out to one of my favorite Bengali restaurants for dinner. "Not spicy," I told the waiter. "No chilies, no pepper, no spice."

"No Indian," he replied cheerfully.

But, like the water that overflows from my bathroom tank, "not spicy" in Kolkata isn't the same as "not spicy" in New Jersey, and my mouth was burning with the first bite. My tongue felt like blisters would slowly begin to bubble up at any moment. I ordered yogurt to cool my palate and my mood.

The next blow to my day was overhearing a conversation that a power cut—or "load shedding," as they call it in Kolkata—had been ordered throughout the city, district by district. But miraculously, the locality where I live was spared.

So I lie in my bed with the overhead ceiling fan obediently revolving its wide, wonderful blades—at high speed. The air feels so good, and the fan's white noise blocks out the sounds of the streets.

Yet, while the fan cools my body, it's not easing my mind. An intrusive thought keeps poking me: "Wouldn't it be easy to give in to family pressure and say, 'Yes, I'm outa here.' I could tell myself—maybe even convince myself—that I need to go home to help take care of Mother."

This argument is so perfect. I could do it—go home, leave the children and the programs in Kolkata—and *not feel guilty* about it.

Then I return to pondering my day: the contradiction of not wanting to give the kids clothes and the gratification of giving it; the pull to stay in Kolkata and the push to get out; the contrast of life in New Jersey and the life of my kids living in the slums.

The hum of the fan is slowly putting me to sleep. Thank goodness there isn't load shedding tonight. I'm shedding enough of my own load.

*Someone is talking on the phone in the other room about different members of the family. When she gets to me, she says, "Rosalie works too hard. Why does she have to work so hard?"*

*I get up to discuss this with her, but when she appears she's smiling broadly, so I decide to let it go. I tell her that, in Kolkata, my clothes are stored in the public library. "Isn't that funny?" I say. "That the library stores clothes. There are books in three sections and clothes in the other." Then I add, "I decided to get rid of a lot them, so now I need new clothes. Let's go shopping."*

*This makes her smile more broadly. She loves to go shopping. We leave together with her arm around my waist.*

I hear the sound of a metal shutter being slammed shut. It's the door to the storage room below my flat where the cauldrons for cooking *biryani*

> *Human life is purely a matter of deciding what's important to you.*
> —Anonymous

are stored. The shattering rattle of its corrugated steel wakes me up.

I look around. The fan is still spinning. I'm still in Kolkata. I feel light and happy.

Professor Jimmy has brought his university students, thirty in all, from Vermont. They're passing through Kolkata on their way to Darjeeling. I've never handled such a big group of volunteers before, and, to make matters even more complicated, they've come on December 31st, during Christmas vacation, when the schools here are closed. I've arranged with Ashit to open Preyrona 2 School, and, surprisingly, neither the children nor the teachers mind giving up a day of their holiday.

Jimmy's group is volunteering for only one day, but I want to make it memorable. I believe that the experience could help shape their attitude toward helping others as they navigate through life after graduation. So I've prepared a special lesson that will connect my students and Jimmy's despite the age difference and language barrier. They'll create sock puppets and then "talk" with each other through them.

The oversized tourist bus is parked a couple of blocks from Preyrona 2, and the university students walk down the narrow lane to the school. The attention they attract in this small slum can't be described. As the students move toward the school, the neighborhood moves toward the school. As the students enter the school, the neighborhood surrounds the school. Through each of the two narrow doors, inquisitive faces peer, eager to share the occasion.

Until a few months ago, these seventy kids had never even seen a foreigner, and now they're crushed into the one small room—24 feet by 24 feet—with a busload of them. Nobody can contain their excitement. Given my sensitivity to noise, I find it overwhelming. I reach into my purse for my ear plugs. "Thank God it isn't summer or monsoon season," I shout to Jimmy, "or the heat in this room would be oppressive."

Before long, the students and the kids are playing with the sock puppets they've made together. Everyone is happy.

The university students want to stay longer, but Jimmy is now shouting, "It's New Year's Eve. I have to get these students back to the hotel before dinner. They'll celebrate for a few hours, and then they must catch a few hours sleep. We leave for Darjeeling at 5:00 tomorrow morning."

"But how can they push through the crowd outside of parents and grandparents and babies? What about their safety?"

"Get me fifteen *rickshaws*. We'll take the students by *rickshaw* to the bus."

This is pretty funny because the bus is only a short distance from the school, but it's a plan, so the *rickshaws* are lined up outside the school. It resembles a religious procession, and, given Indians' love of celebrations—I often say, "Indians are holiday-obsessed"—the atmosphere becomes even more jubilant. The students climb into their "*rickshaw* chariots," and the kids and surrounding neighbors look at them as though they were deities.

As the *rickshaws* move away from the school, the neighborhood moves with them. At the bus, the students board amidst shouts of, "Thank you. Come again. Happy New Year. We love you." The students are reaching out the windows, shaking hands and taking pictures.

I've always said, "You'll never feel more welcome than in India."

I'm getting tired of Shahana's constant assaults. She has a million and one reasons to go to Napier University, but she doesn't have the money. She knows full well that I also don't have it, but she believes I somehow have the key. She's right, of course, but I don't want to disappoint Shahana and, even more importantly, I don't want to disappoint myself. So I hesitate and hesitate until I can't stall any longer.

"Hi, Art." I say cheerily over an international telephone connection.

"Hi," he replies. He's surprised to hear from me. Although we email each other regularly, I usually call him from Kolkata only to wish him a happy birthday, and it's nowhere near his birthday.

"How are you?" I ask.

"Fine."

"What's new?"

"I'm reworking my book."

"Which book? *Heriot* or *The Jewel?*"

"*The Jewel.*"

"Art, you remember Shahana. She cooked scrumptious meals for you on a tiny stove when you were here."

"Of course, I remember her. She's hard to forget."

Borrowing a page right out of Shahana's spiel, I jump in. "Well, guess what? I have good news for you."

"What's that?"

"Shahana is going to school in Scotland."

"Really? That's great."

"There's only one little problem."

"What's that?"

"It costs a lot of money."

"How much money?"

I gulp before I speak. "Twenty-five thousand dollars."

There's dead silence for what seems like hours, which of course is just minutes and probably only seconds, while Art processes the *real* reason for my call.

"I'll lend her the money."

"Art, how can I thank you?"

"Don't thank me."

That's Art. He's straight from the heart.*

* *Shahana graduated from Napier University and works in Edinburgh. Her sister Aatirah later joined her in order to study dental technology.*

*The life I touch for good or ill will touch another life, and that in turn will touch another, until who knows where the trembling stops or in what far place my touch will be felt.*

—Frederick Buechner, writer, theologian

I've been trying to figure out why wealthy Indians seem so insensitive to the poor. Some suggest that there are so many poor people that it's easy to get used to it and become either complacent or overwhelmed or cynical, like watching so many violent films that you become desensitized to violence. But I have a different idea: servants.

Although the caste system is illegal in India, its illegality is only on the law books. It's still in people's minds, like racial or ethnic prejudice that has lingered in the minds of some Americans. In India, one of the lowest castes is that of servants, and there are servants for everything. There's a servant to sweep and swab the floors, and that servant wouldn't dare touch the food, so there's a servant to shop and cook. There's a different servant to wash and iron the clothes and another one to take the kids to school. I once visited a friend, and her two boys, nine and twelve years old, were sitting with their feet outstretched for ten minutes. I thought, "What an odd way to sit." Then a servant came into the room and put their shoes on their feet.

In one respect, having so many people working within a home is a good thing. It provides jobs for lots and lots of people. But think of this: "If all the children of servants became educated and got good jobs and rose out of poverty, who would be the servant?" Then, of course, in marches another thought: "Maybe my friend's boys will learn to put on their own shoes!"

* * *

This morning, I'm tired—really, really tired—and want nothing more than to run away from Kolkata to a place that's cool, clean, and quiet. But instead of running away, I start thinking. No, not exactly thinking but ruminating. All my grievances parade in front of me like mocking ex-boyfriends who have found someone prettier. I start with the Missionaries of Charity in general and then move to Sister Tara in particular.

It doesn't stop there. I keep moving back in history—to the school from which I retired that conveniently forgot to throw a going-away party for me and a job from which I was fired for no apparent reason. Then I start searching through ancient history. I can still recall my hurt at the age of twenty when my best friend had sex with my boyfriend of the time. My brain gives equal weight to ancient grievances as to fresh ones.

The Buddhists say that our minds are like wild monkeys, out of control unless we tame them with meditation. Today, I'm trying a new strategy. I'm saying mantras. They push the thoughts out of my head temporarily, but concentrating on the mantras when I'm tired isn't easy. I start and stop erratically, never getting past the beginning. It seems I can't even remember the end.

I'm taking the Kolkata Metro to RCFC, the children's orthopedic hospital. It's crowded, and the doors are blocked by people leaning against them. I always worry that I won't be able to get off at my stop because there will be too many unmoving passengers in the way. This somehow triggers a flashback about when I was on a train in Italy and Art got off for a few minutes to get some food from a vendor and the train started to move and I panicked because I had no money with me. Why was I so stupid at that time?

This then reminds me of the time when we were running for a train in Yugoslavia as it started to pull away and I jumped on but Art almost didn't get on and I was so worried because I didn't even know which city I was in. Why was I always so dependent?

Before I have a chance to dredge up any more train stories, I push my way to the door and get off.

I'm on an *autorickshaw* and trying the mantras again. They've gotten all mixed up with the *horning* and loud music blaring from the *rickshaw's* radio and the people shouting to each other over the noise. Maybe I'm too tired to fight it or perhaps it's the wrong mantra.

The hospital is off the main road. The trees compassionately shade it from the glaring sun. *Horning* is replaced by children's laughter as they kick a ball with foot or crutch or artificial limb. They have heaps of reasons to be resentful, but their minds seem fresh and light. The ball comes in my direction, and I kick it awkwardly. It's been a long time since I've kicked a ball. I gather the kids, and we move slowly—at their pace—into the classroom. They sit on the floor and smile broadly.

"Good morning, Aunty," they shout in unison. Their voices fill the cavernous room.

Instead of answering, I start to stutter, involuntarily, which sends the kids into gales of laughter.

"What is it, Aunty?" they ask innocently.

"I … I must th … thank you," I reply, but I can't explain what I'm feeling to them as I let their voices and their laughter cleanse my mind. I just discovered the right mantra.

> *Each day comes bearing its own gifts. Untie the ribbons.*
> —Ruth Ann Schabacker

Reena is calling on her mobile, both excited and worried. "Uncle wants to open a school."

"Open a school?" I repeat with disbelief.

"A school for poor kids. His friends sit on a board in London that builds schools all over the world, but the organization does not have any in India. Now that Uncle is back, they are pressuring him to buy a building for a school that will be funded and run by Empower The Children."

Reena's uncle had lived in London for the past sixty years, unmarried, with no dependents. To Reena's delight, he's returned to Kolkata to spend his remaining days. He's living with his elder sister, and Reena is devoted to both of them. She sometimes comments that her uncle doesn't understand the work she's doing with the poor, so this news comes as quite a surprise.

"Is he being forced to do this by his friends?" I ask.

"*He* is not being forced to do this." Her voice is starting to take on worry.

"He's not?" I ask, unconvinced.

"No, *we* are being forced to do this."

"Who are *we*?" I ask guardedly.

"Me and Ashit. Uncle is too old and not keeping well. Ashit is young and healthy. We have to help him."

"Reena, it's nearly impossible to buy a building. Nobody has papers to prove ownership. It's all illegally occupied land. We went through this when we opened Bulbulir Basa Orphanage. Mithu came close to having a nervous breakdown, and it almost destroyed our friendship."

"I know that. But what to tell Uncle? He is our family and he needs us so he can keep his promise to his friends in London."

"But you need your sanity. You and Ashit already work in Preyrona 1 and Preyrona 2. How will you find the time for a third school?"

"I do not know. That is why I am worried."

"Can't you tell Uncle that it's impossible to find land in Kolkata, that you have no time, that you already have enough to do?"

> *If you want happiness for a lifetime, help someone.*
> —Chinese proverb

"No. Uncle needs us."

And that is the sentiment that prevails.

\* \* \*

Ashit isn't having a nervous breakdown, but he's very tired. He teaches all day and searches for a building all evening.

I don't want to put pressure on him, so I don't ask directly. I ask Reena instead. "Reena, any luck finding a building?"

"Ashit found many buildings."

"Good ones?"

"Very good ones."

"So he has many to choose from?"

"Many, but always some problem arises."

"What problem?" I ask, as though I don't know.

"Many that have no papers."

It's always the same story: no papers. Uncle is getting impatient because his English friends are calling him all the time and he has no answer for them. It's too complicated to explain the "no papers" dilemma to the people in London. They are planning to come to see the new school in January, so that gives us less than six months. It took Mithu two years to find a building for Bulbulir Basa, so I don't feel hopeful. But Ashit and Reena won't give up.

After the Kolkata Film Festival in mid-November 2008, Nan, my dear friend in McLeod Ganj, and I take a three-week holiday in Burma, renamed Myanmar by the present military government. I'm so affected by the country that I feel compelled to tell about it.

I write a group email to everyone I know.

Dear friends,

Unfortunately due to the military junta, monks' protest, the Saffron Revolution in September 2007, and Cyclone Nargis in May

> *To see what few have seen, you must go where few have gone.*
> —Buddha

2008, people have steered away from Burma, so Nan and I were a novelty, welcomed with graciousness and curiosity (especially my curly hair). On our very first day in Rangoon, we found the synagogue, a remnant from the days when 2,500 Jews lived there. Now, a mere 20 are left (less than the 30 Jews in Kolkata). I bought a *menorah* with the approach of Chanukah in mind. So, though far from home, we were able to celebrate in the traditional way albeit more than a month early.

Burma is alive with people, and it is always the people who make a trip worthwhile. We managed to find a curly-haired noodle vendor who heaped extra noodles on my plate in recognition of our *sisterhood* and a young boy running alongside our trishaw (a bicycle with a two-seater side car) trying to outrun us, laughing all the way. Then, there was Min who visited us at our teak guesthouse with a gift of a Buddha to carry back to Kolkata.

We spent an afternoon hanging out at a pagoda amidst thousands of Buddhas. The locals prayed but also chatted, ate, and slept. We played Scrabble and that attracted quite a crowd.

A night bus took us to Mandalay to a guesthouse with a roof-top garden. Mandalay is more a sprawling village than a city and also the residence of the Mustache Brothers. Anti-government slander is prohibited even if presented as comedy, but that never stopped the Mustache Brothers. For their offense, they spent years in prison doing hard labor and are still under house arrest and perform only to foreigners. In 2002, Nobel Peace Prize Winner Aung San Suu Kyi (referred to only as "the lady" by the Burmese) sat on one of the chairs to watch a performance. It has been dubbed the "lucky chair," and I was lucky enough to get it.

From Mandalay, a local truck took us into the mountains with the temperature dropping as we continued to ascend. A quiet village awaited us with hill walking, waterfalls, and botanical gardens. No rushing in Burma. It's a laid-back place. Despite the military regime, the people seem relaxed and outgoing and have made the best of the situation. Of course, the babies burst into tears as soon as they saw us (fair-skinned apparitions) but were comforted by their laughing mothers.

A table laid with Burmese specialties was our Thanksgiving dinner. Afterward, the waiter, eager to use his limited English, proclaimed proudly, "You are fresh and active!" Since we are both over 60, we took that as a compliment! On the way back to the guesthouse, we passed a group of people dancing around a campfire singing "Oh, Suzanna."

Back to Mandalay for a quick visit to Shwenandaw Kyaung, an intricately carved teak monastery, looking more like a ginger bread house than a Buddhist temple.

Nan left for Inle Lake, and I took a 5:00 a.m. *rickshaw* to the wharf. Under the star-filled sky,

I passed bicycles laden with goods headed for the markets that were already a hub of activity. The local boat (called the slow-boat) down the Ayeyerwady River was chock-a-block full of Burmese, blanketing the floor with their bodies and belongings. Twenty pink plastic chairs were the "luxury" accommodations for foreigners. At each village, the boat stopped and vendors laden with food and snacks crossed thin planks to board the boat, hoping for a lucky day.

14 hours later: Bagan. What to say? If it isn't one of the wonders of the world, it should be with its over 4,000 temples dating back to 1044. I hired a horse-cart to go "temple hopping" but spent most of the day chatting with the local people.

"Are you happy?" I asked countless times.

And always, "Yes," was their reply.

"Why?"

"We don't have too little or too much. Just 'normal.'" Just like the Buddhist doctrine of the Middle Way.

I heard story after story about their dreams and aspirations as well as their disappointments and struggles. But always spoken with a peaceful, kindly energy and an acceptance of life's events linked to their own *karma*.

A 15-hour ride on a local bus over rutted, dusty, and unfinished roads almost killed me. But it took me to Inle Lake in the mountains. Then a slow boat through lotus blossoms and lily pads ferried us to the hot springs, a balm for a weary traveler's aching back.

The next day, we explored Inle Lake, all twists and turns along canals with houses on stilts and floating vegetable gardens (onions, tomatoes, chilies, beans, cauliflower growing on floating clumps of soil that felt like an unstable water bed when stepped upon). Sunset over the lake was especially memorable because it was sunset over Burma.

While exploring by bicycle, Nan happened upon an orphanage, so we returned there by trishaw laden with food and blankets that we purchased from a local market.

With a sense of sadness, we returned to Rangoon, the end of our holiday fast approaching. With only a couple of days left, we made the best of the situation. We contacted a lovely young woman, Zar Zar, who speaks perfect English, and she guided us to a monastery outside the city limits. We delivered 20 bottles of water purification solution, 10 bottles of iodine and 2 containers of protein powder for children. The monk promised the donation would reach the Delta Region in central Myanmar, which has been devastated by the recent cyclone.

So we left Burma with a sense of *completion* and the desire to return again soon. It is a country not easily forgotten.

Lots of love, Rosalie

\* \* \*

A long layover in Bangkok is just what I don't need. The trip to Burma was fantastic, but now Nan has returned to her home in McLeod Ganj, and I'm eager to get back to Kolkata. I'm sitting next to a Buddhist nun from Australia who's in the same predicament. We strike up a conversation, and she seems friendly enough, so, after a respectable amount of time, I pop the question.

"I'm wondering if you can give me some advice. It's very important to me."

"I'll try."

"I have this problem with my family. They aren't happy that I live and work in Kolkata because they feel overwhelmed with the responsibility of caring for my elderly mother. They're always putting me under pressure to return to my home in the United States. I can't leave my work in India, but I also feel guilty that they're so distressed and unhappy."

"So what is your question?"

"How can I continue my work in Kolkata yet still satisfy them? What can I do to heal our relationship?"

The nun starts to laugh. "Sorry to laugh," she says apologetically, "but unfortunately you've asked the wrong person. My sister resents the fact that I've taken robes. She hasn't spoken to me in years."

We have a cup of tea together and talk about things less painful.

There's a knock on the door. I'm not expecting anyone, so I think it's the kids upstairs who can't walk past my door without knocking, just for the fun of it. After the second knock, I open the door and, to my surprise, I see Nasha, Sultanah's sister, standing there.

"Sultanah is back," she says.

"Come in, come in," I reply excitedly. "Tell me everything."

Inside, Nasha removes her *burka* and wipes her brow. "It is hot," she says, so I fetch a glass of water for her. "We brought her home for Eid al-Fitr at the end of Ramadan, and she refused to go back."

"Eid al-Fitr was at the end of September this year, two months ago. Why didn't you come to tell me this earlier?"

"I did not know when you came from America."

"Oh, I came in September."

"She wants to see you. Can I bring her on Sunday?"

"Of course. I also want to see her."

On Sunday, Nasha carries first the wheelchair and then Sultanah up the stairs to my flat. Nasha is sweating under her *burka* and sits down weakly. Her elder cousin Sabriyah used to do all the lifting and toileting and dressing of Sultanah as well as carrying her up and down the three flights of stairs from their small room to the street level, but now that Sabriyah is married, the responsibility has fallen on Nasha's shoulders. But Sabriyah is tall and strong whereas Nasha has the build of a frail thirteen-year-old. I offer biscuits to Sultanah and Nasha, and they eat hungrily.

"We had no lunch," Sultanah explains. "There was no time."

"You could have come later," I protest gently. "I'm going to be here the whole day."

Sultanah is smiling brightly, but looks very changed from the last time I saw her at Familia Home in Kanchrapara more than a year ago. She's bone thin and very stiff. The daily exercises she was doing at the orphanage had kept her relatively supple, but it seems those effects were short-term.

"They are not good there," Sultanah explains. "They stole from me, and they let me fall. I hurt my leg, where I had the operation four years ago, and it is paining me so much that I cannot do my exercises even though Nasha wants to do them with me. Look." She pulls up her pants leg and shows me an old scar that's swollen and red.

"I'm not a nurse," I tell her, concerned about this lingering, untreated injury. "Let me call Jannie. Maybe she can take a look."

It's Jannie's last day in Kolkata, and she wants a day off, so I don't push my request on her. I just casually mention that Sultanah is in my flat.

"I'll be right over," Jannie replies.

I also call Rosemary and she hurries over.

Everyone is thrilled to have Sultanah back in our lives.

Jannie arrives and sees the pink wheelchair she'd bought Sultanah and smiles happily. "It came back with you," she says.

Then Jannie looks at the scar and says it's infected. "If it's been infected for two months, then it means Sultanah can't fight off the infection by herself. Her body isn't strong enough."

"I want to go to the doctor," Sultanah begs. "It's paining me too much."

"Why didn't you go earlier? Two months with an infection is a serious matter."

"No money," Sultanah replies. "Nasha gives 400 for my tutor and uses 200 for her Spoken English class."

There's no use asking if other family members would help. They're all struggling to survive, squeezed into one small room.

"Also," Sultanah continues, "I have spots all over my body, and they itch. Some of them hurt."

Jannie takes a look and says it could be an allergy. "The ones that hurt are infected because Sultanah is scratching them. She must go to a doctor," Jannie decides empathically. "I'll give the money for the doctor and medication."

Sultanah is obviously relieved. "When will I feel better?" Sultanah asks.

"When the medication starts working," Jannie replies.

Sultanah is smiling at all of us. There isn't a trace of resentment in her face. She obviously has forgiven those who had put her in the orphanage or, perhaps, didn't resent them in the first place. "I'm happy to be home," she says softly.

"Our house seems empty now," Rosemary muses. Sipping tea, I smile. Only in India would seven family members *not* fill up a house. Actually, it isn't even a house, just a small room with a bed, cupboard, TV, and one plastic chair. Sitting here, I feel secure.

As a teacher and storyteller, Rosemary enjoys reminiscing about people she knew years ago, before I arrived in Kolkata. It's a window into her world. My mind drifts as she continues with details I've heard before. I remember when Art and I were traveling in Newfoundland in 1975 and met an old man who invited us into his home to tell us stories about the "old days." Afterward, he said, "People ask, 'What are the poor folks doing tonight?' The poor folks are telling stories."

I'm remembering that old man's laugh when Rosemary says, "He stayed from early morning to late at night, and even my husband was happy when he was here."

> *Whoever is happy will make others happy too.*
> —Anne Frank, Holocaust victim, diarist

"Who? Who is this man?" I inquire, my attention back on my hostess.

"He was a Frenchman. His name was Chevalier. My sister, Magdalene, and I met him at the local market. He was trying to buy some soap, and the vendor did not understand and was giving him the wrong kind. He wanted laundry soap, not body soap. We helped him and then invited him to our house for a cup of tea."

"Did he speak English?"

"Not so much, but it did not matter. We just enjoyed his company. He sat in the chair and said, '*Chai,* bring me *chai.*' and we would laugh. We never called it *chai,* just tea. He was a jolly chap."

I always smile when I hear Indians use British expressions. "What was he doing in Kolkata?" I ask.

"He liked to travel. He went everywhere alone even though he was an old man. He had a daughter, and he talked about her often but stayed away from his home for six months each year. Here in India, we cannot bear to be away from our families for even a day."

"But it seems he found the comfort of family in your home."

"Yes, I guess he did. He would come in the morning and sit on the chair and stay there for hours. Then he would take a walk.

When he came back, he would be tired so he would lie on the bed. He had a hump on his back, so it was hard for him to get comfortable. We would pile up the pillows under his hump until he was almost sitting up. Then he would fall right off to sleep. And we would all gather around the bed and just look at him. We loved him so much."

"It couldn't have been easy for an old man to manage in India."

"He loved India. The noise, the chaos, the crowds. He found France boring in comparison. He would go home but could not wait to get back, and we could not wait either."

"Did his daughter ever visit Kolkata?"

"No, but we used to talk to her from the phone shop on Free School Street. And she sent beautiful gifts when my grandson Anthony was born. She also had a baby by then, and we saw pictures of her baby. It was so nice."

"What happened to him?"

"He came to Kolkata six times. He was with us when my husband suddenly died. Shortly afterward, my brother died and then Magdalene's husband died. We were so heartbroken."

"He must have been heartbroken too."

"He was very sad, but he would tell us, 'Don't be sad. Don't cry. Death is part of life. I am an old man. I will also die.' We hated to hear that."

"So what happened to him?"

"He went back to France to see his new grandchild. He fell ill, but his daughter was taking care of him, so we were not worried, and he promised to come at Christmas. But when he did not come, we called his daughter, and she said he had died. She cried so much on the phone. She kept saying, 'I miss my father. I miss my father.' She knew we loved him and that we would miss him too."

"Your family has suffered so many losses in such a short time. I am so sorry for all of you."

"Yes. It is difficult. My granddaughter Helena has been born and, of course, we love her very much but the house seems so empty now."

Rosemary's story touches my heart. I sometimes feel awkward when staying with friends while in America because I feel like I'm invading their private space. In India, private space doesn't exist, so people are given greater importance. I'm sure that, ultimately, I will grow old in India because, childless, there's no one to take care of me in New Jersey. Neighbors and friends like Rosemary make me feel welcome in Kolkata. That's comforting.

Hindus, Muslims, Sikhs, Jains, Christians, and Buddhists live together in Kolkata, and, for all the years I've been here, there has never been any sectarian violence. I'm told it's because politicians in power a few decades ago made a special effort to give people of all religions a sense of belonging and political authority. Each of these faiths celebrates religious holidays. In fact, they celebrate so many holidays and festivals that I often wonder, "How does any work get done?"

In September or October, Hindus worship the goddess Maa Durga during their major holiday, Durga Puja,[32] which lasts five days in Kolkata. Shortly after that comes Diwali,[33] the Hindu "Festival of Lights," when people light candles throughout the city.

For Jains, Diwali marks the attainment of nirvana or salvation by their ancient sage Mahavira. This is followed soon by Jnan Panchami, the worship of pure knowledge.[34]

In October or November, Sikhs parade to celebrate Guru Gadee, the inauguration of Guru Granth Sahib as the everlasting Sikh Guru. Then, in late November or December, Gurpurab, which can last for several days, commemorates the important events in the life of Guru Nanak.[35] The birthday anniversary of Guru Gobind

Singh falls at the end of December or the beginning of January and also lasts for several days.[36]

For Buddhists, the Elephant Festival on the third Saturday in November uses the symbol of a tame elephant training a young wild elephant, a metaphor for an older Buddhist teaching a younger Buddhist. Bodhi Day in early December honors the enlightenment of the Buddha.[37]

With the Islamic calendar being shorter than the Gregorian calendar, the pageant-filled parades of the Islamic New Year have occurred in the spring and winter in recent years. Eid al-Fitr marks the end of Ramadan,[38] a month of fasting that occurs during the ninth month of the Islamic calendar.[39] Eid al-Adha is the major Muslim holiday, the Festival of Sacrifice.[40]

With so many holidays, businesses and government offices are often closed. During Durga Puja, New Market is practically a ghost market, with very few businesses open but still an over-abundance of diligent market *wallahs.*

Many schools in Kolkata are closed for an entire month for Durga Puja and Diwali. Often the days prior to the holiday are used for shopping and preparation, then extra days are tacked on at the end for cleanup. Many families travel to their native villages for the holidays, extending their festivities even more.

There seems to be *puja* after *puja* after *puja.*

When Ashit casually mentions closing the Preyrona schools for the Banana Leaf Puja, I overreact with a very strong, "No! These children need an education, not another holiday."

But with so many *pujas* throughout the year, it's not surprising that, during the Christmas season, Kolkata's streets are brightly decorated and fake Christmas trees are for sale everywhere. "Ho, ho, ho" is in the air as Santa Clauses, melting under their costumes in the hot, humid air, try to lure people into shops and stores. I'm tempted to go in and buy something just to show pity for the poor Santas.

* * *

"Mr. Khan, on Christmas Day, I have to go to Rehabilitation Centres for Children. Are you free?" I ask jokingly.

In typical Khan fashion, he smiles imperceptibly. "Only busy on Eid," this Muslim man says softly.

"We have a lot of things to carry into the classroom," I tell him. "Can you help me?"

His smile is still imperceptible.

One of the things we have to carry is a fake Christmas tree that's so big it takes up the taxi's whole back seat. We put the boxes in the trunk, and I sit in front with Khan. We don't chat because he's not the small-talk type, but there's camaraderie between us as we drive to the hospital.

The traffic is thick and the *horning* incessant, but, for the first time in a long time, my impatience is tempered. It's a lot shorter to Tollygange from Sudder Street than from the North Pole, I figure.

At the hospital, Khan and I unload the car to the wide-eyed wonder of the children and staff.

Then my wonderful taxi driver goes far beyond his role of driving and *schlepping*. To my surprise, Khan starts putting up decorations while I, ever the teacher, begin to read to the children from a Dutch pop-up book sent by Willeke who first came from her home in The Netherlands to volunteer in 2005. Khan strings gold garland across the walls while I show the kids a picture of a small goat that wants to help Santa pull his sleigh. Khan tapes shiny balls to the classroom walls while the story book reveals that Santa's sleigh suddenly breaks down and needs repair. Khan hangs colorful bells from the fan just as the little goat, now a hero, finds a missing screw. Khan finishes and looks on with his typical non-smile that displays as much emotion as the Mona Lisa when Santa's sleigh becomes airborne again—with the little goat pulling it, of course.

The big kids don Santa Claus hats while the little ones get reindeer antlers. There's one small Santa suit, and seven-year-old Rajat is the right size. He's from a very interior village far from

Kolkata so possibly they don't celebrate Christmas there. That might be fueling his enthusiasm as he forces his twisted, deformed arm through the sleeve and awkwardly steps into the pants. The teachers look on proudly as Rajat does everything independently.

"The hat? The beard? What has happened to them?" I ask, looking about.

Khan finds them under a pile of boxes. Rajat stands proudly for a picture. All the kids start to clap.

"The room looks so pretty, but the tree," I say to the kids, "is bare. Would you like to make the decorations?"

We distribute scissors along with old Christmas cards that I carried from New Jersey, and the kids very meticulously cut out the designs: snowflakes, reindeer, Santa Clauses, candy canes, little elves. Next, they punch a hole at the top, attach a small string, and hang their creations on the tree. Those who can't walk drag themselves to the tree and hang their decoration on the bottom branches.

Then we distribute small gifts, each attractively wrapped. "These gifts are from Willeke Aunty. You know she loves you," I tell them.

Khan and I are headed to Sudder Street. The traffic hasn't abated. Neither has the noise, but we aren't complaining. We're *kvelling!*

"Khan, do you realize what we did today?"

Khan shrugs his answer.

"A Jew/Bu and a Muslim brought Christmas cheer to Hindu children."

Mr. Khan smiles imperceptibly.

> *As we let our own light shine, we unconsciously give other people permission to do the same.*
> —Marianne Williamson, spiritual activist, author, lecturer

There's a knock on the door. I'm not expecting anyone, and the small, mischievous kids in the building continue to delight in disturbing me by knocking and running, so I don't answer it. A second knock—a good sign. I get up and unlatch the door. I can't recognize the couple standing in front of me in the dark stairwell, but their greetings, heavily laced with an Irish brogue, give them away.

"We're just checking up on you," says Donneca in jest.

"You can do that anytime you want. Sinead, Donneca, come in. What a surprise."

Sinead and Donneca are Roisin's mother and father. After Roisin recovered from malaria, she returned to Ireland and began studying gardening. I'm thrilled to see them and get news about their daughter.

"Sit down. Sit down," I urge them. "Tell me about Roisin."

"She loves nature, so she is happy," Donneca replies.

"We just came from visiting Rosemary. She wants to open a tutorial center. Just fifteen small kids, to teach them the basics," interjects Sinead. "You're a teacher. What do you think?"

"I think it's a good idea. She's been teaching all her life. She's very kind-hearted and loves the children. I'm sure she'll make a success of it."

"We also met Patrick, Magdalene's son. He told us he wants to go to college," Donneca continues. "He's a clever boy. I think he can give it a go."

"Yes, it would be good for him," I agree.

"But Sultanah," Sinead says cautiously. "She also needs to go to school. Rosemary tells us she's in the house all day."

"What happened to the idea of free education?" asks Donneca sarcastically.

"Unfortunately, disabled kids don't get the same chance as non-disabled kids," I reply, telling him something he already knows.

"And poor kids in the village also don't get the same chance," he laments. "Don't get me started or I'll go on for hours."

Sinead, who has been lost in thought, says, "There must be a way for Sultanah to go back to school. If only Sister Cyril would let her re-enroll in Loreto School."

"It's the transport, always the transport," I remind her. "Sultanah isn't a small kid anymore. She's a teenager now, and Nasha can't push her wheelchair across Kolkata."

"Then maybe Sultanah can become a boarder at Loreto School. They do accept a number of boarders. That would solve the wheelchair problem. And on weekends, she could take a taxi home and visit her family. I'll speak with Sister Cyril today."

"Let me know if there's something I can do," I respond. "You know I'd do anything for Sultanah."

The following day, Donneca and Sinead are back with the news that Sister Cyril agreed that Sultanah can become a boarder student after she fulfills the requirements. They also announce that they're leaving Kolkata for a couple of weeks, going to southern India. They ask if I'll help Nasha enroll Sultanah. "She needs a letter, a formal request. Then she can fill out the application form," they say. "It shouldn't be too difficult."

*It shouldn't be too difficult.* Whenever I hear those words, I shudder!

I write a very detailed letter explaining the situation: Sultanah can't come from her house each day because she is wheelchair-bound and the distance is too great. Therefore, the family is requesting that she become a boarder at the school.

I give the letter to Nasha, and she goes to Loreto School to deliver it.

Unfortunately, Sister Cyril isn't there, and no one else will take the letter. She's told to come back in the evening.

Unfortunately, Sister Cyril is in a meeting in the evening, and Nasha is told to return in the morning.

Unfortunately, she goes again in the morning, and again she is turned away.

Nasha has become frantic and asks for Rosemary's help. After all, Rosemary is a teacher and speaks fluent English, so that should add some weight to the request.

Rosemary and Nasha go to Loreto School together. Sister Cyril isn't available, so they leave the letter with someone in the office.

Donneca and Sinead are back in Kolkata and have met with Sister Cyril. They were *not* turned away, a situation that I find interesting.

They bring the news that Sultanah will become a day student because Sister Cyril believes her family is now against the idea of her becoming a boarder. I'm shocked. The letter I wrote was very explicit and clearly stated that the family wants Sultanah to become a boarder.

Sinead and Donneca try to persuade Sister Cyril to change her mind, but she won't budge. So arrangements are being made for an *ayah* who will bathe and dress Sultanah in the morning, carry her down the three flights of stairs, and take her to school. The *ayah* will wait the whole day and then take her back home.

This sounds a lot more complicated than Sultanah becoming a boarder but, to my amazement, the arrangement works and Sultanah starts school.*

* *Sultanah attended Loreto School for several years, then transferred to the Indian Institute of Cerebral Palsy in 2012.*

Jubilation! Ashit has found a building. A building with papers. The sense of accomplishment is well-mixed with relief. Uncle is very proud of Ashit and now treats him like a son. For Reena, that caps the victory. They're eager for me to visit, and I give Mr. Khan general directions.

But now, Mr. Khan has the job of actually finding our new

school, Preyrona 3, which is in Krishnapur, a village outside Kolkata. Driving his beat-up, old, white Austin Ambassador taxi, once the luxury car of dignitaries but now rattling and sorely in need of new retread tires, he twists and turns down picturesque lanes lined with coconut trees and banana trees. The road is quiet and the people friendly, waving at a foreigner suddenly amongst them. The sense of community isn't lost on me. The people appear relaxed and content. I wonder to myself, "Why is Empower The Children opening a school here?" In Kolkata proper, the kids are dirt-poor and extremely needy. But the tranquility in Krishnapur belies a hidden, unspoken societal condition: illiteracy. Everyone may be happy, but no one can read or write.

Ashit and Reena are in a celebratory mood. They greet me with hugs and kisses. They toss flower petals onto my hair and force sweets into my mouth. They can't stop grinning as they show me around the still-empty, two-story building. They speak as one, pointing out all the features. "This will be one classroom and here is another classroom and there are two kitchens and two bathrooms and a covered, flat roof for drama practice and a small patch of land for a garden and the local people all want to help."

I keep congratulating them, but it doesn't seem like my approval means much to them. They keep giving me credit for the new building even though I had nothing to do with finding it or funding it.

"Thank you, thank you, thank you," they keep saying.

"I haven't done anything," I protest. "All the credit goes to Uncle and Ashit," which makes Ashit blush and turn away shyly.

"Without you, Ashit would not have searched for the new building," says Reena.

"Without *Uncle,* Ashit wouldn't have searched for the new building," I counter.

"Yes, of course, Uncle was most important, and we are so grateful to him, but, without your support, Uncle would not have trusted Ashit. You gave Ashit the chance to work with the poor children and prove himself. Now Uncle is happy with Ashit. The credit goes to you."

I can't dissuade them, so I accept their thanks graciously.

We're still dizzy with excitement as we go from room to room and plan the programs. There's one door that hasn't been opened yet. I assume it's a storage room or, in some way, not fit for a classroom, so I don't mention it.

Khan and I get ready to leave, and I finally ask the question that's been nagging at my mind all afternoon.

"Reena, what about Uncle? Has he been here yet? Is he happy with the building?"

"Uncle has not been here yet. We have been preparing for him. We are almost ready."

They guide me to the unopened door and, almost ceremoniously, open it. It's beautifully decorated and adorned with garlands. Incense is burning in front of a small altar. It's lovely.

"Uncle's room," they announce proudly. "He can stay here whenever he wants."

January 31, 2009. A big banner is draped across the door: "Welcome to Preyrona 3 School."

Without restraint, the conch is loudly sounded, pronouncing the importance of the occasion. Two small girls dressed in gold *saris* are waiting impatiently.

*When we do the best we can, we never know what miracle is wrought in our life, or in the life of another.*
—Helen Keller, author, political activist, lecturer

One tiny girl dips her finger into a paste and puts a *tilak* on the forehead of Willeke, our special guest. In 2006, a year after her first volunteer trip to Kolkata, Willeke founded Help2Help in The Netherlands to raise money for the children here. She's a terrific fundraiser, and the generosity of the Dutch people has enabled her to enrich the children's lives in countless ways.

On this trip, Willeke's husband, Erik, has accompanied her. He's so tall that he has to fold almost in half to receive the blessing. The other girl struggles to place a garland around his neck. Again, Erik bends down, almost to the floor. The only sound is the conch and, of course, the clicking of our cameras.

All volunteers receive this traditional welcome when they visit the schools, and they're thrilled and touched. The children give the volunteers from abroad due respect because they understand they are there to help them, and the volunteers realize that their contribution to the programs is taken seriously. The children also want to touch the volunteers' feet.

Volunteers bring with them a vote of confidence and communicate to the kids a new idea—that they are valued. When I tell the children that a volunteer came all the way from America or, in the case of Willeke and Erik, The Netherlands, they feel prized. Perhaps for the first time in their lives, they're the focus of someone's attention, not just another mouth to feed in a large family struggling to get by.

* * *

Samaya is young, just eight years old, but already she has absorbed social values about what is considered attractive. She was injured at the age of three-and-a-half when an unattached window fell on her head while she was playing with friends at a construction site. Her head is slightly flat on one side, and there's a distinct indentation near her ear. She complains of headaches, but mostly she's self-conscious.

"They think I am ugly," she tells Reena, often looking dejected.

But whenever volunteers come to the school, she suddenly brightens.

Reena is so happy to see the change. "Samaya, is your head feeling better?" she asks.

"No."

"Then why are you so happy today?"

"The visitors came from America."

"That makes you happy?"

"Yes."

"Why?"

"They love me, don't they?"

"Of course they do, Samaya."

I've heard this remark from the children many times. This is the uplifting power of a visit from a friend or even a stranger from a far-off land.

The drums echo through the coconut groves, audible from quite a distance. It doesn't sound like we're in India because these drums are deep and resonant whereas the *tabla* drum, traditionally used in Indian performances, has a quick, melodic quality.

Shelley Chatterjee, who created and funded women empowerment groups using her salary as a social worker, has brought me to Khamargachi, a tribal area in West Bengal about fifty kilometers east of Kolkata. I rode a local train an hour-and-a-half to get here.

The place is picture-postcard perfect—if you discount the underlying poverty and illiteracy. It's taken Shelley two years to gain the trust of this community, and now she wants Empower The Children to open a school for the tribal children.

I'm here because I trust Shelley. We teamed up six years ago, in 2003, to open Dankuni Tutorial Centre in Dankuni, a town one-half hour north by train from Howrah Station. Shelley identified for me a situation that, unfortunately, is widespread in India—many children attend a local school but, because of parental illiteracy, receive no support at home. Shelley proposed that Empower The Children rent a small room and hire teachers to assist students with their homework and exam preparation. The Dankuni Tutorial Centre proved to be so successful that, in 2005, we added a morning session.

I also trust her to lead me through the darkness that has enveloped Khamargachi. Walking slowly and carefully along narrow paths, we approach a large, open field where everyone is waiting for me. I'm used to this: "Rosalie is coming. Get ready for her presentation, her photos, her story." But this time, it's different. They don't want to hear about me. Instead, they want me to understand something about them and their unique Santali culture.

The girls and women are dressed in colorful traditional tribal dress, their necks adorned with garland leis. Some men wear *lungis*; some are sporting shirts; others have bare chests. The drums are enormous, hung by leather thongs around the men's necks, but the men seem comfortable carrying them. The excitement is palpable as I approach. The members of the community recognize that the fate of their new school rests with me. This adds to my excitement—and pressure—too.

After a few *short* speeches, also unusual at Indian performances where lengthy speech-making has become an art, the men start to play. The drums have such a powerful sound that it makes the whole area pulsate with a repetitive beat that seems to affect the rhythm of my heart. After quite a long time, the women and girls emerge from a shadow. They dance a very simple, rhythmic, repetitive step, moving slowly in a circle as the drummers move with them.

I sit spellbound, hypnotized by the traditional music and the fires burning brightly. The students are singing in Santali, which sounds nothing like Hindi or Bengali. I try to pick out anything in the scene that seems familiar, but this is definitely a unique experience. I feel privileged to be here.

It doesn't take me long to make my decision. The presence of the entire community tonight has told me what I need to know—that the school will not run in isolation but has the backing of the tribe. The children will receive

> *If you think in terms of a year, plant a seed; if in terms of ten years, plant trees; if in terms of 100 years, teach the people.*
> —Confucius, teacher, politician, editor, philosopher

encouragement and support from a strong, close-knit society. These are the ingredients for success. This future school in Khamargachi, with Shelley as the director, has the blessings of Empower The Children simply because the children have the blessings of their parents.

# Greater Horizons
## Early 2009–Early 2010

Fiona, a Scottish volunteer, emailed me a few months ago that a serendipitous thing had happened. While distributing flyers for an upcoming fundraiser, a colleague told her, "My wife would be interested in what Empower The Children is doing in Kolkata. She grew up there." Fiona contacted her colleague's wife, Liz, and found that she was interested in more than just the fundraiser. She hoped to start a cross-cultural exchange between Perth/Kinross schools in Scotland and Empower The Children schools in India.

So, off I go to Scotland, flying from New Jersey, in May 2009 to meet Liz and the Scottish students. Liz is a Councillor of the Perth and Kinross Council in Scotland, and she has vision. She wants the world to be a better place and understands the necessity of everybody doing their share to make that happen.

"We strive to inspire our children to be more than good students, to also be good citizens and rights-respecting individuals," Liz explains. "The United Nations has prescribed four specific standards: values, the whole school community, ethos, and child empowerment.[41] If a school meets those standards, it can become a rights-respecting school. That has become our goal."

I'm impressed by Liz's passion. It's easy for me to become impassioned living in a developing country, but it may be equally easy to become complacent in a rich, thriving country where most people's needs are met with relative ease. I smile as I listen. Liz is my age and has the same ideals that drove many of my college friends to join the Peace Corps and go on Civil Rights marches.

"Liz, I must tell you. When Fiona emailed me that you'd grown up in Kolkata—or Calcutta as you called it then—I thought you were Indian."

"Indian? With a name like Liz Grant?"

"Well, I thought maybe Liz was a nickname for a difficult-to-roll-your-tongue-around Indian name and that you had married a man named Grant."

Liz chuckles at my logic.

"So how is it you grew up in Kolkata?"

"My father was the manager of a jute mill. At that time, the British were the managers and the Indians were the workers. I'm glad that has changed."

"Yes, now, the rich Indians are the managers, and the poor Indians are the workers. Unfortunately, for the poor people in India, not a lot has actually changed."

"That's why I'd like our students to help your students. You know Jan Caldwell, our citizenship coordinator, spoke to our students a few months ago and asked them if they

*Before you embark on any path, ask the question: Does this path have a heart?*
—Carlos Castaneda, author

thought they could make a difference in the world, or not. Almost all of them said, 'No.' Maybe something will change after exposure to your students' lives."

"We'll send your students photos and artwork and videos of

dramas and alphabet books," I ramble on enthusiastically. "Our kids love making all those things."

"We'll do the same and we'll raise money. Maybe *our* kids can feed *your* kids," Liz says idealistically. "Then they will realize they *can* make a difference."*

* *Starting in 2009, the cultural exchange project between the Perth/ Kinross students and the Kolkata students continued for more than three years.*

\* \* \*

The music at Preyrona 3 School is blaring, but for once I don't mind. Fiona, and her friends Kirsty, Richard, and Kim have come from Perth to bring a bit of Scottish culture into the lives of our kids, starting with a jig.

"Step, step, clap. Step, step, clap. Turn, whirl, turn. Whirl, turn, clap. Now you try it," says Fiona as Reena, who loves to dance, demonstrates and translates into Bengali.

The kids, ages five to fifteen, line up two by two and follow Fiona's lead. It's hard to hear her directions over the music, so eventually everyone's efforts dissolve into gales of laughter.

"This is a kilt," Kirsty continues after everyone is seated on the floor. "The men wear a kilt when they play the bagpipes. Would anyone like to try it on?"

Of course, everyone wants to try it on even though it's made of heavy-weight wool and Kolkata is hot and humid.

"And here are some pictures of Perth," says Kirsty. "The telephone booth is red, and the streets are lined with baskets of flowers. It is very pretty in Perth."

The kids stare at the pictures in awe. The streets are clean and wide, with only a single car on the road—an impossible sight, both the cleanliness and the single car, in Kolkata.

"In the winter, snow falls," continues Kirsty.

Reena realizes that the kids have no experience of cold weather, so she isn't exactly sure how to translate snow. She tells them, "Scotland is covered with ice cream in the winter."

The kids react with disbelief.

"Look at the picture," she persists. "There is vanilla ice cream over everything."

That brings whoops, shouts, and probably a fair measure of jealousy. Ice cream? Over everything?

"This is a picture of a castle," says Kim. "The king and queen live in a castle."

There's no king or queen in India, so Reena changes those terms of royalty into *raja* and *rani*. Many Indian men are named Raj, a short form of Maharajah, a Sanskrit word that means "great king," so the kids understand.

"And here is a Highlands cow," says Kim. "It has long horns and thick, shaggy hair. It looks very different than cows in India. The Highlands cow would feel very, very hot in Kolkata."

Richard gets up in front of the class. "Now, we will look at a pop-up book. It has many different stories. The first is about the Loch Ness Monster. It lives in a lake called Ness, and its name is Nessie. Do you believe Nessie really exists?"

With a show of hands, the kids give Nessie a vote of confidence. The kids pass around the book, not realizing something very significant—if they hold the book flat, the pictures won't pop up. It's such a simple thing and taken for granted in Scotland or America, yet we must show each individual child in this small classroom in Kolkata how to hold a pop-up book.

"We must dress this Scottish lad," Kim says when Richard completes his part of the lesson. "He will be cold in Scotland without his hat and kilt." She distributes a piece of paper with the outline of a boy and a piece of plaid material. "Glue the material on his head and body, then draw the Scottish hills in the background and even a castle if you have time."

Everyone gets to work immediately. Afterward, they hold up

their pictures proudly and shout, "Aunty. Aunty. Uncle. Uncle."

These wonderful volunteers from Scotland repeat this lesson in seven schools over the next seven days. Each time, the children and teachers reward them with the same enthusiastic response.

The kids in Kolkata are opening their minds to the wonders of another culture. Hopefully, the kids in Scotland are opening their hearts to their less fortunate Indian friends.

All the volunteers love the kids at Preyrona 2 School. Though the children are poor, living along the railroad tracks in impoverished conditions, they've retained a sweetness and innocence that's endearing. They come to school early every day. As they wait for the door to be opened, their queue snakes along the narrow lane and spills out onto the road.

In the single classroom, now more than 70 children sit on the floor shoulder-to-shoulder. When both teachers are teaching at once, they divide the children by age and teach different subjects. The cacophony of languages includes Urdu, Hindi, Bengali, and English. The atmosphere is rich, but the school is as poor as the kids. And this is the subject of endless discussions among myself, Reena, and Ashit.

"The kids at Preyrona 2 are the only ones who eat a cold lunch," I mention for the tenth time.

"There is no kitchen and no room to build one," Reena replies. "It is a very congested area."

"They get only bread, an egg, and a banana each day. No variation. It must be so boring," I remind them even though they need no reminder.

"They never complain," Ashit answers proudly.

"The kids at Preyrona 3 School get rice and a different vegetable each day. It isn't fair," I continue.

"We asked for permission to bring cooked food in from outside, but the local authorities did not agree. They said it was too dangerous to carry hot cauldrons through a crowded neighborhood." Reena says, knowing that I'm already aware of this.

Yes, we're rehashing an old conversation, always hoping that a new solution will emerge.

"And the room? It's cold in the winter and wet during the monsoon. The poor kids. In school, they should enjoy better conditions than they must endure at home," I lament.

This is like preaching to the converted because Ashit and Reena are almost obsessed with finding a new building for the school, so my complaints are unnecessary. But when I teach at Preyrona 2, I feel for the kids there. Women cook for their families in the narrow lane, and the smoke comes in through the gaps in the roof and the open doors. The smoke is irritating, so the kids rub their eyes and noses throughout my lesson, and I keep clearing my throat.

I hate to put Ashit and Reena under pressure, but I keep thinking that if we brainstorm enough we can come up with an answer. We always have before—with other schools.

"We can't give up," I say. "We have to keep putting it out to the Universe that we want a new building, and, eventually, we'll get it."

"It will cost a lot of money," Ashit mentions almost inaudibly.

"It's true, but somehow we'll get the money. I know it."

\* \* \*

Willeke cries easily, so when she sees the conditions at Preyrona 2 School, her eyes fill with tears. "It's just the smoke," she says quickly. "It burns when I wear my contact lenses." She looks around at the children and, although she knows we're helpless to do anything, she feels compelled to ask, "How much would it cost to build a new school?"

"A lot of money," I reply. "More than Empower The Children can afford to spend."

"What's a lot of money?" Willeke is an accountant, so numbers don't frighten her.

"About twelve *lakh*," I answer. "That's 27,000 dollars. More than 17,000 euros. This is a very congested area, so our building options are limited."

She replies, "There's a town in Holland called Grjipskerke where the people select one project each year to receive the money they raise at their annual bazaar. This is a small community of only about 1,000 people, so it is a huge endeavor, months in the planning. People come from the nearby communities and donate thousands of items to be sold. Everything is categorized and organized inside a gymnasium. It's a gala event, and food and beer add to the festive atmosphere. Last year, a charity in Kenya, Mama Mzungu, received a donation of about that amount to drill water wells. On September 11, 2010, the people of Grjipskerke are having their thirtieth annual fundraiser. The town gets a lot of proposals, so maybe we don't have a good chance, but why don't we try? Send a proposal for a new building, and I'll translate it into Dutch."

Willeke may be an accountant, but she's also as creative as an artist. Her photos catch the longing in the kids' eyes, their yearning for a better life. So, I interject, "Attach your Kolkata photos. Don't forget. They tell the whole story."

"I'll work on it as soon as I get home," she promises.

"But do you have time?"

"I'll make time," she assures me. "These kids are as important as my clients' balance sheets."

I can see that Willeke is buoyed by the idea of submitting the proposal.

> *I always feel if you do right, right will follow.*
>
> —Oprah Winfrey, media proprietor, talk show host, actress, producer, philanthropist

"When's the deadline for the proposal?" I inquire.

"It has to be submitted by October 31."

"And when do they announce the selection?"

"On November 16."

"When do I start praying?" I ask. "Now or on November 16?"

"Start praying now!"

*I'm being lowered from a cliff onto a narrow ledge. I'm terrified. Below is a deep cavern, certain death if I were to fall. I'm told to say, "I am beneath God." I say the words in a trembling voice.*

*I walk along the ledge, clutching the rock, searching for indentations or bulges, anything for my fingers to grasp. If I succeed in walking along the ledge, then someone gets a gift.*

*I walk in a daze until I reach the end. I repeat this again. It's no easier the second time. I'm breathless with fear.*

*I try a third time, but I can't move. I can't find anything to hold onto. I feel paralyzed. I call out, "I can't do it. I can't walk."*

*Someone pulls me up off the ledge, back onto the cliff.*

I wake up. My mind is confused. Usually, I'm able to interpret my dreams, but this one is so powerful that I don't know where to begin.

My friend Carole, who is a counselor in the fields of psychotherapy, mind/body medicine, and metaphysics, sends an email from America and gives her interpretation. She writes: "You feel like your life depends upon your success. That you can't fail under any circumstances, but you're terrified that you will fail. Perhaps this is how you feel about your work. You must succeed in order to help the children. Failure isn't an option. You're compelled to succeed because then someone gets a gift. That must be the children in the programs. They receive the gift of a better future." Then she delivers the good news. "But when you can't do it anymore, then someone rescues you, saves you. So you aren't alone."

"It takes a long time to say hello at Prabartak Home," I explain to Kathy, a volunteer from Alaska, as we get out of the taxi. Before we even reach the front door, the residents are gathering around us, hugging us, shaking our hands, and pantomiming as they speak to us excitedly in Bengali.

"They always have a lot to say since we started bringing the outside world into their lives," I explain to her. "On Monday, they have music; on Tuesday, they have art; on Wednesday, drama; on Thursday, vocational training; on Friday, literacy; and on Saturday, my class. Their schedule is as busy as mine," I add laughing.

"They're so happy," Kathy says.

"Yes, everyone notices the same thing. The Prabartak team— Mr. and Mrs. Ganguly, the staff, and Empower The Children—have made an investment in these kids' lives and it's paid off."

The kids are tugging at our arms and pulling us into the classroom. They're pointing at the pictures of the drama they'd recently performed, which are displayed on a bulletin board.

"Me, me," says one boy, pointing to a picture of a king in an elaborate robe and dramatic make-up.

"Beautiful," Kathy tells him.

Each one, in turn, proudly points to his or her picture, smiling broadly.

"They certainly are full of life," Kathy comments.

"When I first came here nearly six years ago, they were just as sweet and loving but not independent. During my lessons, I had to help them with everything. Of course, some of that was because they wanted attention, but a lot of it was lack of self-confidence. Then, one day, I told the class, 'I have a bad back and can't keep bending down to help you. It hurts too much. Please complete the lesson without any help today.' And guess what? Except for the really disabled students, they all worked independently, and that's how it's been since."

"You must be really pleased," Kathy says.

"I am." Then, to the residents, I call out, "*Bosho, bosho.* Sit, sit."

It takes a while, but finally everyone is sitting on mats on the floor, and we're ready to start the lesson.

Alok has become very busy with many other responsibilities so my every-Saturday translator now is Nandu who taught herself English by watching television. When I call her "teacher," she blushes with pride.

I walk over to the wall map and point to Alaska, then tracing with my finger, make a long arc to Kolkata. "Kathy has come all the way from Alaska to be with you today," I tell them. They laugh and clap appreciatively. They're always thrilled when someone from far away cares enough about them to come and visit.

"*Chup.* Quiet. Listen to Rosalie Aunty," Nandu gently admonishes.

"Today, we will talk about snakes," I continue, and they nod and smile. I read a fact book about snakes, and they add to my lesson with information they've already learned on the Discovery Channel and Animal Planet. Then they make snakes by covering cardboard tubes with colored tissue paper and finish them by gluing pieces of ribbon to make long red tongues and adding black wiggly eyes.

"*Khub bhalo*, very good," I tell them and they swell with pride.

"The snakes are really cute," Kathy notes.

"All the lessons were developed by speech teachers in America, my colleagues. They're the ones who deserve the credit."

"But you bring the lessons to life for these young people. You make them want to learn and participate. That's the most important thing."

We're both right, of course. Educating young people in any nation where schooling is not a universal norm requires the knowledge of experts in cultures that value education as well as the local teachers who work hands-on with the children. In other words, for greatest success, it takes an international team.

Now Amit brings out his *tabla,* a pair of drums of contrasting size and timbre, and starts to play. One by one, the kids get up to dance, each in his or her own way. Kathy dances with them, which I really appreciate. Here, on this day, Kathy is part of that international team.

"Okay, time for us to leave," I announce.

Everyone gathers around as Kathy takes a digital picture and shows it to them on the camera screen. Then she lets them take pictures of her, which they do very carefully, respecting her camera.

"*Byas.* Enough," I say again and again, but everyone, including Kathy, is reluctant for our departure. "*Chalo,* let's go! Let's make a move," I insist and finally we start from the classroom.

The kids hug us even as we walk, which makes descending the stairs almost impossible. They like to carry our bags to the taxi, so we let them. They ask Kathy if she will return, and she pantomimes that she will fly home next week. The kids are disappointed, but they don't let that news ruin their mood. They've seen dozens of volunteers come and go. They understand that I'm the only one who will be there every Saturday. We finally get outside and into the taxi. They pick some flowers from a nearby bush and press them into our hands. They wave wildly as the taxi pulls away.

"I haven't felt so loved since my husband proposed to me," Kathy says with a wink. "They are so attentive."

"Yes, they are." Then, smiling with satisfaction, I add, "It takes a long time to say good-bye at Prabartak Home."

"This woman is different!" This is what I would say to myself each time I attended a committee meeting at A.I.W.C. Buniadi Bidypith High School where I noticed an attractive woman in her late fifties wearing a fashionable *salwar kameez*—and *sneakers* rather than the usual stylish sandals. Her name is Arundhati, and she's principal of the school's pre-primary section. Over the years, we've become close friends.

Her family hails from Gopalnagar, a village three hours south of Kolkata. She has very warm memories of weekend outings to her familial home—memories of picnics, eating fruit picked fresh from the trees, swimming in the pond with her cousins. "I almost drowned because I was forced to swim with a *sari,*" she tells me with a chuckle. "It was dead weight when it became wet. No bathing suits in those days!"

It's been a long time since anyone except Professor Mitra, Arundhati's father, has taken an interest in going to the village. Arundhati's siblings have scattered to Australia and Luxemburg, and her own children are living in Delhi and Mumbai. For this reason, her father donated the land and house to the village so that it can be used for a school.

Driving through lush countryside, Arundhati, her father, and I easily forget the noise, pollution, and chaos of Kolkata. Even though I've been in India more than I've been anyplace else for nearly a decade, the contrast between city and country is never lost on me. Each time I step outside the city, I feel like I'm joyously stepping into a completely different world. The sensation seems to amplify, not diminish, with time.

Here, the trees are hung with bananas and coconuts. Red flowers punctuate the gardens. People walk effortlessly with huge bundles balanced on their heads. Water is drawn from the community well. Animals roam aimlessly. Serenity comes to mind.

The car carries us as far as possible, and then we walk. But, unlike Kolkata, it's a pleasure to walk here. The air is fresh, and the footpath isn't crowded. Arundhati's father is aged, so two men come to his assistance. Very tenderly, they guide him to the house and help him into a chair. We are hot and thirsty, so the school principal whacks six coconuts from a nearby tree and offers them to us. The milk is sweet yet thirst-quenching. A simple, satisfying lunch has been prepared, but first we want to see the school.

Even with very meager funds, the villagers have managed to renovate the building. They've plastered the walls, hung ceiling fans, and stuffed several bookcases with school supplies. The six blackboards in this one-room schoolhouse delineate the classes: first blackboard is Class 1, second blackboard is Class 2, and so on.

The students are surprised to see a foreigner and stare at me, but not rudely. They have an innocence that was lost long ago in the West. They welcome the guests in the usual way: sing their songs, recite nursery rhymes, and play the harmonium. I've seen it countless times. In fact, we do the same when visitors come to our Preyrona schools—it's nothing original or imaginative; it's their custom. We applaud appreciatively and then leave for lunch.

After we finish eating, Arundhati and I take a walk, and she shows me a small stone temple, quite deteriorated but still used by the local people during *pujas*.

Our walk is cut short because the students have prepared a special program for us. I'd rather wander around for a while longer, but, of course, we can't disappoint them. The program is taking place behind the school in a large field. Chairs have been set up so we can watch it comfortably. A large mat covers an area of grass.

The school principal tells us that twelve students will participate. "They have been studying gymnastics. They want you to see what they have learned," he says.

The students perform for twenty minutes, easily manipulating their bodies into pretzel-like positions and somersaulting across the mat, sometimes in tandem. To add a dramatic finish, they form a human pyramid, and those on top twirl their bodies like kites twisting in the wind.

"I'm impressed," I exclaim. "And it's been a long time since I've said those words. The children are doing something innovative and unique."

The students' gymnastic teacher is humbly suppressing a smile but is obviously proud.

We congratulate the students wholeheartedly, and they touch our feet.*

*\* Because of my visit to Gopalnagar and my subsequent conversation with the same Indian businessman who supported Mitali's Girls Coaching Centre and Bulbulir Basa Orphanage, he came forward to fund the educational program in this village.*

\* \* \*

It's getting late, so we have to go. We're given gifts of local handicrafts and made to promise that we'll return again soon. I haven't felt so relaxed in months. I hope to take that feeling back to Kolkata and hold on to it for as long as possible, but, as we approach the city, the noise starts to build, the pollution blows through the windows, and the traffic forces our car to crawl.

Suddenly, we pull off the road, and the driver informs us that we have a flat tire. We get out of the car, and he begins to fix it. Slowly but steadily, we are surrounded by local people, staring very intrusively.

My patience is growing thin and, very snappishly, I ask Arundhati, "Haven't these people ever seen a tire being changed before?"

She speaks with them in Bengali then begins to laugh.

"Why are you laughing? What did they say?" I ask rather rudely.

"They aren't staring at the tire. They're staring at your hair. They want to know if it's real or a wig."

Then my tension breaks, and I start to laugh too. When I do, the people surrounding us also laugh. When the tire is fixed, we get back in the car, and this crowd of impromptu spectators waves us off enthusiastically.

"You know, Arundhati, it's hard to stay mad for long in Kolkata. The noise, pollution, and traffic are maddening, but the people, like the children, have retained their innocence."

"The star is an amputee. She wears a wooden leg but is very graceful in her movements," says Kakali, who is preparing a dance recital to be performed by the patients at Rehabilitation Centres for Children. Although they're all orthopedically disabled, they love to dance. So when they hear that special donors are coming, they seize upon the opportunity to perform. "It will be held in the auditorium," Kakali informs me. "That location makes them feel important."

I arrive in time for the traditional greeting: the wail of the conch shell, a dab of *tilak* on my forehead as a blessing, and a garland of flowers around my neck. No matter how many times I receive this greeting, I'm always touched. It's so personal because it takes time, it takes preparation, and it takes effort. In contrast, the Western tradition of a handshake or hug is so fleeting and casual.

Children who are able to walk, no matter how clumsily, escort the guests one by one to the auditorium. Then, together, they slowly ascend a flight of stairs and find a seat. There's a group of donors from Holland and a group from Scotland who fill the front row. A board member from RCFC stands on the sidelines, prepared to go to the podium with a speech. Teachers and other invited guests occupy the rest of the seats. In the last row, the mothers of the babies who underwent surgery sit and wait, ready to leave suddenly if the baby starts to fuss. There's an air of excitement in the room but also a degree of seriousness. We all wish for the kids to succeed.

The star is the first to perform. She's dressed in a startling beautiful costume of red and gold. Her wooden leg is covered with a white sock and looks a bit thicker and rounder than her other leg.

The music starts, and she begins. She is lovely on the stage, and, even though the music stops twice because of problems with the sound system, she doesn't falter. She receives thunderous applause.

The rest of the kids hobble onto the stage. They're dressed in simple but charming costumes. Club feet, twisted limbs, crooked spines—nothing stops them from performing. Each child has a chance to move in a loosely choreographed style as the others follow along in the background, swaying their arms and hips. It takes a long time for each solo, but no one minds.

We think that the performance has ended, but there's a surprise waiting for us. The kids quickly remove their costumes and in their everyday clothes perform a pantomime centered around the daily activities of a balloon seller. The child who is the balloon seller mimes each action so intricately and with such attention to detail that the audience is spellbound. The rest of the children hold their wind-swept imaginary balloons with delight. It's a beautiful scene.

The audience is so happy for the kids that we each feel a personal sense of achievement. Their success has become our success. Their triumph is our triumph.

There's a big advantage to having a large school building like Preyrona 3. We can offer many more programs—even one for mothers. So now voices of adult women are echoing throughout the classroom as they sit around a table, clutching their notebooks filled with measurements, patterns, and sample clothing. Their goal is to learn tailoring skills and eventually become independent, but at the moment it's their self-esteem that speaks to me.

"If you have faith in me, then I have faith in myself," says Banni. "I cannot believe I am getting this training for free."

"You are giving me respect, so now I have self-respect," adds

Pyle. "Earlier, only my husband and his family got recognition. Now they are giving me recognition."

Everyone nods in agreement. The women proudly show me what they've learned to make: *sari* blouses, petticoats, men's shorts, *salwar* pants, undergarments, baby sets. They stitch the clothes by hand and then on the sewing machine. I praise them profusely and my praises are sincere.

"Because I'm helpless with a needle and thread, that has made me dependent upon tailors and darners my whole life," I tell them, and they laugh.

"We will teach you, Aunty," they promise.

It's 2:00 in the afternoon, and my stomach starts to growl. Everyone hears it. This generates more laughter, of course.

"We get our household work done, and then we come to class," one woman tells me. "Sometimes we have no time to eat, but we do not mind. We so much like to learn that we do not miss the food."

My rumbling stomach reminds me that I do the same thing. When work occupies my mind, I forget to eat. But I don't encourage this and, instead, say, "Try to eat before you come. We want you to stay healthy. You are important members of your families."

This idea—that the women need to be respected as important members of their families—was exactly Reena's sentiment when she proposed the idea for this adult vocational class. "There is plenty of room at Preyrona 3. Let us start a program for the women. This will be good not only for them but also for their children."

I had looked at her skeptically, so she persisted.

"Imagine how much this will help the children, knowing that their mothers are going to school. This gives importance to education. It will affect the whole family."

I didn't argue with her then, but I wasn't convinced that a tailoring program can change a life. Now, six months later, I realize that Reena was right, and as I'm leaving the vocational room, a young woman grabs my arm and her words give me final confirmation.

"If you have no money or means of earning, then you are dependent upon others and you feel bad. Through this training, I will become independent. Then I will be a *perfect woman.*"

> *There is room at the top for everyone.*
> —Anonymous

Almost with shock, I realize that these words encapsulate everything that I came to India on my own to learn—to be a perfect woman. When I traveled with Art and he made all the decisions, I was far from perfect, nothing more than a willing, mostly silent tagalong. Somewhere deep inside, I knew something was missing from the experience. In the past, when I carried no money and was dependent on Art, I felt bad and, at times, even panic-stricken. With her words, this woman has reminded me that I have become independent. Though not a perfect woman, I'm further along in that direction than ever before. And if I can help these women become independent, then … well, then we're all a little bit closer to perfection.

Shalom Israel. I can't think of a more Jewish name. Shalom is a *landsman,* a fellow Jew, living in Kolkata. How did he come to be written up in a newspaper in Philadelphia? My friend Bernice sent the article to me, and I'm reading it with pleasure. So far, the only contact I've had with Jews in Kolkata has been when buying an occasional sweet bun at Nahoum & Sons Jewish Confectioners in New Market.

Shalom Israel. I can't stop *kvelling* over his name and the significance of his presence here. When the nation of Israel was created in 1948,[42] 6,000 Jews were living in this city. But the vast majority soon left for Israel, as well as the United States, Canada, and England. Today, Shalom Israel is one of only thirty Jews who remain.[43]

He looks after synagogues, once splendid but now echoing with emptiness. I remember meeting a Jewish woman in Vancouver, British Columbia, who grew up in Kolkata. She told me wistfully, "At that time, the synagogues were full."

Shalom also takes care of the remaining Jews, all elderly, and he handles their burial when that time comes. But here's something disturbing. The article says Shalom lives in the Jewish cemetery. I picture a hovel amidst the gravestones. *Oy vey!*

I quickly call my Jewish friend Nan who lives in McLeod Ganj but visits every November for the Kolkata Film Festival. "Nan, when you come this year, we have to do something to help this man I just read about, Shalom Israel. He's living in poverty, dedicating his life to others." I read the article to her.

"We can find the Jewish cemetery and ask him what he needs," she says sensibly.

"Don't you think we should be prepared before we meet him?" I ask apprehensively. "Bring him something immediately?" I suggest.

"What are you thinking about?"

"I can spare a few thousand rupees. He can use it for himself."

"And I can bring a brass holder for a *yahrzeit* candle. That would be appropriate because it's the candle lit in memory of the dead. If there are only elderly Jewish people left in Kolkata, it will get more use than sitting in my cupboard."

When Nan arrives, we go in search of Shalom Israel. Mr. Khan isn't available, so we hail a roaming taxi. "Jewish cemetery. Jewish cemetery," we call out through the window of the taxi. The driver circles around and around, hopelessly lost. By the time we get there, our nerves are frayed. We had assumed that the cemetery would be a small place, but, to our surprise, it's spacious. The graves are well maintained and clearly marked, quite unlike the Jewish cemetery in Yangoon, Burma, that I attempted to visit last year. The caretaker at the synagogue there discouraged me from walking or exploring; he said the cemetery was so overgrown with uncleared weeds that the gravestones had become buried beneath the entangled vegetation.

To our relief, Shalom lives in a large stone house on the grounds. I give him the article, Nan gives him the *yahrzeit* candle holder, and we chat. I decide not to give him the money I brought; it no longer seems necessary.

He shows us around the cemetery, pointing out the newest grave, that of his father who died a couple of years ago. Shalom shows no emotion, but I can't help wonder, "What will become of the cemetery and his life after the few remaining Jews are also dead and buried?"

"The Jews came to this city from Syria, Iran, and Iraq and thrived as traders," he tells us. "They once held important positions and were well respected. There was never any prejudice because their numbers were so small that they weren't even considered a minority." He pauses a moment. "Now, the number has dwindled to near extinction," he says with resignation. "I feel a responsibility toward them. How else can they manage?"

I know it's a bit cheeky, but I can't resist asking, "If the only Jews left in Kolkata are elderly, how will you marry?"

Shalom doesn't answer, but shrugs his shoulders and blushes.

He asks about Nan's activities in McLeod Ganj and my work in India. Nan doesn't offer much in the way of reply, but I answer with some embellishment about my early days at Daya Dan that brought me to Kolkata and now the Preyrona schools and others. So, as we're getting ready to leave, we do the usual: exchange mobile numbers and email addresses and promise to stay in touch even though there's no apparent reason to do so.

But just out of curiosity, without being intrusive, I casually ask,

"Shalom, how do you support yourself?" I'm embarrassed to tell him that we'd pictured him as destitute.

"I'm a teacher of the deaf. Call me if you need me."

* * *

"They're not deaf. They're not deaf. They can all hear *something.*" Shalom Israel is speaking quickly and excitedly. With the opening of Preyrona 3 School, we enrolled four deaf students, and I realized immediately that they would need special attention. I still feel guilty that we couldn't help Subhagya's partially sighted brother, and I don't want to make the same mistake with these children. I thought of Shalom and asked if he would help.

He had taken the four students from Preyrona 3 School and two residents from Prabartak Home for audiological evaluations to determine if they have any residual hearing and is now delivering his report.

"I wish I could have been there to see their eyes when they heard the first beep," I reply elatedly.

"It was a long day. I picked up the kids from Prabartak and brought them to the doctor's office. It took more than a half hour for each one to be tested, but they waited very patiently. Tarala was acting like a typical teenager and wanted to know every detail of what was happening before she would cooperate. Sunil, who is mentally limited, was nervous and, at first, couldn't follow the directions, but eventually he relaxed."

"And what about the kids from Preyrona 3 School?" I ask.

"They were fine. They understood what was expected of them."

"And when do they get fitted for the hearing aids?"

"They've already been fitted. As long as they were at the office, we didn't want to waste any time. Jannie is here from Holland for only two weeks and this is her special donation, so we want everything completed. We'll bring the kids on Monday to have the aids placed in their ears."

"Yes," I agree. "Jannie deserves to see it completed. She spent the last year tirelessly fundraising."

"The kids became more animated when they were fitted with the aids," Shalom continues. "You could see it in their eyes. They became brighter."

"Will the kids use them properly? Do they understand the importance of the hearing aids to their lives?" I ask nervously. "After all, they're very expensive. We don't want them wasted."

"They understand the importance already and they haven't even received them yet. You know that radio that Sunil carries around with him?" Shalom asks.

"Yes, it's never on the station properly. It's mostly static. I keep fixing it, but he doesn't seem to know the difference," I reply.

"Well, after Sunil was fitted with the sample, he kept repeating, 'Music, music, music.' He was never able to enjoy the radio before, but with the hearing aid, he'll hear music instead of static."

"A simple thing like that, bringing music into the life of a child. We're lucky, aren't we?" I ask of Shalom.

"Yes, we are," he replies. "We are very lucky."

I see two small words in an email—*We won!*—and my heart starts to pound. It's amazing how the simplest phrase can carry so much meaning and evoke such strong emotions: He died. Get lost. Be mine. Try again. I care. *We won!*

I stare at those words, and I feel like Willeke has sent a huge bunch of colorful balloons all the way from Holland. "We won" was all she wrote, but that's enough to conjure up images of a new school in Dakhindari to replace the decrepit Preyrona 2 School: a school with a bathroom, kitchen, classrooms, vocational equipment, and computers; a school with a roof that doesn't leak, windows that close properly so that cooking smoke from outside doesn't waft in, and children sitting on benches instead of shoulder-to-shoulder on mats on the floor. Oh, how two small words can fire up the imagination!

I try to reign in my excitement. "This is India. Anything is possible," everyone says. It's possible we'll have a new school, and it's possible we won't. It's possible that this new school will have these wonderful features, and it's possible that it won't.

I lean back, away from the computer screen, to think.

Thanks to Willeke, the people of Grjipskerke have promised to raise money for a new Preyrona 2. Now we have to either locate the owner of the land and building or find a different plot nearby.

But what about the papers? We know the futility of finding land with proper papers.

Willeke's two little words have sparked so much—What? Joy? Hope? Despair? All at the same time? How is *that* possible?

> ***Trust your hopes, not your fears.***
> —David Mahoney, author

Too many questions are racing like mischievous monkeys through my head. I call Reena.

"Reena, Willeke's proposal was accepted. The people in Holland will send money so we can replace Preyrona 2."

"I am dancing," she says joyfully. "This is very good news for us."

"But who owns the land?"

"Oh, ho. That is the problem. It is used by the club authority, but, actually, it is occupied land. They have no papers."

"So how will we buy it from them?"

"Very difficult. If the club authority gives us papers, they will be false documents."

"So what do we do?"

"We must find the owner. If we do not have proper papers, then, in the future, someone can come along and claim the land and close our school."

"Is that possible? To find the owner, I mean?"

"I think it is not possible."

"What should I tell Willeke?"

"That is very difficult. Willeke has worked so hard, and we do not want her disappointed, but she has to know the truth. The land is occupied, and it is impossible to trace the original owner."

"I hate to do it, but I'll write to her. This isn't going to be easy."

I sit in front of a blank computer screen. I had planned to replace her two words, "We won," with two words of my own, "I'm thrilled," but instead I'm forced to write, "No hope."

\* \* \*

Ashit refuses to accept "no hope." He also doesn't want to move Preyrona 2 to a new location. "Muslim parents do not allow their children to go too far from their neighborhood," he says. "I want to find the owner and build where we are now, for the children who are now attending."

> *If you want to get something,*
> *you have to know where you want*
> *to go and how to get there.*
> *Then never, never, never give up.*
> —Norman Vincent Peale, minister, author

In the late fall of 2009, he starts a search of the municipal records going back sixty years to the time of India's Independence in 1947. At that time, due to sectarian violence across the country, people traveled in opposite directions: Muslims to Pakistan and East Pakistan (now Bangladesh) and Hindus to India. They left their legally owned land and settled on whatever land was available just to be among people of their shared religion. The question of who owned the land was moot.

Fortunately, since the late 1940s, the Indian government saw a need for all transactions to be duly recorded and recorded and recorded again into what is a bureaucratic maze of over-abundant paperwork. For example, when Art and I went to a bank in Mysore in 1982 to cash a traveler's check, the transaction was carefully entered into ledger after ledger after ledger. The bank's back wall, from floor to ceiling, was completely hidden by stacks of dirty, moldy, mouse-eaten ledgers. It seems they are never discarded.

Ashit is hoping that this obsessive retention of documents will help him uncover the land's owner and, hopefully, that person isn't living in Bangladesh, Pakistan, London, or New Jersey.

So Ashit teaches in the morning, teaches in the afternoon, and searches after school—just as he did when he was looking for a building for Preyrona 3 School. But now he's confined to a municipal office, the work is tedious, and, because the journals cover a span of more than sixty years, it takes a long, long time. With his young, restless nature, being stuck in an office isn't his cup of tea, but he doesn't complain. Through his efforts, Preyrona 2 School could be razed and replaced.

After months of searching public records, Ashit finds an ownership document that matches the location of Preyrona 2 School. He is very careful to be sure he hasn't confused this property with an adjacent piece of property or something similar, so he checks and rechecks until he is convinced the document is accurate. Looking at the owner's name, he is surprised to see it is familiar. The family owns a factory, Indian Alkalis Ltd., in Kolkata and hasn't moved to Pakistan, Bangladesh, London, or New Jersey.

I'm in New Jersey for the summer when he makes his discovery and sends a long, convoluted email, which I condense to three simple words: "There is hope."

"Happy Anniversary," says Eva, lifting a glass of champagne.

I don't drink so I'm holding a glass of water. "To our years in Kolkata."

It's 2010. We've passed the ten-year mark. We recognize the significance of the occasion and want to share it. Over the years, volunteers have come and gone, but, to my good fortune, Eva is still here, managing her own projects.

"We have a lot to celebrate," I tell her.

"There's enough suffering in Kolkata. It's important to have things to celebrate."

"True, the city is generous with its pain, but it also brings moments of happiness."

"So you've been happy here?"

Because I've often asked myself this question, I answer quickly, "On the whole, I've been very happy. Just think. When I started, there was only a rooftop school with Reena, a small orphanage, and a girls' tutorial center. Now, Empower The Children has educational, vocational, and lunch programs in ten locations in India as well as projects in Mexico and Africa. Steadily, we've been able to help more and more children."

"You have a lot to be proud of."

"I'm not proud of myself. I'm proud of the kids, and I'm grateful to the people who are helping me. It takes a strong team to get anything done in Kolkata. The wheels move slowly. But when I see the look on the kids' faces, all my impatience disappears. They're young, so they have the rest of their lives to reap the benefits of their education. I'm getting old. That's why I want things to move fast."

"You're not so old. It seems you get younger and younger each year that you're here."

"That's true. The kids give me energy and motivation. They're an inspiration to me. But the city is very challenging. It's mainly the noise. I have a hard time handling that. Without my earplugs, I'd be on the next plane back to New Jersey."

"The noise doesn't bother me as much as it bothers you."

"I know. Sometimes I envy you. At night, the dogs bark and bark and bark. Yet, during the day, they're so passive, lying on the sidewalks and roads exhausted from fighting all night."

"I'm on the same schedule," Eva jokes. "I stay up all night, fighting with my friends on Skype."

I laugh, then continue my litany of complaints. "And the *horning*. The incessant blowing of horns is totally senseless."

"The drivers can't help it. It's India."

"And the pollution," I continue. "Kolkata is the third most polluted city in the world. I'm sure it's taking years off my life."

Now anxiety shows on Eva's face. "You're not planning to leave, are you?" she asks hesitantly.

"Of course not," I assure her. "I keep saying, 'Kolkata is killing me but I can't leave without a sign. A sign dropped me here, and only a sign will whisk me away.'"

I pause. She smiles. Then we raise our glasses in unison, in triumph.

"To ten more years!"

And that's when I realize that so many of us are here doing exactly the same thing: stopping at nothing. I'm bent on empowering children, reclaiming their lives. But, of course, I'm also, really, reclaiming my own.

The journey hasn't been easy. At each juncture, I was beset with fears and doubts, never given room for complacency or ease. Though scarred by mistakes and misgivings, the journey has been made and I can look back with consolation that not a single step has been wasted.

I like to think that I made the journey willingly.

> *Fate leads the willing soul but drags along the unwilling one.*
> —Seneca, Roman statesman, philosopher

# Empower The Children
## Ongoing

Empower The Children has grown substantially since its inception in 2001 but still operates on a shoe-string budget. Only 4.5 percent of donations go to administrative costs with the remaining 95.5 percent going directly into programs. This allows Empower The Children to fully fund Atmaraksha, Nivedita, and Nehru Colony preschools, Preyrona 1, Preyrona 2, Preyrona 3 schools, Dankuni Tutorial Centres, and Khamargachi School. Empower The Children provides lunches and holiday clothes for the students at Benoy, Badal, Dinesh (BBD) School.

I am strongly connected to Prabartak Home and Rehabilitation Centres for Children where I partner with other organizations to bring music, drama, art, and dance into the residents' lives. Vocational training has become a cornerstone of our programs so that teenagers and women can become independent-minded and self-sufficient.

A world-wide network of volunteers and donors has made all this possible. As a statement of gratitude to them, I will donate fifty percent of all proceeds from *Reclaiming Lives* to Empower The Children.

\* \* \*

Photographs on the following pages appear in black-and-white. To view these same photographs in color, order the e-book version of *Reclaiming Lives* online. Search for keywords: "Reclaiming Lives Giffoniello"

Find more Empower The Children photographs at empower-children.org

# New Preyrona 2 School
## 2012–2014

Thanks to Ashit's perseverance, the Preyrona 2 School project was able to continue and succeed. Demolition of the old building, which was done by hand labor,

> *The secret of success is constancy of purpose.*
> —Benjamin Disraeli, British Prime Minister, statesman

began in March 2012. By the end of May, the slate tiles had been removed from the roof and the bricks that comprised the walls lay in large piles for salvage and use as foundation material for the new building. Construction began in August, and concrete was poured for the floor of the upper level at the end of September. In October 2012, even though the building lacked walls, teachers and students assembled for classes. By April 2013, the walls had been erected and the interior painted in bright, child-like colors.

Preyrona 2 School is an example of partnership in action. The initial donation came from the community of Grjipskerke in Holland, through Willike's organization Help2Help. Then Kolkata Seeds·Japan provided a sizeable amount for construction costs and also bought school uniforms. Empower The Children played the role of project facilitator, with Ashit being responsible for on-site project management.

Because of these organizations in the Netherlands, Japan, United States, and India, children who live in a slum in Kolkata now feel more like real students in a school that is more like a real school.

Most of the 70 to 90 children, ages 5 to 16, who attend Preyrona 2
School assemble in the empty lot next to the original building.

Rosalie Giffoniello poses with girls at Preyrona 2 School who model
their new holiday clothes, given annually by Empower The Children.

Workers begin to disassemble Preyrona 2 School by hand
in March 2012.

Workers remove the slate tiles from the roof to expose the bamboo
trusses and rafters.

In July 2012, the new two-level Preyrona 2 School building takes
shape on the same lot where the old single-level school
had once stood.

Even before the school has walls, students and teachers assemble
for classes.

This page and the following two: Preyrona 2 students now receive
their education while sitting on colorful new rugs, surrounded
by walls painted bright yellow and blue.

# Acknowledgements

My heartfelt thanks to:

Reneé and David Drucker, my parents, who were models of sacrifice and compassion. The importance of good parents cannot be underestimated.

Roy Drucker, my brother, who unselfishly took care of my mother, giving me the freedom to live and work in Kolkata. I know it was a great sacrifice and I am forever indebted to him.

Art Giffoniello, my former husband, who taught me to be strong in the face of adversity. His enduring friendship sustains and nourishes me, and he continues to be an important member of our family.

Janet Grosshandler, co-founder of Empower The Children, who plays a very important role from her home in New Jersey, USA. Although she's half way around the world, Janet has proven her commitment to the children and women in Kolkata by making sure the organization runs efficiently. Together we've accomplished so much.

Barbara Cohen, my dear friend, who read through the manuscript with fresh eyes. Her attention to detail was impeccable and her input invaluable. It would be impossible to find a truer friend.

Becky, an American volunteer at Daya Dan in 2000, who suggested the title *Reclaiming Lives*. Unfortunately, she died in a car accident while still in her 20s. I wish she had lived to see it published.

The success of Empower The Children would not be possible without the love-filled efforts of many people in the U.S., India, and other nations: board members, program directors, teachers, volunteers, fundraisers, donors, partner organizations, and many others too numerous to mention.

Myself for undertaking this book project, completing it in fits and starts, but in the end making it a labor of love.

And Robert Weir, editor of *Reclaiming Lives,* without whose assistance this book would not be possible. He took my diverse stories and crafted them into a cohesive manuscript. He added description and detail so that the stories became rooted in time and place. But more importantly, he came to the project with a humanitarian's heart. Before starting to edit, he visited Kolkata, explored the city, met the people, and listened to the children's voices. For his contribution to the manuscript, I am very grateful; for his guidance, support, and love, I am forever blessed.

*Robert's Acknowledgment:* Rosalie Giffoniello is tuned into people. Even in her initial draft, her dialogue and descriptions of human emotions captured Kolkata's daily life. She cast her characters well, and it was my privilege to construct the literary stage, set, and scenery on which their stories unfold. Rosalie sacrificed what could have been a comfortable life in the U.S. to become a part of frenetic Kolkata for so many years. Her reflections of past and present relationships provide insight into her fears as well as her courage. Her lesson, taught by example, is that we can—if we dare—make a positive difference in our world. And do it with laughter, compassion, patience, and love.

# Glossary

*adhan* (Arabic): Islamic call to prayer, broadcast over loud speakers by a *muezzin* five times each day

*autorickshaw* also called *tuk-tuk* (English): A small, three-wheeled, motorized vehicle that is designed to carry five passengers plus a driver but can be seen holding more than that, a common means of public transportation in urban India

*arre* (Hindi): an expression equivalent to "oh"

*aste* (Bengali): slowly

*atall* (corrupted English): "at all" as in "not at all" but pronounced as "a tall"

*ayah* (Hindi): a native maid or nursemaid

*baba* (Hindi): literally, father or other male members of a family; often used as an exclamation of surprise as in "oh, *baba!*"

*baksheesh* (Persian): tip or bribe

*bandh* (Hindi): work stoppage, strike

Bar Mitzvah (Yiddish): A Jewish rite-of-passage ceremony that marks a young boy's coming of age at 13 and 12 for girls

*basa* (Hindi): home, house, door, dwelling

*basti* (Bengali): slum

*beshert* (Yiddish): an inevitable, preordained event

*biryani* (Urdu): a meal that consists of meat, potatoes, rice, onions, and spices, often cooked in large cauldrons over an open fire *bonsai* (Chinese, Japanese): A Japanese art form of miniature trees grown in small planters

*bosho* (Bengali): sit

*bulbulir* (Hindi): small bird

*burka* (Urdu): a full-body cloak worn by some Muslim women in public

*byas* (Bengali): enough

*chachkies* (Yiddish): knickknacks

*chai* (Urdu): black tea flavored with spices and herbs

Chanukah (Yiddish): an eight-day Jewish holiday commemorating the rededication of the Holy Temple in Jerusalem

*chalo* (Bengali): "Let's go!" or "Get moving!" Often repeated— "Chalo. Chalo."—to express urgency.

*chapatti* (Urdu, Hindi, Bengali): thin, unleavened wholemeal bread

*chaupal* (Hindi, Urdu): the commons; a shared, public part of a neighborhood where people pump water, bathe, toilet, cook *biryani*, and converse

*chup* (Bengali): quiet

*cycle rickshaw* (English): a human-powered, tricycle taxi designed to carry one, two, or maybe three passengers on a bench seat in addition to a driver who pedals and steers the vehicle

*dal* or *dahl* or *daal* (Sanskrit): a common meal in India and neighboring countries consisting of dried lentils, peas, or beans often eaten with rice or chapattis

Dharma (Sanskrit): duty or virtue as it pertains to law in the universal or abstract sense; behavior necessary to maintain natural order

*dhobi* or laundry *dhobi* (Hindi): laundry worker

Geshe and Geshe-la (Tibetan): an advanced academic degree for Tibetan Buddhist monks equivalent to a doctor of philosophy degree in the Western world; *la* is a term of greater position or respect *ghat* (Bengali, Hindi)*:* steps leading to a body of water, such as a lake or river, particularly a holy river; a place where people gather, bathe, and wash clothes and cooking cauldrons

*godown* (Malaysian): a warehouse or storage room

*gompa* (Tibetan)*:* monastery, nunnery, university, or meditation room or hall

Haggadah (Hebrew): a Jewish text that sets the order of the Passover Seder

*hashi* (Bengali): smile

*henna* (Arabic)*:* a tropical shrub whose leaves are used as a red dye to tint hair or apply temporary tattoos, usually to the hands and feet

*horning* (English): the Indian term for honking a vehicle's horn

*karma* (Sanskrit)*:* fate, destiny based on experiences in previous lives

*khata* (Mongolian): a traditional ceremonial scarf; a Tibetan blessing shawl

*khub bhalo* (Bengali): very good

*kishka:* (Yiddish) stomach

*kora* (Tibetan): a type of pilgrimage or walking meditation in the Tibetan Buddhist tradition

*kvelling* (Yiddish)*:* to be happy or extraordinarily proud; rejoice

*lakh* (Hindi, Urdu, Sanskrit et al): a unit of numbering in South Asia equal to one hundred thousand

*landsman* (Yiddish): a fellow Jew, a compatriot, a countryman

*lassi* (Bengali, Urdu, Punjabi)*:* a yogurt-based drink

*lungi* or *sarong* (Bengali, Hindi et al): a traditional garment worn by Indian men around the waist to cover their hips and waist; a simplification of the *dhoti*

*maisie* (Hindi): aunt; a person responsible for attending to the needs of a child or dependent adult; a caregiver

*mandala* (Sanskrit, Hindi): a circle or circular diagram, a symbolic depiction of and instruction about the way to Enlightenment in Hinduism and Buddhism

*mani* pills (Tibetan): herbal pills made by Buddhist monks

*menorah* (Yiddish): a candle holder for either seven or nine candles used for Jewish holidays

Middle Way or Middle Path: in Buddhism, the insight into emptiness that transcends opposite statements about existence

*muezzin* (Arabic): The person in an Islamic mosque who leads and recites the *adhan* (call to prayer), chosen for his ability to recite the *adhan* beautifully

*oy vey!* (Yiddish): an exclamation of dismay or exasperation

*paan* (Hindi): a psychoactive stimulant made of betel leaf combined with areca nut and cured tobacco

*pallu* (Sanskrit): the loose end of a *sari* that's draped over the shoulder

*pandal* or *puja pandal* (Hindi): a temporary temple constructed for Hindu holy days or *pujas*

*paneer* (Hindi, Urdu): fresh cheese

Passover Seder or Seder (Hebrew): order or arrangement; a Jewish ritual feast that marks the beginning of the Jewish holiday of Passover

*pranāma* (Hindi): touching of the feet in Indian culture as a sign of respect

*preyrona* (Bengali): inspiration

*puja* (Sanskrit, Urdu, Hindi): adoration, reverence, prayer, religious devotions

*raja* (Sanskrit): king

*rani* (Sanskrit): queen

*rickshaw* or pulled *rickshaw* (English): a form of human-powered transportation consisting of a two-wheeled cart with a pair of pulling forks, pulled by a person on foot, and with a bench seat for one or two persons in the rear

*rinpoche, Rinpoche* (Tibetan): "precious one;" an honorific used for senior monks in Tibetan Buddhism (capitalized if used as a title for a particular person)

*salwar kameez* (Urdu): a long tunic and matching loose trousers favored mainly by girls in North India and by both genders in Pakistan and Afghanistan

*samsara, samsaric* (Sanskrit): circle or wheel; in Buddhism, the continual, repetitive cycle of birth and death

Sangha (Sanskrit): a community or association; a Buddhist monastic community

*sari* (Sanskrit): a strip of unstitched, woven, colorful fabric, worn by Indian women, that ranges from four to nine yards in length that is draped around and over the body

*schlep* (Yiddish): to carry clumsily or with difficulty; lug; to move slowly or laboriously

*stupa* (Sanskrit): a mound-like structure or temple containing Buddhist relics; an ancient form of *mandala*

*tabla* (Hindi et al): a pair of small Indian hand drums used as accompaniment in Hindustani music

*thangka* (Tibetan): Buddhist tapestries of deities, consisting of a painting on silk with embroidery

*tiffin* (British): a lunch or light meal

*tilak* (Sanskrit): the sacred mark of protection on the center of a Hindu's forehead

*wallah* (Hindi, Urdu): a person involved in some kind of activity or labor; a worker, often associated with a particular profession such as a *rickshaw wallah,* a person who pulls a *rickshaw,* or a *dhobi wallah,* a person who washes clothes

*yahrzeit* (Hebrew, Yiddish): soul candle; in Judaism, a candle lit to commemorate the dead

# Endnotes

1.  1980 population estimate for Bombay, India, http://books.mongabay.com/population_estimates/1980/Bombay-India.html, (cited October 10, 2011).
2.  "Mumbai," Wikipedia, http://en.wikipedia.org/wiki/Mumbai, (cited October 10, 2011).
3.  "Buddha Field," Satrakshita, http://www.satrakshita.be/a_buddha_field.htm, (cited October 10, 2011)
4.  "5th Dalai Lama," Wikipedia, http://en.wikipedia.org/wiki/5th_Dalai_Lama (cited October 10, 2011)
5.  "Tsuglagkhang, Dharmashala," Native Planet: Explore Your World. http://www.nativeplanet.com/dharmashala/attractions/tsuglagkhang,/(cited October 1, 2012)
6.  Andrew Harvey, Sacred Therapy: Jewish Spiritual Teachings on Emotional Healing and Inner Wholeness by Estelle Frankel, page 16. http://books.google.co.in/books?id=MnMma2_JtP4C&pg=PA16&dq=Andrew+Harvey+when+the+heart+is+broken+open&hl=en&ei=ADKUTv_oAaWNmQW13sj4Bg&sa=X&oi=book_result&ct=result&resnum=2&sqi=2&ved=0CDgQ6AEwAQ#v=onepage&q=Andrew%20Harvey%20when%20the%20heart%20is%20broken%20open&f=false, (cited October 10, 2011).
7.  "Nobel laureate of India," Wikipedia, http://en.wikipedia.org/wiki/Nobel_laureates_of_India, (cited October 14, 2011).
8.  "Waist-strings on Indian children," http://www.indiamike.com/india/health-and-well-being-in-india-f2/waist-strings-on-indian-children-t70173/3/, (cited January 17, 2013
9.  Amanda Briney, "India Place Name Changes: Significant Place Name Changes Since Independence," About.com Geography. http://geography.about.com/od/specificplacesofinterest/a/indianames.htm, (cited March 23, 2012).
10. "Kolkata," Wikipedia, http://en.wikipedia.org/wiki/Kolkata, (cited March 23, 2012).
11. Ibid.
12. "Durga," Wikipedia, http://en.wikipedia.org/wiki/Dorga, (cited October 20, 2011)
13. "Durga Puja," Wikipedia, http://en.wikipedia.org/wiki/Durga_Puja, (cited October 20, 2011).
14. "Lakshmi," Wikipedia, http://en.wikipedia.org/wiki/Lakshmi, (cited October 20, 2011).
15. Ibid.
16. "Ganesha," Wikipedia, http://en.wikipedia.org/wiki/Ganesha, (cited October 20, 2011).
17. "Murugan," Wikipedia, http://en.wikipedia.org/wiki/Kartikeya#Symbolism, (cited October 20, 2011).

18. "Durga Puja," Wikipedia, http://en.wikipedia.org/wiki/Durga_Puja, (cited October 20, 2011).

19. "Indian Independence Act 1947," Wikipedia, http://en.wikipedia.org/wiki/ Indian_Independence_Act_1947, (cited October 29, 2011).

20. "Partition of India," Wikipedia, http://en.wikipedia.org/wiki/Partition_of_India, (cited October 29, 2011).

21. "Dominion of Pakistan," Wikipedia, http://en.wikipedia.org/wiki/ Dominion_of_Pakistan, (cited October 29, 2011).

22. "Howrah station," http://en.wikipedia.org/wiki/Howrah_station, (cited October 14, 2011 and updated February 6, 2013).

23. "Kolkata," Wikipedia, http://en.wikipedia.org/wiki/Kolkata, (cited October 14, 2011).

24. Ibid.

25. "the calcutta samaritans," http://thecalcuttasamaritans.org/aboutus.htm, (cited October 27, 2011).

26. Rehabilitation Center for Children literature.

27. "Bihar," Wikipedia, http://en.wikipedia.org/wiki/Bihar, (cited October 21, 2011).

28. David Kenneth Waldman, "Walk for Education Worldwide," (speech, Kampala, Uganda, East Africa, November 25, 2004,) http://www.tolovechildren.org/ files/41742790.pdf, (cited Oct 29, 2011).

29. "Victor Banerjee," Wikipedia, http://en.wikipedia.org/wiki/Victor_Banerjee, (cited October 29, 2011).

30. "Sarada Devi," Wikipedia, http://en.wikipedia.org/wiki/Sarada_Devi, (cited October 29, 2011).

31. "Dinesh Gupta," Wikipedia, http://en.wikipedia.org/wiki/Dinesh_Gupta, (cited January 1, 2012).

32. "Durga Puja," Wikipedia, http://en.wikipedia.org/wiki/Durga_Puja, (cited October 29, 2011).

33. "Diwali," Wikipedia, http://en.wikipedia.org/wiki/Diwali, (cited October 29, 2011).

34. "Major Jain Holidays & Dates," india-religion.net, http://www.india-religion.net/ jain-holidays.html, (cited October 29, 2011).

35. Sukhmandir Khalsa, "All About Sikh Holidays Festivals and Gurpurab Celebrations: Sikh Celebrations and Festivities," About.com: Sikhism, http:// sikhism.about.com/od/commemorativecelebrations/tp/ Celebrating_Sikh_Holidays.htm, (cited October 29, 2011).

36. "Gurpurbs," Shiromani Gurdwara Parbandhak Committee, http://www.sgpc.net/ festivals/index.asp, (cited January 1, 2012).

37. "Buddhist Festivals and Holidays," UrbanDharma.org, http://www.kusala.org/ udharma3/holidays.html, (cited October 29, 2011).

38. "Eid al-Fitr," Wikipedia, http://en.wikipedia.org/wiki/Eid_ul-Fitr, (cited March 30, 2012).

39. "Ramadan (calendar month)," Wikipedia, http://en.wikipedia.org/wiki/Ramadan_ (calendar_month), (cited March 30, 2012).

40. "Eid al-Adha," Wikipedia, http://en.wikipedia.org/wiki/Eid_al-Adha, (cited October 29, 2011).

41. "RRSA Standards," Unicef: United Kingdom: Rights Respecting Schools Award, http://www.unicef.org.uk/Education/Rights-Respecting-Schools-Award/RRSA-Standards/, (cited October 29, 2011).

42. "History of Israel," Wikipedia, http://en.wikipedia.org/wiki/History_of_Israel, (cited October 28, 2011).

43. "Ethnic communities in Kolkata," Wikipedia, http://en.wikipedia.org/wiki/ Ethnic_communities_in_Kolkata, (cited October 28, 2011).

# Your Response

Please tell us:

    What you think of:

        Empower The Children's work in Kolkata

        Rosalie's story

        *Reclaiming Lives*

    Send your comments to:

        Giffoniello@gmail.com

        Robtweir@aol.com

Learn more about Empower The Children at empower-children.org

* * *

*Reclaiming Lives* is also available as an e-book. Search online for keywords: "Reclaiming Lives Giffoniello"

This was an inspiring account of the author's life and love of children. Witty, personal, touching, and filled with adventure and hope, I highly recommend this book for anyone who has dreamed of helping others have a better life, filled with love. Five Stars. A must read!

— Volunteered review on Amazon.com

Made in the USA
Charleston, SC
26 May 2015